Hannah has produced a book that will be a gift to the church. He doesn't get bogged down with unnecessary scholarly debates but ably and simply exegetes the text always looking to the larger context and contemporary application. This reads like it is from the hand of a seasoned pastor-scholar who has continually thought through these texts and crystalized his explanations without being simplistic. Hannah lets his theology and big picture of the Bible guide his exegesis in the best way. This book is faithful to the text and thus puts our eyes on our Shepherd-King whose return we continue to long for.

Patrick Schreiner

Associate Professor, New Testament and Biblical Theology,
Midwestern Baptist Theological Seminary, Kansas City, Missouri;
author, *Matthew: Disciple and Scribe.*

Dr. John D. Hannah has gifted the church with an admirably concise and insightful exposition of Matthew's Gospel. Providing his reader with clear and helpful charts and with thoughtful questions for reflection, Dr. Hannah helps his audience to understand, digest, and apply Matthew's message. This work belongs on the shelf of every serious student of the Bible.

Guy Prentiss Waters

Professor, New Testament, Reformed Theological Seminary,
Jackson, Mississippi; author, *For the Mouth of the Lord Has Spoken:
The Doctrine of Scripture*

D1740073

MATTHEW

A call for unity and responsibility in the church

John D. Hannah

CHRISTIAN
FOCUS

John D. Hannah has been a professor at Dallas Theological Seminary for forty years, specialising in theology and history. He is also an author, and frequently speaks at churches and conferences.

Copyright © 2024 John D. Hannah

ISBN 978-1-5271-0887-5
E-book ISBN 978-1-5271-1117-2

10 9 8 7 6 5 4 3 2 1

Printed in 2024
by
Christian Focus Publications Ltd.,
Geanies House, Fearn, Ross-shire,
IV20 1TW, Scotland, U.K.

www.christianfocus.com

Cover design by Daniel van Straaten

Printed and bound by
Bell & Bain, Glasgow

Contents

Dedication

I wish to dedicate the publication of this commentary to Mrs Beth Motley, my sister-in-law, who has been a faithful, diligent, and competent secretary for over thirty-two years. Her expertise in management, in editing numerous manuscripts for me, as well as her dedication to the Lord through service to others, has been a constant encouragement and delight, making the task of teaching so much a pleasurable experience over the years. It is impossible to adequately express my thankfulness to you, though on countless occasions I failed to do so.

Preface

I often enjoy simply holding the Bible in my hands seated in a comfortable chair, meditating on the wonder of it all. It is a book beyond comparison to any others; it is the voice of the infinite triune God condensed into literary form so that we might not only read it but listen to the instructions, admonitions, and encouragements of God the Spirit speaking through it. Simply to ponder the reality that the sovereign creator of the universe would condescend to communicate to blighted, rebellious earthlings is a treasure; it is the 'pearl of great value' (Matt. 13:45), the 'treasure hidden in a field' (Matt. 13:44). One is not only astonished by the fact that God would desire to communicate Himself to us but also by the manner of doing so. It came over forty centuries ago in the form of a promise to Abraham (Gen. 12:1-3) and unfolded in subsequent promises through the Hebrew Scriptures. As the writer to the Hebrews tells us, the self-disclosure of God took a quantitative leap forward with the revelation of a person, God's Son, from heaven: 'Long ago, at many times and in many ways, God spoke to our fathers by the prophets, but in these last days he has spoken to us by his Son ...' (Heb. 1:1-2a).

The Gospel According to Matthew tells us much about the sheer majestic reality of God's revelation of Himself through the Lord Jesus. It reveals to us that the revelation of God has come through God Himself (who but an infinite, righteous, holy, and truthful being conveys such a divinely impeccable revelation but one who is perfectly all that in being and truth ('the Word became flesh and dwelt among us, and we have beheld his glory, the glory as of the only Son from the Father, full of grace and truth' [John 1:14]). Further, throughout the gospel, Matthew recorded from his experiences with Jesus, lifted without error by the controlling and superintending directives of the Spirit of God, the evidence of His claims through His words and works, His miracles. However, the composition of Matthew's account is more than a historical narrative of the words, claims, and ultimate accomplishments of Jesus in bringing to our world hope by reversing the condemning blight on the human soul through His atoning death, evidenced by His deliverance from death in His resurrection. Let me explain. This particular writing, like all the Holy Scriptures, is grounded in the realities of human existence, in Matthew's context, the early church, the realities of the post-pentecost effusion of the Holy Spirit. And even beyond that narrow context, it is a timeless book that has brought instruction, hope, perspective, and comfort throughout the centuries. Let me say a word about the timelessness of Matthew's work.

First, one unmistakable truth that surfaces through the pages of the gospel is that the One who came to disclose the way to the presence of God did so with unincumbered clarity. Simply put, the salvation that Jesus announced, this 'Immanuel' (Matt. 1:23), this One who 'will save his people from their sins' (Matt 1:21), is not free in that it had to be purchased (God's consistency of character, being just and righteousness, demands payment for sin), but that it has been purchased and is free to us. The Pharisees and Sadducees were simply wrong in thinking ethnicity granted privilege, position reward, and effort obligation. The error of the religious leadership in Jesus' day has been and is being repeated today.

Second, the book is also a manual of instruction for the proper conduct of social relationships, as well as individual demeanor. It is a book written to the early church that was, at that time, predominately Jewish but needed to be awakened to the reality that through Abraham 'all the families of the earth shall be blessed' (Gen. 12:3). Here you will find the deepest meaning and intent of the Law of God, how to handle interpersonal conflict in the community of the faithful, the importance of spiritual character that is more fundamentally essential than the productivity of our spiritual giftedness in service. It explains the nature and origin of human choice-making, and it clearly speaks of the obligation that emanates from the privilege of the experience of divine grace. The list of instructive benefits is inexhaustible; it is as relevant today as when Matthew's first readers heard it read in the assemblies of the saints.

Third, this gospel will grant to its perceptive readers an understanding of the cause of the difficulties that confront all of us at times as Jesus' devotees. It is that persecution, and it comes in various forms and circumstances, that is our lot; however, the promises that accompany such of divine provision, protection, and deliverance are more than overwhelming. Pause to imagine the grace and mercy of God! A reoccurring theme in this regard is the warning of the presence of false teachers who not only make it difficult to enter the kingdom, but provide untrustworthy, inaccurate instruction at times.

As we approach the commentary that follows, a few qualifications and clarifications seem appropriate. First, the audience that I am seeking to address is the people of God, the interested learner who attends Sunday worship, not the scholarly community. I make this particular comment, not because I have been derelict in reading considerable scholarly material, but because I wish primarily to speak to the larger community of those interested in biblical studies. I have chosen this approach for several reasons. While formally trained in biblical studies, my burden is to translate scholarship, so important and so very needed, for the learned and eager laity of the churches. While we often hear a dirge-like denunciation of illiteracy in the pew, I find a limited number of sources that are accessible and relevant to a basic, practical understanding of the Bible and devoid of defensives of particular prejudices manifesting such minutiae that it proves incomprehensible for the average enquirer (both in content and interest). I have sought to write a practical, biblically accurate commentary that focuses on applying the text (in years of teaching teachers the books of the Bible, I have often heard them say that sometimes finding appropriate applications that are both textually sensitive and accurate, without repetitious generalizations, is hard). Thus, what follows is an attempt to engage in a serious endeavor to understand Matthew's work, but I have included few footnotes and only a brief bibliography. While the views expressed in the commentary are a result of serious work, any shortcomings in representing our conservative scholars accurately are entirely my own, which I will willingly confess as my own ignorance, interpretative errors rooted in misperception and, therefore, misrepresentation.

It is my prayer that God will use this small attempt to explain the wisdom and wonder of our faith. The Apostle Paul expressed much the same desire in writing to the Ephesian believers (3:14-21):

> ... I bow my knees before the Father, from whom every family in heaven and on earth is named, that according to the riches of his glory he may grant you to be strengthened with power through his Spirit in your inner being, so that Christ may dwell in your hearts through faith—that you, being rooted and grounded in love, may have strength to comprehend with all the saints what is the breadth and length and height and depth, and to know the love of Christ that surpasses knowledge, that you may be filled with all the fullness of God.
>
> Now to him who is able to do far more abundantly than all that we ask or think, according to the power at work within us, to him be glory in the church and in Christ Jesus throughout all generations, forever and ever. Amen.

JOHN D. HANNAH

Introduction

Authorship

While the title of the book, 'The Gospel According to Matthew', was probably not attached to the original document, the universal witness of the early church, as well as suggestive internal evidence, indicates that Matthew, a disciple of our Lord (10:3), composed it.[1] We are not specifically told that Matthew composed the original scroll, he being mentioned without distinction only twice within it (in the enumeration of the disciples he appears eighth in the list [10:2-4] and also in Jesus' call to join His emerging band of intimate followers [9:9]).

What we know from internal evidence is that the author's former profession was that of a tax collector who operated under the client king, Herod Antipas, in the service of the Romans. He resided in Capernaum, a city on the northern shore of the Sea of Galilee, situated on the highway called the Via Maris (the Way to the Sea) that ran from Mesopotamia in the East through the Fertile Crescent to the Mediterranean Sea.

Capernaum was the residence of Jesus and the center of His ministry after He left Nazareth (4:12). In Matthew 9, after describing the healing of the paralytic in Capernaum (9:2-7), the text states that 'as Jesus passed from there, he saw a man, named Matthew, sitting in a tax booth ...' (9:9). This places Matthew both as a resident of Capernaum, a frequent

---

1. Compositions at the time were made upon lengthy scrolls that would be rolled up when not in use. When multiple scrolls were in the possession of a church, in order to prevent unnecessary openings, which would damage the fragile document, it became customary to place pieces of paper in the fold of them for accurate identification and ready access.

topic in the gospel (4:13; 8:5; 9:1; 11:23; 17:24), and as a tax collector (it is interesting that the topic of money comes up more frequently in Matthew than in any other gospel [e.g. 17:24, 27; 18:24]).

So the author resided in the Galilee, a region inhabited by Jews and Gentiles ('Galilee of the Gentiles,' [4:15]) and wrote using some Aramaic loan-words suggestive of Gentile influence. Perhaps his pro-Galilean bias becomes most evident when he alone records, in his account of Jesus' post-resurrection appearances, the instructions of Jesus that His disciples should meet with Him in Galilee (28:10).

It can also be inferred with confidence that the author was Jewish as well as Galilean. Although he does reveal a regional preference for Galilee in contrast to Judea and, while his bias is demonstrated by his stress on what Jesus did in Galilee with little reference to Jerusalem – he records only one journey there, the Passion Week – he is aware of Jewish customs (1:18-20), of the nation's social experience and political context (2:1, 22; 14:1), of social classifications within Jewish culture (2:4; 26:3, 57, 59; 27:2), and a depth of knowledge of its history (1:1-17). Perhaps most telling is his immense knowledge of the Hebrew Scriptures evidenced by the plethora of citations throughout the text.

Jesus found Matthew in a tax office pursuing a career in the service of the Roman empire (9:9). Generally, tax gatherers accumulated significant wealth because, while they collected required taxes that the Roman law stipulated, they were also allowed to collect more. For both reasons, they did not ingratiate themselves to their countrymen. The tax that Matthew collected was likely a poll tax. It was used for internal improvements, though its distribution was subject to the wishes of the political establishment connected to the client king, Herod Antipas.

The external evidence for Matthean authorship in the early centuries of the church is abundant. Without specifically ascribing authorship to the disciple, there is evidence that the gospel was not only attributed to Matthew but was also quoted by second-century writers. *The Epistle of Barnabas* (c. 117–c. 132) contains a quotation from Matthew 22:14 ('many are called, few are chosen'), words only found in this particular gospel.[2] *The Didache* (c. 140), also denominated as 'The Teaching of the Twelve', an early church manual of discipline, quotes the Lord's Prayer of Matthew 6:9-13 (identifying the source as 'a gospel').[3] While Papias' work, *The Sayings of Our Lord* (c. 130), has been lost, it is quoted in *Ecclesiastical History* by Eusebius, bishop of Caesarea (c. 260–340). Papias, who was bishop of Hierapolis, is quoted as follows: 'So then Matthew wrote the oracles in the Hebrew language, and everyone interpreted the oracles as he was able' (3:39:16). We have clear evidence that Papias understood that both Mark (3:39:15) and Matthew wrote accounts of the words and works of Jesus. The earliest unambiguous assertion comes from Irenaeus (c. 130–202), bishop of Lyon, who stated that Matthew wrote a gospel account for the Hebrews when Peter and Paul were preaching in Rome.[4]

To state the case succinctly, in every instance where a subsequent writer or later council in identifying a list of canonical books, the 'first' gospel, the book is attributed to *Matthew*, the disciple of our Lord. The earliest listing of books to be read in the churches, the Muratorian Canon, dated in the late second century is available only in fragments; however, the listing of New Testament books begins, '[1] ... at which nevertheless he was present [a reference to Mark], and so he placed [them in his narrative]. [2] The third book of the gospel is that according to Luke ... [9] the fourth of the gospels is that of John [one] of the disciples.'[5] Athanasius, bishop of Alexandria, in his Easter or Festal Letter of 365/366, in which he enumerated the canonical writings, lists Matthew's gospel first among the New Testament books. Later he wrote, 'Again, it is not tedious to speak of the [books] of the New Testament.

---

2. *The Epistle of Barnabas*, 4:14.

3. *The Didache*, 8:1-9.

4. Irenaeus, *Against Heresies*, 3.1.1: 'Matthew also issued a written Gospel among the Hebrews in their own dialect, while Peter and Paul were preaching at Rome, and laying the foundations of the Church.' Additionally, Irenaeus' statement documents his understanding that the gospel was written prior to the outbreak of hostilities that led to the destruction of the Temple in Jerusalem.

5. The Muratorian Canon, 1-9.

These are the four gospels, according to Matthew, Mark, Luke, and John.'[6]

Matthean authorship was not doubted until the rise of the Enlightenment in the eighteenth century. Unbelief, shrouded in academic and intellectual achievement, then rejected the integrity of the witness of Holy Scripture and regarded as false the assumed divine superintendence of human authorship that overcame the oft-blighted perceptions and distortions. The interpretative clues of the biblical writers were increasingly regarded as the mere observable qualities common to human authors. A spirit of skepticism descended upon rigorous scholarly attainment, leading increasingly to transmuting providence into natural law and limiting divine participation to the distant margins of consideration.

Recent scholarship has put an interesting twist on Matthean authorship postulating that, while the disciple did gather remembrances of the teachings, claims, and accomplishments of Jesus, he did not do so in the form as we have it today. The claim finds traction in a comment made by Papias and recorded by Eusebius. He is quoted as adding the phrase, 'and the same writer uses testimonies from the Epistle of John and from that of Peter likewise'.[7] If the statement is valid, it is not a denial of Matthean authorship, but is a matter concerning the sources and the manner of compilation.

Date

The dating of Matthew's gospel, as is true of literature as a whole, is important because social context provides valuable insight into the meaning of the text. Simply put, entering into the immediate world of the writer tends to increase the understanding of what is read (a position rejected by postmodern literary critics). Within the gospel itself several clues narrow the time of its composition. It is justifiable to suggest that the gospel was written at a distance in time after the events recorded. For example, when Matthew tells how the betrayal fee paid to Judas was used after it was returned to the nation's religious leadership (the purchase of a field

---

6. Athanasius, *Letter*, 39.4.

7. Eusebius, *Ecclesiastical History*, 3.39.16

for the burial of the poor), he states: 'Therefore that field has been called the Field of Blood *to this day*' (27:8), suggesting a lapse of time since the purchase, but yet before the city was destroyed by the Romans. Again, Matthew says that the religious leaders fabricated a lie to cover up the implications of the empty tomb of Jesus by telling those who should have guarded it securely to say robbers stole its contents while they slept (28:11-14). Then he adds this comment: 'And the story has been spread among the Jews *to this day*' (28:15), which suggests a significant period between the event and its recording.

Further, Matthew assumes that the temple and its services were still in operation at the time of writing. For example, when he prefaces Jesus' first discourse, the Sermon on the Mount (5:1), the temple was still in existence. In speaking of the need for purity of heart and its relationship to interpersonal behavior as the criteria of worship, Matthew recorded Jesus as saying, 'So if you are offering your gift there before the altar, and there remember that your brother has something against you, leave your offering there before the altar … and then come and offer your offering' (5:23-24).

There are clues within the gospel that suggest the city had not yet been ravished by the Romans. In the temptation-of-Christ narrative we are told that Jesus was taken by the devil to the holy city and set on the pinnacle of the temple (4:5); in Christ's instruction in the Sermon on the Mount concerning false oaths we should not swear by Jerusalem because 'it *is* the "city of the great King"' (5:35); in 24:1-2, Jesus was departing from the temple when the disciples reflected upon its stunning beauty; in 24:15, Jesus speaks of the inner sanctuary of the temple complex, the Holy Place; and in 27:53 we are informed that when the deceased came out of their tombs with Christ's great victory over death 'they went into the holy city'. Though an argument from silence, the writer gives us no hint that the city and temple have been destroyed.

The range that several conservative scholars provide for its composition is sometime in the 50s and 60s. Graham Scroggie stated: 'Matthew's record was written probably about A.D. 58.'[8]

---

8. Graham Scroggie, *A Guide to the Gospels* (Grand Rapids, MI: Kregel Classics, 1948), p. 234.

Leon Morris concurred, saying that 'There is good reason for seeing it as appearing before A.D. 70, perhaps the late 50s and early 60s.'[9] D. A. Carson states rather succinctly both the lack of scholarly conclusiveness and the acceptance of a pre-70 date: 'While surprisingly little in the gospel points to a firm date, perhaps the sixties are the most likely decade for its composition.'[10] If the occasion for the gospel was, at least in part, related to the issue of Jewish-Christian duties to carry the news of Jesus to the Gentiles (28:18-20), the new constituency of the people of God, an implication of the promises made to Abraham, it would make sense that the gospel was composed prior to the fatal Jewish uprising in A.D. 66–70.

Place of the Writing

The locale of the composition of the gospel is uncertain as well. Generally, those who hold to a pre-70 date suggest that the location was in Palestine.[11] Those who hold that the composition took place there often designate the specific area as Judea, particularly the city of Jerusalem, but the claim lacks supporting evidence. On the contrary, given Matthew's bias for the Galilee, it seems strange to do so. Among the options of recent scholarship is the suggestion that the gospel was written in Antioch in Syria (which the Romans considered a part of Palestine), where there was a large Christian community (Acts 13:1-2; 14:26-28). There are indications within the gospel of Aramaic influence, which would accord the possibility of Antioch, for that language was widespread in the 'Galilee of the Gentiles' (4:15) also. There are numerous other suggestions in this regard, yet the evidence for each is slender.

---

9. Leon Morris, *The Gospel According to Matthew* (Grand Rapids, MI: William B. Eerdmans Publishing Co., 1992), p. 11.

10. D. A. Carson, *Matthew, The Expositors Bible Commentary*, vol. 1 (Grand Rapids, MI: Zondervan Publishing Co., 1917), p. 21.

11. The name by which the geographical area was re-designated by the Emperor Hadrian after the failed Bar Kochva revolt (A.D. 132–34). By so doing, he suggested that the ancient homeland of the Jews was a ruse, the true possessors of the land being the ancient Philistines (hence, 'Palestina'). The British used the designation, the Palestinian Expeditionary Force, following the capture of the city during World War I, a period called the British Mandate. The city of Jerusalem was also renamed Aelia Capitolina by Hadrian in honor of the emperor's family, but that has been lost in time.

Distinctive Characteristics

As with the discussion of the writer, date, and location of the composition, other topics assist the reader in the interpretative process because it helps to narrow the focus, and, thereby, assist in understanding. In that light, a summary of the emphases within the gospel becomes the motive for indulging in a thematic discussion. What can we learn from the contents of the gospel itself? While Matthew shares much in common with the other gospels, there are unique characteristics in his account, as is true of the other three.

For example, notice has already been made regarding Matthew's focus on Jesus' ministry in the Galilee, noting only one journey, the climactic one, to Jerusalem. John, in contrast, tells of several trips of our Lord to Jerusalem, and he also mentions several post-resurrection appearances in the city, whereas Matthew records only one. He mentions the encounter of 'Mary Magdalene and the other Mary' (28:1) with an angel at the empty tomb who instructed them to tell the disciples that 'he is going before you into Galilee; there you will see him' (28:7). When the two women met Jesus subsequently, He repeated the same instructions: 'go and tell my brothers to go to Galilee, and there they shall see me' (28:10). The disciples followed the instructions. Matthew ended the narrative with Jesus' further direction to carry the message abroad (28:16-20).

So, what are those emphases? First, that the original audience was largely, if not exclusively, Jewish as opposed to Gentile is clearly evident from the perfusion of quotations from the Hebrew Scriptures. There are over sixty direct quotations from them in the gospel, a significant contrast to about thirty in Mark, twenty-five in Luke, and only sixteen in John. Matthew's purpose, at least in part, was to demonstrate that Jesus is the long-promised Messiah, the Christ. Christian faith is 'true Judaism'; it is the culmination of what the prophets of the nation promised, pondered, and awaited. Further, the Jewishness of this gospel is brought out in Jesus' frequent references to the Mosaic Code. The 'Sermon on the Mount', Jesus' great commentary on entrance into the kingdom of God (chs. 5–7), contains a declaration of the misuse of the Law by the religious leaders of His day: 'Do not

think that I have come to abolish the Law and the Prophets;
I have come not to abolish them but to fulfill them ... For I tell
you unless your righteousness exceeds that of the scribes
and Pharisees, you will never enter the kingdom of heaven'
(5:17, 20). The same negative evaluation of the use by the
scribes and Pharisees of their own sacred texts is found in
the seven woes of Matthew 23. In the controversy with the
Pharisees, when approached concerning His thoughts of the
most important commandment of the 613 that they advocated
(Matt. 22:34-40), Jesus distilled the Law into one word (love)
expressed toward two entities (God and mankind). The very
preamble of the gospel suggests much about the audience:
'The book of the genealogy of Jesus Christ, the son of David,
the son of Abraham' (Matt. 1:1). The good news for the early
Jewish constituency of the church is the good news of the
Jewishness of Jesus!

Second, even as Jesus is the person promised in the Hebrew
Scriptures as the Christ, or the Messiah, so Christianity is
the fulfillment of God's promise of redemption for mankind.
The promise made to Abraham (a 'land' prefigured
materially yet ultimately fulfilled in heaven); a 'seed' being
Jesus (Gal. 3:16), the one who made the divine promise a
reality, and a 'blessing' which is the eternal existence of
God's people in His presence [Gen. 12:1-3]), a promise often
repeated to His ancient people, finds its ultimate fulfillment
in a manner the Jews hardly could have imagined. While the
Jewish people, as a whole, failed to embrace the promise in
Jesus, grace has been granted without ties to ethnicity or to
proselytism into Judaism. The key concepts in Matthew's
gospel are (1) 'the Christ' (used seventeen times) to highlight
the identity of the redeemer and (2) 'the kingdom of heaven'
(thirty-two times), 'the kingdom of God' (five times), 'the
kingdom' (six times), and 'the kingdom of the Son of Man'
(six times) to emphasize the 'world' that He secured for
His people. The long-awaited kingdom has drawn near in
Christ and His followers, who are a new entity, the church.
Thus, the kingdom, the church, the realm over which Jesus
is recognized as Lord, is both a present reality in the church
(4:17; 12:28), in shadowed form, and a future reality to be
revealed in magnificent splendor. Jesus, by virtue of His

enthronement in heaven now, but also someday on the 'new' earth, as in heaven, will be without opposition. Jesus offered His rule, and it came by virtue of His triumph. It waits its fullest manifestation when His enemies become the footstool under His feet in the final judgment.

Third, Matthew lived, at least when we first encounter him, in the Galilee, an area of Jewish and Gentile constituents, which in part explains Judean attitudes to the region ('Can anything good come from Nazareth?' asked Nathaniel [John 1:46]). The word 'Gentile' is used in two ways: ethnically meaning non-Jews, and religiously meaning the lost. When Jesus began His public ministry, Matthew quotes an Old Testament text (Isa. 9:1) indicating it as a fulfillment of prophecy in the 'Galilee of the Gentiles'. Matthew has an interest in Gentiles, noting Jesus' healing of a Roman centurion's servant (8:13), the Gadarene demoniac (8:32), and the Syro-Phoenician woman's daughter (15:28). Most interesting is that, following the rejection of Jesus by the religious leadership for violating the Law (12:9), Matthew quotes a passage from Isaiah claiming that Jesus' embrace of Gentiles was a fulfillment of prophecy (Isa. 42:1-4, the lengthiest Old Testament citing in his composition).

It is apparent that Matthew had an interest in the legitimacy of expanding the constituency of Christ-followers. He is the only gospel writer to use the term 'church' (16:18; 18:17). The gospel famously ends with Jesus' command to carry the good news to the nations: 'Go therefore and make disciples of all nations …' (28:19). In context, it seems to be a not-so-subtle insight that God's people are not limited to His ancient people! It is also interesting that in the two passages where the church is mentioned, we have instruction about the issue of authority and about interpersonal conflict management with procedures for resolution. This gospel is meant for and reflects, in part, the needs of the embryonic church.

Fourth, Matthew's gospel displays a very hostile view of the religious leadership of his day, particularly of the Pharisees and the Sadducees. The Sermon on the Mount (chs. 5–7), for example, is a declaration of the kind of righteousness needed to enter the kingdom that Jesus was offering to the nation. Jesus makes it clear that Pharisaic righteousness is both inadequate and spiritually destructive. The seven woes of chapter 23 speak for themselves. The Pharisees, in Jesus' and Matthew's view, were 'blind leaders of the blind' (15:14). Matthew cites comments about both religious parties in statements quoted from John's preaching ('You brood of vipers …' [3:7]). The leadership of the nation, the Sanhedrin, was composed of Sadducees, Pharisees, and elders. Sadducees were of the aristocratic priestly caste; they were a minority party, but they held the power. Pharisees were not priests; they were teachers of the law; they were laymen, and they composed the majority party. Elders were powerful lay nobility. There were serious theological differences among the three groups, but they shared a common hostility towards Jesus. He did not reject all that the Pharisees taught; in His view, their teachings were sometimes more accurate than their lifestyle; he said, '… do and observe whatever they tell you, but not the works they do. For they preach, but do not practice' (23:3).

Fifth, Matthew's literary technique and style is worthy of reflection; he displays the marks of a careful craftsman, as well as of a master teacher, in the arrangement and presentation of material throughout the gospel. Matthew builds his argument around five discourses of Jesus (chs. 5–7; 10; 13; 18; and 24–25). The teacher in Matthew is brought out in at least two ways: first, he arranges things in threes and sevens. For example, Joseph receives directions from the Lord in three dreams (1:14; 2:13, 19); three times Peter denies the Lord (26:69-74); seven parables are in Matthew 13; and seven woes in Matthew 23. The number fourteen, the double of seven, is a rhetorical device prominent in chapter 1 (1:17). Further, Matthew employs clever teaching devices such as organizing information in trilogies, likely for memory ease (six comments on Pharisaic misuse of Scripture divided into two units of three each [5:21-48], three errant religious practices [6:6-18], and three errant matters of moral conduct [6:19–7:5]).

Additionally, he repeats phrases or tenses of verbs to frame sections. For example, Matthew 4:23-25 is repeated in 9:35, stressing that Jesus taught and performed miracles. Chapters 5–7 comprise a major discourse and chapters 8–9 a major section of miracles. Of the eight beatitudes, the first and last are in the present tense while those in between are in the future tense. Again, Matthew is revealed to us as more than a former employee in a tax office in the service of a foreign power; he is a master writer-teacher.

Occasion of the Writing

Matthew's gospel, judging from its internal content, clearly suggests several purposes in its composition arising from the situation at the time. First, and perhaps foremost, the original audience was composed of Jewish Christians (the argument for this view is stated above). It may be safely surmised that the rehearsing in literary form of the person, claims, and accomplishments of Jesus Christ had several functions. It would have provided organized data to help those Christians in their witness to their Jewish compatriots, and, in that sense, as is true of the other gospel accounts, it served as an evangelistic manual with apostolic eyewitness authority. Second, the gospel certainly functions to strengthen the early church in their embrace of the good news, and, as such, was a manual on the spiritual life, their walk in the faith.

The gospel was written, it seems, to address a reoccurring problem of adjusting to a new social situation that relates to the constituency of the people of God. In this sense, the issue may have been to address Jewish-Gentile relations in the new entity, the church (this you find as a theme in several New Testament books, but especially in Romans where Paul makes the point that all ethnicities are equal in Christ and we must learn to live in harmony with one another [12:1–15:21]), the theological basis stated in the chapters precede the exhortations. The thought seems to be that Matthew senses the urgency to remind Jewish Christians that they have an obligation to reach out to Gentiles because the promises made to Abraham were for them, though the channel of delivery was through 'true' Israel. This becomes clear in the selection of material in the account, as noted above, such as the centurion's servant, the Gadarene demoniac, and the Canaanite's daughter in the former territory of Phoenicia. A gospel heavily Jewish in orientation ends with the command from Jesus to carry the good news to the nations. Another hint to possible early Jewish/Gentile tensions in bringing the two groups harmoniously together in the unity of the body of Christ is the specific instruction in handling interpersonal conflicts in the assembly of saints (17:15-20), as well as the stress of the cardinal Christian virtue of humility (18:1-4).

Beyond the possible issue of Jewish-Christian hesitancy to carry the good news to the non-Jew, or at least to display small bias in social discourse and worship, it must not be missed that the gospel contains a great volume of instruction for the general deportment of Christians, truths that are timeless insights. For example, while Jesus repudiates the Pharisaic manner of giving (6:1-4), prayer (6:5-15), and fasting (6:15-16), He gives us valuable instruction on those subjects. In like manner, Jesus contrasts the moral conduct of the religious leadership on such important topics as wealth-management (6:19-24), worry (6:25-34), and a judgmental spirit (7:1-5) in a way that is certainly timeless.

Theme of the Writing

The central theme of the gospel is twofold. First, Jesus is the fulfillment of the promises in the Hebrew Scriptures; Jesus is the Messiah! This seems validated by the more than fifty direct citations from the Old Testament and some 262 allusions or parallels to it. Further, a unique feature of Matthew is the ten formula-quotations in the gospel, five in the initial two chapters. 'All this took place to fulfill what was spoken by the Lord through the prophet' (1:22; 2:15, 17, 23; 4:14; 8:17; 12:17; 13:35; 21:4; 27:9), followed in each case by an Old Testament citing. Second, the consequence that Jesus is the Christ is to be lived out practically in the churches and proclaimed to the nations (the gospel ends with a plea for the nations!).

Structure of the Writing

There are three general ways commentators have approached the gospel. The first is to organize the gospel around the five discourses of Jesus (each of the five discourses ends in a similar phrase as the narrative continues ['And when Jesus had finished these sayings ...' 7:28; 11:1; 13:53; 19:1; 26:1]). If one

outlines the gospel in this fashion, the work of Michael Green
may serve as an excellent example:[12]

1–4	Introduction (Genealogy, birth narrative, beginning of ministry)
5–7	Teaching #1(Sermon on the Mount)
8–9	Miracles
10	Teaching #2 (Mission instruction)
11–12	Rejection of John and Jesus
13	Teaching #3 (Parables)
14–17	Miracles and controversies
18	Teaching #4 (The church)
19–22	Journey to Jerusalem
23–25	Teaching #5 (Judgment and the end of the world)
26–28	Death and resurrection

Green takes the view that the gospel has two parts, the division
being geographic. Chapters 1–13 take place in the Galilee,
14–28 in Jerusalem. In the telling of the story, Matthew has
Jesus leave the Galilee and make a single visit to Jerusalem.
The gospel ends with Jesus in the Galilee where Matthew
records His post-resurrection appearance. Again, the gospel
writers are quite selective in material-choice, seeking to view
the events and teachings of Christ from their point of view
or a theme they each seek to develop.

A second approach, suggested by the Anglican scholar
R. T. France, follows a biographical/geographical/thematic
approach.[13] France sees the gospel divided into six parts with
introductory phrases like 'When he heard that John was
arrested, he withdrew into Galilee' (4:12) or 'From that time
Jesus began to show his disciples ...' (16:21) marking each
section (except for the first and last sections): the introduction of
the Messiah (1:1–4:11); the Messiah in Galilee revealed by word
and deed (4:12–16:20); the Messiah leaving Galilee for Jerusalem

12. Michael Green, *The Message of Matthew: The Kingdom of Heaven* (Westmont, ILL: InterVarsity Press, 2020), p. 30.

13. R. T. France, *The Gospel of Matthew* (Grand Rapids: MI: William Eerdmans Publishing Co., 2007), pp. 2-5.

with pending conflict (16:21–20:34); confrontation with the religious authorities in Jerusalem (21:1–25:34); the Messiah rejected, killed, and vindicated (26:1–28:15); and in Galilee the mission launched (28:16-20). Thus, France emphasizes the instructional aspects of the gospel with a view to the spread of the good news through the early churches by the apostles. In this approach, at least as it is presented, is the downplaying of Jesus' clash with Jewish leadership leading to His death. This influences how one reads, for example, Matthew 5–7.

This approach is followed by Craig Blomberg with slight modification in that he recognizes the phrase 'from that time Jesus began to …' (4:17; 16:21) as structural dividers in the gospel.[14]

The Introduction of Jesus, 1:1–4:16
The Claims of Jesus Presented, 4:17–16:20
The Rejection and Triumph of Jesus, 16:21–28:20

A third way is to see the gospel more thematically, as a retelling of Jesus' life-events and teachings progressing from His birth to the post-resurrection appearance in the Galilee. The development in the gospel would be then as follows: birth and preparation for His ministry (chs. 1–4), the verification of His claims through preaching and the performance of miracles (chs. 5–10), the rejection of the nation's leadership (chs. 11–12), private teaching in preparation for His departure (chs. 13–18), journey to Jerusalem (chs. 19–20), official presentation and rejection (chs. 21–27), and His appearance in the Galilee (ch. 28). Through this grid, the gospel of Matthew appears to pivot on the events of chapter 12 with the official verdict of the nation's leadership about the validity of Christ's claims as Messiah that were confirmed by His miracles ('But the Pharisees went out and conspired together against him, how they might destroy him' [12:14]. 'It is only by Beelzebul, the prince of demons, that this man casts out demons' [12:24]). From that point Christ turns from public proclamation to either private instruction of His disciples or teaching through parables so that the masses would not understand what He was saying (13:11). As Christ instructs the disciples, and

---

14. Craig Blomberg, *Matthew* (Brentwood, TN: B&H Publishing Group, 1994), pp. 24-25.

increasingly manifests hostility to the religious hierarchy, the leadership becomes increasingly hostile to Him. While this approach is biographical, it focuses upon Jesus' claims as the Christ, His national rejection, the preparation of His disciples for His departure, death and resurrection, and His command to be mission-minded. This proposal will be the structure of the commentary that follows.

I. **The Claims of Jesus: The King 1:1–11:1**
   - A. The Presentation of the King, 1:1–4:11
   - B. The Proclamation of the King, 4:12–7:29
   - C. The Miracles of the King, 8:1–9:34
   - D. The Instruction of the King to the Disciples, 9:35–11:1

II. **The Rejection of Jesus: The King, 11:2–27:66**
   - A. The Responses to and Rejection of the King, 11:2–12:50
   - B. The Consequences of Rejecting the King's Teaching, 13:1-52
   - C. The Final Ministry of the King in the Galilee, 13:53–16:12
   - D. The Final Instructions of the King in the Galilee, 16:13–18:35
   - E. The Journey of the King to Jerusalem, 19:1–20:34
   - F. The Official Presentation and Rejection of the King, 21:1–27:66
   - G. The Conclusive Proof of the King's Claims and Person: The Resurrection, 28:1-20

Applications

1. The grace and mercy of God is seen in Jesus' choice of Matthew. He was a disgrace in his culture, being a tax collector for the Roman oppressors. Yet, in His grace Jesus called him to be a disciple and then to write a gospel about Him for His own people, the Jews. God calls and uses people as He wills, but not according to

merit for we have none without Him! There is hope for all of us that God will show His kindness toward us. Are you not glad that His ways are not ours?

2. Being with Jesus, listening to His words and observing His life, made the disciples willing to tell others about Him. Matthew even authored a gospel to share with others his understanding of Jesus' claims and accomplishments. Does Jesus inspire you to tell others? Are you impressed with who He is?

3. The perception of Jesus by the educated religious leadership is a witness to the darkness and blindness of our faculties. Though the leadership had the Old Testament, they missed the whole point of it. They said that His powers were of supernatural origin, but they said the devil and his colleagues energized Him. Is that not a testimony to the human condition? Knowledge of the Bible does not suggest the correct interpretation of it.

4. The theme of the gospel is so significant it cannot be missed. Jesus is the promised king of God's people, the Jews as well as the Gentiles. He is royal to His people far beyond that of any earthly potentate. He is Lord over all creation and rules the nations. Do you know Him as your sovereign?

5. Matthew did not purpose, nor did the other gospel writers, to write biographies of the life and times of Jesus. Though they are biographical in a secondary sense, their real purpose is to explain Jesus' claim that He came from heaven to become the savior/king over the entire earth. Does He reign in your life?

6. As we study the gospel, think about the Lord as He is presented. He is the king; He is loyal and compassionate toward His people. He is the greatest of all the rulers in the world and yet His kingship is so different from that of other monarchs and potentates in our world. He came in humble circumstances, He spoke words of wisdom and mercy, His miracles affirmed that He was a unique

person, He died through cruelty and political injustice, and then rose victoriously and is enthroned forever as 'King of kings and Lord of lords'.

7. Is there insight to be gained concerning how to motivate people towards their religious duties by looking at Matthew's method? Certainly, the gospel ends with a command accompanied by a wonderful promise of God's provision, but he first explains to us the person of Jesus and His accomplishments. He spoke to us of grace and mercy before obligation and duty because the root motivation should be appreciativeness for the gift of Jesus. Do you find yourself motivated by guilt and command before explaining the reason that should motivate all of us?

The Claims of Jesus: The King (1:1–11:1)

I

The Presentation of the King
(1:1–4:11)

1. The Subject of the Gospel (1:1)

The opening sentence confronts the reader with the focus of the gospel. It begins with the phrase, 'the book of the genealogy ...'; the phrase, being variously translated, could be rendered as 'the record of the generation ....' The term translated 'generation' is also found in verse 18 where it seems to be uniformly rendered as 'birth'. If we understand the term in light of its usage in verse 18, the immediate reference would be to what follows in 1:2–2:23, the entire birth narrative from His heritage to the settlement of the family in Nazareth. If we render the phrase as 'the book of genealogy' the reference would be to what is found in 1:2-17. What is clear, in light of how the term is translated within the initial chapter, is that it does not refer to the entire gospel as a sort of subject statement. Rather, 'generation' in verse 1 encompasses the extended birth narrative of 1:18–2:23. It would seem most logical that 1:1 should be read as introducing the heritage and advent of Jesus.

It is uncommon in the gospel accounts for Jesus to be referred to as 'Jesus Christ'; more commonly 'Christ' is employed as a title (Jesus who is the Christ, the Messiah, the Anointed One) as is the term 'Lord'. Subsequently the titles, 'the Christ' and 'the Lord', became part of His name, the Lord Jesus Christ. Outside the gospels, the designation Jesus is rarely used, the exception being in the Book of Hebrews. Of the eight occurrences of the designation 'Christ' in Matthew's gospel, this (1:1) is the only instance where it is used as a name (the name given to Him is Jesus, 'you shall call his name Jesus, for he will save his people from their sins' [1:21]). In the epistles, *Christ* becomes a name as well. By the use of the double name, Matthew is seeking to show that from the beginning of the incarnation Jesus is the promised One announced by the prophets, the Messiah; prophecy reached its penultimate in Jesus, the ultimate deliverer from the consequence of human blight inherited from the failure of the first Adam.

Our Lord is further identified with two Old Testament figures to whom God made significant promises, to Abraham who received the promise of blessing and to David who received the promise of royal succession. It is interesting, as well as insightful, that Matthew mentions David before his chronological predecessor Abraham, who lived a millennium prior to David. Jesus, the ultimate fulfillment of both, emerged on the scene of human history a millennium after David (1035–970 B.C.). The title 'Son of David' is found seventeen times in Matthew's gospel, more than by any other gospel writer. What does this suggest? It is a reminder that chronological sequencing was not as important to the ancient eastern mind as it is to westerners (another indication of this is that there are gaps in the genealogy that immediately follows). Quite frequently, thematic issues are what an author traces and the presentation of the historical setting is subservient to his literary goals. With this in mind, it would seem that Matthew mentions David first because one of the primary arguments in the gospel is the sentence placed by Pilate about the cross, 'This is Jesus, the King of the Jews' (27:37b). Jesus, the son of David and the son of Abraham, is the one who is the ultimate Messiah-figure, the Christ, the deliverer of His people.

It is through the royal reign of Christ that the promises made by God to Abraham are fulfilled. God made significant assurances to Abraham that unfold in the narrative recorded in Genesis. In Genesis 12:1-3, he was blessed with the promise that he would become a great nation and would bring blessing to the world. Three chapters later he is promised an heir, a son, and innumerable descendants; the promise became a unilateral covenant. In chapter 17, God changes Abram's name to Abraham ('... your name shall be called Abraham, for I have made you the father of a multitude of nations' [17:5]). The 'seed' promised was Jesus (Gal. 3:16) who in the capacity of a son of David, the 'Lion of the Tribe of Judah, the Root of David' (Rev. 5:5), though appearing as 'a Lamb standing as though it had been slain' (Rev. 5:6), would not only bring judgment to the rebellious, but the redemption promised through Abraham. In the progressive unfolding of the details of the promise to Abraham, the final fulfillment was through a son of David. Thus, promise, royalty, and provision meet in Jesus Christ, the topic that constrained Matthew to compose the gospel that bears his name. The gospel is about the one who fulfilled all that is meant in being the descendant of Israel's greatest king-deliverer.

The gospel begins with a hint that God's intention is to bless the multitudes through Abraham and ends with the command to tell the nations, the Great Commission (28:19), the fruition of the blessing through Jesus Christ. As a son of Abraham, He is not only an Israelite; He alone is the 'true Israelite', the one who would bless the nations! Thus, Jesus is the 'true' Adam in light of the redemption that He secured based on His ethical, moral, and religious integrity; He is royalty, a true king for believing Israel, and for Gentiles as well; and He is the one who came in fulfillment of God's promise to Abraham to bless the nations. He is the Son of David, the Son of Abraham, the Second Adam! That the genealogy extends back to Abraham, not to Adam, indicates the Jewish orientation of the gospel. It is also interesting that Matthew uses Abraham, not Abram (in Genesis 12:2 Abram is granted a promise, but in Genesis 15 and 17 God declared the promise in the form of a covenant, changing his name (17:5) and extending the promise ('a great nation' [12:2], 'a multitude of nations' [17:5]).

The Coming of the King (1:2–2:23)

Three themes are discernible in this section: first, Jesus is the fulfillment of Old Testament prophetic expectations as evident by Matthew's five quotations from the Hebrew Scriptures (1:2; 2:6, 15, 18, 23); second, Matthew emphasizes the identity of

Jesus with the ascription of Messianic titles; third, the author argues that Jesus is a true king in contrast to the illegitimate Herodian dynasty (on that point many contemporaries would have agreed). The point of the genealogy is to mark out the identity of the one who defines the advance of the divine disclosure of redemptive history. A new era has dawned!

Parenthesis: the meaning of the Bible as a whole

The Bible has one central, all-encompassing story; it is the inter-trinitarian love of God expressed through creation with the divine intent of the greater display of God's glorious personhood garnering the praise of His people. This is the basic reason for the divine creation of all things. The Bible begins with the creation of a habitation, a garden, and of a couple placed within it (Gen. 1–2); it ends with a much more expansive dwelling, not with two individuals, but with myriads singing God's praises forever (Rev. 21–22). Between the two 'gardens' is a catastrophic tragedy that brought the devolution of all creation (Gen. 3). With that information, and the assurance that Genesis 3 is not the end of the drama, the Bible is the story of how God will triumph over all that is contrary to His character while exuding that which displays His beauty. God will not fail to bring His desires to fruition.

The Bible is the story of three things: creation, de-creation, and re-creation. It is a book about redemption: redemption promised and anticipated in the Old Testament Scriptures, a volume of shadows; redemption revealed in the person of the redeemer in the gospels; redemption applied in the books of the New Testament from Acts 1 through to Revelation 20; and actualized in the 'New Garden', 'the New Jerusalem,' forever (Rev. 21–22).

Thus, the Bible is structured around three eras of history; scholars commonly speak of the Old Testament era, the New Testament era, and the Kingdom; or, a period that was, the period that is, and a period that will be. Hebrews 1:1 speaks of a time long ago when God spoke 'to the fathers in the prophets' ('the times of ignorance,' Acts 17:30), and now has spoken 'in these last days' through His Son. Most Jews thought of only two ages: the former times and the latter times. They thought they were living in the former times, because they did not think the 'latter times' had come in the spiritualized kingdom inaugurated by Jesus. The 'latter times' are divided into two parts – the time between Christ's two advents and the period of His full, perfect reign after His second coming. Hebrews 9:10 refers to the closing phase of the 'last days' as the 'time of the reformation' or 'consummation of all things' (9:26). Peter, in his sermon recorded by Luke (Acts 3:19-24), says that the prophets from Samuel onwards announced 'these days', the latter days, and that Jesus will not return to earth 'until the period of the restoration of all things' (v. 21), or the latter part of the latter days. The Jews envisioned only two eras in all of history: the former days and the latter days, the promise of the Messiah and the advent of the Messiah. They saw the Messiah as reigning politically and religiously, not crucified and resurrected. They did not see the latter days in two parts, with the Messiah reigning most fully beyond the limitation of time ('when time shall be no more').

The Structure of the Bible: Three Great Eras

The Era of Promise and
    Anticipations: The era that 'WAS'

The Era of Partial Fulfillment,
    Inaugurated in Christ's
    Exaltation: The era that 'IS'

The Era of Complete
    Fulfillment, Eternity: The era that 'WILL BE'

At the very centre of God's great redemptive purpose is Calvary, the cross-sufferings of Jesus our Lord. He alone has the qualities and the willingness to restore the 'garden'. This brings us to Matthew's gospel wherein the author reveals to us why Jesus can accomplish such a feat, destroy all His adversaries, and reign victoriously forever.

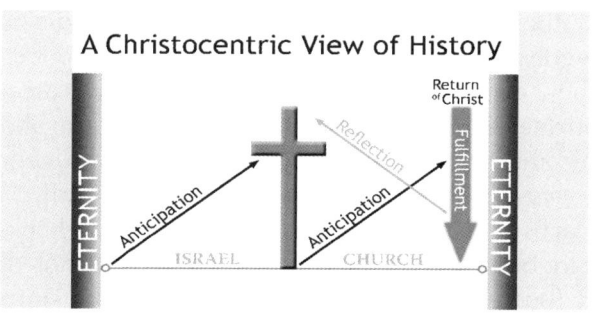

A Christocentric View of History

The Genealogy of the Promised One (1:2-17)

In this section, Matthew claims that Jesus is within the lineage of the promised One, a son of Abraham and a son of David; these verses demonstrate that this Jesus, among the many of the time, is a legitimate claimant of Messianic prediction (His words and His works will demonstrate it). It explains how this Jesus could be from Nazareth, an obscure place, yet a royal son. Further, it helps the reader to understand that, though Jesus was not Joseph's literal son, He was a son of David through his stepfather.

These verses give us the legal (father-to-son) right of Jesus as the son of Abraham, son of David, and the 'son' of Joseph to be the long-anticipated One. This is a royal genealogy, rooted in the most fundamental promise of God, the Abrahamic Covenant, and unfolded in subsequent covenants (most particularly in conformity to Matthew's theme, the Davidic Covenant [Jesus is the Davidic promise fulfilled!]) combined with the New Covenant (Jer. 31:31-34; Heb. 8:1-13) as captured by Matthew in the words, '... he shall save his people from their sins' (1:21).

A second genealogy of our Lord is found in Luke's narrative (Luke 3:23-38) where he reverses the order and argues from son to father, suggesting Jesus' physical, legal lineage to Adam. Luke, in keeping with his theme of the humanity of Jesus, does not stress His right to be king; legality is established through fathers. The differing purposes of the two genealogies account for the 'discrepancies' in the two lists. While both lists trace Jesus' lineage through Joseph, Matthew writes that Joseph was the son of Jacob who was descended from David's son Solomon (Matt. 1:16); Luke 3:23 says that Joseph was the son of Heli who was descended from Nathan, also David's son and Solomon's brother. Matthew gives us Jesus' kingly heritage from David, Luke his physical heritage through Mary, since Jesus had no earthly father. Both Joseph and Mary shared Davidic heritage.

The genealogy is fascinating from a structural point of view as Matthew explains in verse 17. The genealogy is arranged in three fourteen-name units covering time periods of about 1000 years (Abraham to David), 400 years (David to the deportation), and 600 years to Christ respectively (2000 years in all). Matthew has put artistic design into his account. This, perhaps, would account for omissions in the genealogy (as will be noted below). Further, fourteen may have numeric, symbolic significance

for his Jewish readers. It is the double of seven, the number
of completion or perfection! Here may be an anticipatory clue
to the uniqueness of Jesus' person! If fourteen has a numeric
significance indicating the perfection or sovereignty of God,
three suggesting order and neatness, and seven fullness, you
have a stunning instance of artistic power.

As to the omissions in the genealogy, they would suggest
that Matthew did not intend to present a complete ancestral-
heritage sequencing. It is evident that there were more than
fourteen generations between Abraham and David, the span
of a millennium, while the second group, encompassing about
400 years, contains the same number. The second section omits
four kings in Judah's dynastic history. Judging from the kings
who are absent from the list, one commentator has observed that
they were notoriously wicked (Ahaziah, Joash, and Amaziah
followed the dictates of Ahab in the Northern Kingdom, as
well as Jehoiakim who was deposed), postulating that as a
possible reason.[1] Also, the kingdom's fifth king is designated
as Asaph (v. 7), but he is also known as Asa, a godly king; and
the thirteenth king is designated as Amos (v. 10), but is perhaps
better known as Amon.

Matthew lists seven people in the period from the exile to the
birth of Jesus while Luke lists twenty-two. The word translated
'father of' does not require a strict father-son sequencing; it
can mean grandfather, for example. Between Perez, the twin
born of Judah (Gen. 38), and Aminadab, who is found in the
wilderness narratives (Exod. 12-40), is 400 years (vv. 3-4). Rahab
(v. 5) appears as David's great, great-grandmother. However,
between entering the land and the ascension of David to the
throne is a period of about 400 years. Boaz is David's great-
grandfather in the genealogy (vv. 5-6). It is unlikely that in
400 years there would be only four generations. It seems clear
that the genealogy is compressed and that the word 'father' is
not always to be taken literally. Thus, in the list of the Judean
kings, the construction is more artistic in design than strictly
literal. Further, Matthew may be engaging in numerics. Seven
is the number of perfection and twice that number, which is the

---

1. D. A. Carson, *Matthew* (Grand Rapids, MI: Zondervan Publishing Co.,
2007), p. 67. This argument for exclusion seems to stumble in light of the inclusion
of Manasseh and Amon, who were horribly wicked (v. 10).

numeric value of David ('dwd,' 4+6+4=14 – the Hebraic use of associating letters with numerical value), would mean that the author may be saying that Jesus, who is the Christ (the Messiah, the Anointed One), is greater than David.

Though not unusual, five women are found in the genealogy (cf. 1 Chron. 2:4; 3:5), though they are not included in the count. Tamar (v. 3, Gen. 38), wife of Er, disguised herself as a prostitute to enter an incestuous relationship with Judah, saving the nation (though not aware of it); Rahab (v. 5; Josh. 2; 6:25) was a prostitute who married an Israelite, Salmon; Ruth (v. 5; Ruth 1:1-5) was a Moabitess who married Boaz, David's great-grandfather, his father being Jesse. Bathsheba (v. 6; 2 Sam. 11:2-5) was Uriah's wife after whom David lusted; and Mary was a godly Galilean peasant girl of Davidic lineage. Here we have a clue as to the constituents of the kingdom (without social barriers, Jew and Gentile; without gender barriers, male and female; and without sin barriers, a pagan prostitute and respectable Jews). The inclusion of these women, most coming from non-Israelite origins, prepares the reader for the inclusion of Gentiles into the Messiah's realm of rule (a clue to one of Matthew's focuses in writing his gospel).

It is interesting that in each of the three divisions of our Lord's genealogy a major covenant was given: Abrahamic (Gen. 12, 15, 17), Davidic (2 Sam. 7:14), and New (Jer. 31:31-34). Matthew weaves together the three great promises to introduce the one deliverer. The Abrahamic Covenant is the seminal promise in the Bible wherein God promised to Abraham a land, a seed, and a blessing that are ultimately fulfilled in God's redemptive promises (heaven, Christ, and life eternal). The Davidic Covenant unfolds the Abrahamic Covenant to explain that the 'son of Abraham', who would fulfill the promises, would be of royalty. The New Covenant explains how the 'son of Abraham' would accomplish the redemption of His people by the shedding of blood.

It is also interesting that Abraham (v. 2), David (v. 6), and Jechoniah (v. 11) begin one of the three 'fourteens'. Each was less than ideal. Abraham sometimes displayed a lack of faith; David was adulterous with a person referred to as the 'wife of Uriah', perhaps to stress David's failure; and Jechoniah was idolatrous, and his nation collapsed. This seems to emphasize that the

Christ, a 'true' son of Abraham, would not fail morally; He would redeem the nation. Twice the phrase 'and his brothers' (vv. 2, 11) appears. This seems to highlight the corruption in the genealogy of Jesus. Joseph's brothers were like their sibling Judah, as well as Josiah's other offspring like Jechoniah (Jehoiachin).

Another way to think of the tripartite genealogy, three units of fourteen names, is an up-down-up line. From Abraham to David things get better, progressively revealing the grace of God (this would explain the inclusion of Gentile women in this section). The second section plummets from the grand era of David and Solomon to Jeconiah and the Babylonian Captivity. The northern kings were all wicked, the southern a mixture. It looks as though the promises of God are futile! The third section begins Israel's recovery from captivity, a new beginning, culminating in the advent of the deliverer, the promise to Abraham unfolded in a new stage in the progression of divine redemption.

It is important to note that verse 15 breaks the literary pattern of the genealogy. Throughout the genealogy to this point a re-occurring phrase is 'the father of'; however, in verse 16 the phraseology is not 'Joseph the father of' but 'Joseph the husband of Mary of whom was born ....' The feminine preposition ('of whom') declares that Mary was alone the human parent, not Joseph.

THE
LIFE
OF
JESUS
CHRIST

Birth	Beginning of Ministry	Death
5/4 B.C.	A.D. 29	A.D. 33

The Promised One Conceived (1:18-25)

In 1:1-17, Matthew claims that Jesus is within the lineage of the promised One, a son of Abraham and David, the promise of redemption through a king; those verses demonstrated that this Jesus, among the many of the time – Jesus being a common name – was a legitimate claimant of Messianic prediction. It explains how this Jesus could be from Nazareth, an obscure place, and yet be a royal son. Further, it helps the reader to understand that though Jesus was not Joseph's literal son, He was a son of David through his stepfather. It explains how the genealogical record of verses 1-17 connects to Jesus Christ (1:1).

It is important to note that, in this section of the birth of Jesus, the emphasis is on Joseph, not Mary, and divine guidance for him through dreams. The narrative is written from his viewpoint. Further, Matthew does not describe the birth of Jesus; rather, he describes the circumstances of his conception!

Parenthesis

There has been considerable inquiry into the question of the necessity of Jesus' birth without a father providing the twenty-three chromosomes through insemination. Several things are clear. First, Jesus was born of a virgin. Second, Jesus did not avoid the blight of Adamic unity by being virgin born, though He was the sinless One (the attempt to avoid this conundrum in some traditions of Christendom is to proport that His mother was born immaculately [i.e., without sin]). The God that created the genetic structure of Adam, composed of forty-six chromosomes, could have also supplied the twenty-three that Joseph did not in the conception of Jesus. This leads to a finite regression of Jesus' maternal heritage back to Eve and the unwarranted assumption that she did not participate in the fall state). Perhaps, a plausible explanation is found in the resurrection and the ascension. Could it be that the event of His birth and His departure are 'bookends' for us to understand that Jesus was truly unique? He came to us to be clothed in humanity, but with a difference that marks Him out from all others (John 1:14). He left this world in a manner unaccomplished by any in humanity, the great resurrection. He alone conquered death in dying to assure us of the accomplishment of His purpose in coming. Could it be that Matthew wants us to know how special Jesus is, that He stands apart from all humanity in His identity with us?

The circumstance (v. 18)
Matthew uses few words to describe what on the surface was a tremendous and catastrophic turn of events. Formally, Jewish marriages were contracted, considered legal, sometime before the husband would come to his wife's home and take her to his father's house where the marriage would be consummated (remember the parable of the Ten Virgins which describes this cultural tradition [Matt. 25:1-11]). The marriage appeared to have been destroyed by unfaithfulness.

The plan of Joseph (v. 19)
Being a compassionate man, even in those horrific circumstances, Joseph wanted to settle for a quiet divorce so as not to further embarrass Mary. Matthew places a good deal of emphasis on the character of Joseph since he was the legal, though not biological, father. He was a 'just' man (godly or righteous, meaning that he was zealous in observance of the Law, v. 19). Further, he believed the word of the angel that was communicated through the dream, dropped the notion of a private divorce, and married her. His character also appears in his demeanor towards the pregnant Mary, not fulfilling his role as a husband until after the birth of Jesus. Likely, he was older than Mary; he appears to have died before Jesus began His public ministry, certainly before the end of Jesus' public ministry (John 2:1; 19:26-27).

The intervention (vv. 20-23)
Joseph was informed by an angel that Mary had not been unfaithful to her marriage promise and there would, therefore, be no grounds for his planned marital dissolution. While Mary was certainly pregnant, the conception was a divine intervention. There are several statements in the passage that point to Jesus' miraculous conception. Mary, not Joseph, is the one 'of whom' (a feminine pronoun, v. 16) Jesus was born; Joseph was His legal father, not His physical father. 'Before they came together' (v. 18), 'knew her not until' (v. 25), and 'from the Holy Spirit' (vv. 18, 20) clearly imply our Lord's

virgin birth. Later, the couple would have several children together (Matt. 12:46).

The purpose of the pregnancy is stated. This 'son of David' (v. 20) would be given a son who will be the deliverer of His people. The 'clock' of the drama of redemption was about to take a giant forward step in its realization! The role of the child is clarified in verse 21: '... he will save his people from their sins.' He will be a spiritual redeemer first, fulfilling the Abrahamic promise; later He will fulfill the Davidic promise of ultimate rulership. He will accomplish this by what is stated in Matthew 20:28, by becoming a ransom for us. Israel's consistent failure to be God's true servant to the nations was their inability to see their role among the nations as spiritual, rather than political and material.

Matthew states that the virginal conception of Mary was a fulfillment of a prophecy of Isaiah (Isa. 7:14). Jesus is the promised One of the Old Testament Scriptures; He is the fulfillment of prophecy, the long-awaited One. The threat to the house of David, like that of Ahaz's day, will be met by an Immanuel figure.[2] The context of the quotation from Isaiah is that the wicked king Ahaz sought solace from God through the prophet; an invasion was pending. To comfort the king and assure him of God's promise of deliverance, the Lord gave a reassuring sign. Ahaz, however, feared the Syrians more than he trusted the Lord. The issue in the Isaiah passage is Ahaz's need to trust; the sign is about the surety of relief through trusting. The Lord gave Ahaz assurance by indicating that before a woman could conceive and birth a child he would be delivered (7:14-15). The Hebrew term *almah* can mean a literal virgin, being used in that way in the Hebrew Scriptures (Gen. 24:43), though the range of meaning can be broader. Matthew interprets the term narrowly. While the word *almah* is the feminine, the masculine equivalent, which means a 'young man', appears in 1 Samuel 17:56 and 20:22. The point

---

2. It is important to grasp how Matthew uses references to Old Testament passages. His method is typological; that is, Old Testament events are seen as shadows, pre-figures, or patterns that come to fulfillment in a later event. Such a way of reading the Old Testament-fulfillment-in-the-New Testament does not require for him a strict literalism; sometimes Matthew uses an Old Testament passage because of its theme.

of the word has more to do with a time element than sexual experience. Within the time frame of conception and birth, a deliverance is promised. In context, that was relief from the invasion of the Syrians. Matthew projected from the Ahaz-Syrian crisis to a greater deliverance through one born of a literal virgin who would truly be the 'Immanuel-figure,' Jesus.

The outcome (vv. 24-25)
When Joseph awoke from the dream, he took Mary into his home, but did not consummate the union until after the child was born. His obedience in taking Mary is as remarkable as her obedience (Luke 1:38). By taking a pregnant woman into his house, people would judge him morally suspect; in a society dominated by the value of honor, he would be a communal object of shame. It could have brought into question his moral integrity, or at least had the potential of stirring the gossip mill.

In conformity to the angelic instruction, Joseph named his son Jesus. It is important to note that Joseph named Mary's offspring (v. 25), making him the legal father, cementing His official status as an heir.

Applications

1. Jesus as the son of Abraham and the son of David is the fulfillment of Old Testament promises. He is the long-awaited One! The Old Testament ends with a promise that the Messiah is coming; Matthew begins by looking back to the Old Testament as completed in Jesus. Jesus is the meaning of the Hebrew Scriptures. It is Jesus who will reverse the tragedy of the human condition; He alone is gathering a people to dwell in His new garden with Him. Have you met this long-promised One?

2. Jesus is the long-awaited king! He is royalty, the One to bless the nations (1:1). The gospel begins with a declaration that Jesus is the promised deliverer; it ends with a command to declare Him to the nations (28:20). Jesus is the promised One, the true king, and the only Lord. Do you know Him as the Lord over your choices?

Does He inform your morality? Kingship and Lordship are combined in our redeemer. His right to rule over us is rooted in His redeeming mercies. He is our true king, and the only Lord.

3. Wicked people cannot prevent the plans of God from coming to fruition, nor can the sinful actions of His children. Jesus' heritage was composed of godly and ungodly. This brings to mind acts of righteousness and acts of sin. Yet, God's plan was accomplished. Evil cannot prevent the actualization of the divine will in your life or mine. Our days may appear dark, but above the clouds the sun is always shining! Appearances can be deceiving! Have you learned to trust that God has a master plan even when it cannot be seen or understood?

4. From the very beginning of the gospel, God wanted us to know how very special Jesus is, so He came to us through a unique, one-of-a-kind way. He came from heaven! He came from there to bring us there. Are you ready? Is it your desire to be with Him there? Can you think of ways that God has intervened in your life story to bring about His will and purposes that at the time seem strange, if not troubling, but now appear wonderful? Does this not teach us that to understand some things may require an understanding of its outcome?

5. Joseph is a case study of a faithful man who acted righteously in a most troubling situation (1:19). The character qualities of a person are not as often revealed in good times as in distressful ones. Can you imagine the pain of hearing that your spouse has been unfaithful? What do you reveal about yourself in hard times? What steps are you taking to ameliorate the worst of it?

6. Jesus was not only royalty; He was also the redeemer (1:21). His name and His mission matched! What great assurance of salvation we can have because of the greatness of the redeemer. He is a powerful sovereign as well as all-caring! Have you met this redeemer? Do you know the meaning of the incarnation?

7. God works through sinners to accomplish His purposes;
    He blesses apart from human merit. Think of Rahab,
    a harlot. Think of the heroic, grimy circumstances of
    the acts of Tamar, a Philistine, to preserve her heritage
    and, in doing so, help fulfill the promises of God. God
    uses whom He pleases to accomplish His will. The only
    explanation for God's willingness to use broken people
    is His mercy and grace. There is hope for all of us because
    God has a purpose that dereliction cannot prevent. The
    emphasis in the Bible is upon the faithfulness of God.
    What comfort does this bring to you?

8. An unmistakable assumption in the Holy Scriptures
    is that there is a world of reality far more magnificent,
    enduring, and beautiful than the one that surrounds
    us. The sum of what we can see and understand is
    far less than what truly exists. To access that world
    of infinite glory and peace, someone from that world
    must come to reveal it to us. Simply put, finitude cannot
    approach infinitude, but infinitude has come into the
    realm of finitude. Infinitude came in the person of the
    Lord Jesus Christ and to us in the person of the Spirit
    of God. Finitude, however great, is not infinite and the
    greater world can only be ours through the One who
    came into our world so that we could enter the greater.
    Our greatest need is not help to find our way, but rather
    to find One to be our way, and that One alone is our
    divine substitute, Jesus!

2. The Promised One Recognized (2:1-23)

The emphasis in this chapter is upon the divine protection
of the child; God determines and executes His will in spite
of the opposition of powerfully sinister people. Here the
emphasis is not on Jesus' origins, but the recognition of His
royalty (positively and negatively); the chapter highlights the
various responses to the advent of the Messiah, anticipating
the variety of reactions to Jesus throughout the centuries.
Some visited from a great distance, others knew the Hebrew
Scriptures but had no interest in searching into the matter, and
still others were simply threatened into a paranoid reaction.

The visit of the wise men (vv. 1-12)

Since Jesus seemed to be from Nazareth, a non-Davidic and obscure village in the Galilee, how did He fulfill the prediction about the Messiah's birthplace, which said that He would come from Bethlehem? There is a Bethlehem in the Galilee (Josh. 19:15), so Matthew is careful in designating the birthplace as 'Bethlehem of Judea' (v. 1).

This paragraph can be profitably divided for teaching around three responses to the birth of the Christ-child. Some recognized His uniqueness and came to worship, some were apathetic, and others were alerted and hostile. Another perspective would be to see the chapter through the lens of the three quotations Matthew cites from the Hebrew Scriptures that not only identify His birthplace, but also His office and opposition. Thus, Matthew is confirming for his readers that Jesus is the fulfillment of the prophets of old:

- Micah 5:2: the birthplace of the king
- Hosea 11:1: the calling of the king
- Jeremiah 23:15: mourning because of the king

The theme of Gentile relationship to Jesus is an important one in Matthew's gospel; it ends with a call to go to the nations. While Herod is threatened by news of the birth of a potential rival, Gentiles come from the land of exile, Babylon, to worship Him! (Perhaps another hint that the gospel was composed at a time when the role of the Gentiles in the Messianic community was unclear.)

The arrival of the wise men to Jerusalem (vv. 1-2)

It is important to note that the arrival of the wise men was 'after' the birth of the child (v. 1); the town was less crowded, and Mary and Joseph were then residing in a home (v. 11). Since Herod destroyed the children in the environs of Bethlehem who were less than two years of age, it is reasonable to say that Jesus was at least several months old, perhaps over a year (v. 16), at the time of the magi-visit.

The wise men were probably Gentile astrologers/ astronomers from Babylon or Persia (based on the length of travel-time to Jerusalem) who believed the Scriptures.

Possessing a knowledge of the Hebrew Scriptures, they may have understood the appearance of the star as a fulfillment of the Balaam oracle. Instead of cursing the nation of Israel, he blessed them by saying, 'A star shall come forth from Jacob, and a scepter shall arise from Israel' (Num. 24:17). Perhaps a clue to the celestial phenomena can be found in Stephen's epic message ('The glory of God appeared to our father Abraham and said …' [7:2]). Could that have been the visible presence of God, the shekinah glory?

It is interesting that Matthew notes the spiritual insightfulness and action of Gentiles at the inception of the narrative. Since his gospel also ends with a command to go to Gentiles with the same message (28:19-20), could this be another clue for dating the composition of the gospel prior to the destruction of Jerusalem and for recognizing that there was a growing awareness that the church is more than redeemed Judaism?

There has been considerable discussion about the star phenomena. It would seem that it was a unique, divinely-directed, luminary in the sky. It appeared as the wise men left Jerusalem and stopped over a dwelling (v. 9). It simply was not an ordinary light in the sky! Could it have been the glory of God appearing in the sky, a bright light, a divine celestial appearance, as Abraham experienced according to Stephen (Acts 7:2)? Thus, 'his star' (v. 2) may have been a stellar manifestation of God's glory (because its actions are unique [v. 9]). Compare Acts 7:2-3.

Matthew refers to Herod as 'Herod the king' (v. 1) until the magi worship Jesus; thereafter, he is referred to only as Herod. The subtle significance of the shift is the implication that with Jesus' advent Herod was no longer a king; Herod was symbolically dethroned.

The child born in obscurity, and not in the royal capital, is recognized as the 'King of the Jews'; readers of the gospel should know that the One born under suspicion of illegitimacy is, indeed, a legitimate Davidic son! Note also that the magi say, 'Where is he who has been born king?', not 'born to be king'. Jesus was king upon His coming! Additionally, they offer another designation for Jesus, 'King of the Jews,' a fourth title.

The reaction of Herod in Jerusalem (vv. 3-8)
Threats to Herod's hegemony over the region are well recorded. Herod, a client ruler under the authority of Rome, was an Idumean (his mother was Arabian) who married into the Hasmonean dynasty and ruled Judea from 37 B.C. He was more interested in his own throne than in his own soul. His response reveals that his attachment to the Jewish faith was superficial; instead of rejoicing in the advent of the promised One, he responded in fear and retribution. Herod was known for his extravagant building projects (Caesarea, the Herodian, Machaerus, Masada, the Temple) as well as his cruelty. He murdered his favorite wife Mariamne and three of his sons for plots against him. On his deathbed, he ordered the murder of the Jerusalem nobility in the Roman hippodrome (an action not consummated).

Since Herod died in 4 B.C., our Lord was most likely born in 6 or 5 B.C. (our current calendar establishing the time of Christ's advent was developed in the sixth century A.D. by Dionysius Exiguus [c. 470–c. 544], an eastern monastic). The time divisions of B.C. and A.D. have now been redesignated, reflecting a general secularization in western culture, into B.C.E. (Before the Common Era) and the C.E. (the Common Era) in much current literature.

The religious leadership of the nation was alarmed and apathetic. They knew the Scriptures intellectually without any interest in investigating such a startling claim. Formal knowledge is not heart affection. The leaders of the nation, largely Sadducees, were pro-Herodian, pro-Roman politicians who feared the loss of their position in a nation under the authority of a foreign power. The term 'chief priests' is applied to the ruling high priest, but also to living predecessors in the office. Scribes were professionals in the study of the law, so they could be referred to as lawyers; many of them were Pharisees. 'Scribe' indicates a profession; Pharisees and Sadducees were religious parties.

In quoting Micah 5:2, Matthew makes it clear that the ruler will fulfill the promises to David. The king will be a shepherd for His people (2 Sam. 5:2)!

The journey of the wise men to Bethlehem (vv. 9-11)

It is common in Christmas pageants to represent the magi as three in number since they brought three types of gifts. However, the entourage was likely greater than that; people traveled in caravans for protection, and these were men of considerable wealth suggested by the length of the journey over the Fertile Crescent and the expensive gifts. Further, the visit came after the actual birth of Jesus because the text indicates that the family were residing in a home in Bethlehem. The numerous visitors that had come to comply with the mandated registration had certainly returned to their homes (Luke 2:1-7), leaving better options for the accommodation of a new-born and a recovering mother.

The gifts brought by the magi would have financed the flight to Egypt (v. 11). They tell us much about their perception of the baby. Gold speaks of His royalty; frankincense of His priestly role; and myrrh (perfume for embalming the dead) of His death. In these gifts we see who He is, what He came to do, and the cost He paid! There is, perhaps, an allusion here to the visit of the Queen of Sheba (1 Kings 10:1-10) to a son of David, Solomon, bringing gold in great quantities and spices. Later, Matthew will tell us that a king greater than Solomon is here (12:42).

The return of the magi and the escape to Egypt (vv. 12-15)

God sovereignly took action to preserve His Son through a dream, the third in these two chapters and the second in which direction comes by an angel. Egypt was a well-ordered Roman colony outside the jurisdiction of Herod. According to Josephus, there were about a million Jews living in Egypt at that time.

The quotation from Hosea 11:1 contextually is about Israel's return from Egypt at the Exodus. Jesus' return fills this text with deeper meaning in that He is the 'true Israel' figure. Jesus is the 'new Moses' who would deliver His people! Moses delivered the nation from bondage, but he failed in the wilderness and could not lead the people into the Promised Land. The 'new Moses' will experience the 'wilderness', rise above temptation and solicitation, and lead His people to the 'Promised Land'; He will not fail! In the case of both 'Moseses', powerful monarchs failed in their plots to kill them. Both founded nations: Moses through the Exodus and Jesus through the 'New Exodus'. As Hosea tells us, God's great love for His people was at the root of the first exodus; so much more was that love revealed in the coming of Jesus from Egypt as the 'new Moses-figure'.

The way New Testament writers, such as Matthew, employ Old Testament passages is important to grasp. Sometimes the words quoted apply literally to Jesus and are fulfilled in Him. In this case, Matthew took a concept from a verse, the motif of deliverance, and applied it to Jesus. Jesus fulfilled the role of Moses in that He was called from Egypt to affect a great deliverance (Matthew's method is typological, the recognition of parallels between Old Testament themes and Jesus).

The treachery of Herod (vv. 16-18)

Since the age limit on the killings was two years, Herod must have gleaned information from the wise men and probably extended the time to be sure Jesus was included. Thus, we have a clue that Jesus was born about 6/5 B.C.; Herod died in 4 B.C. That Herod would be evil enough to exterminate the children in the environs of Bethlehem is well attested in the works of Josephus.[3] Upon marriage into the Hasmonean dynasty, he murdered all his Hasmonean rivals for the throne, including his brother-in-law, mother-in-law, and his favourite wife, Mariamne. Those were only a few examples of his murderous plotting.

There is a question concerning the quotation of Jeremiah 31:15. Rachel wept for the exiles from Ramah, the location of the deportation in the time of the Babylonian exile, which was not an event in Bethlehem. Rachel is symbolically seen as the mother of the nation; weeping is the universal language of grief. Prophecy has many fulfillments, but one ultimate fulfillment when time shall be no more. In the Jeremiah passage, Rachel is comforted with a promise of the restoration of her children; the child born of Mary fulfilled it. Matthew is saying that a new deliverer, a 'New Moses', will ensure the deliverance of His people, and bring weeping to an end. With the advent

---

3. Josephus Flavius, *The Antiquities of the Jews*. Trans. William Williston (public domain, 1737), pp. 15-17.

of Jesus, a new era dawned, and the blight of captivity and deportation was gloriously resolved. Apart from verse 15, Jeremiah 31 is a chapter of hope expressing the promise of the return of the Babylonian exiles. The point is that there is hope beyond immediate tragedy. Also, even as mothers shed tears at the Babylonian deportation and God promised a return of the captives, so there was hope for the Bethlehem mothers because the Messiah had escaped and would inaugurate His kingly reign in His ministry, most fully at the end of times.

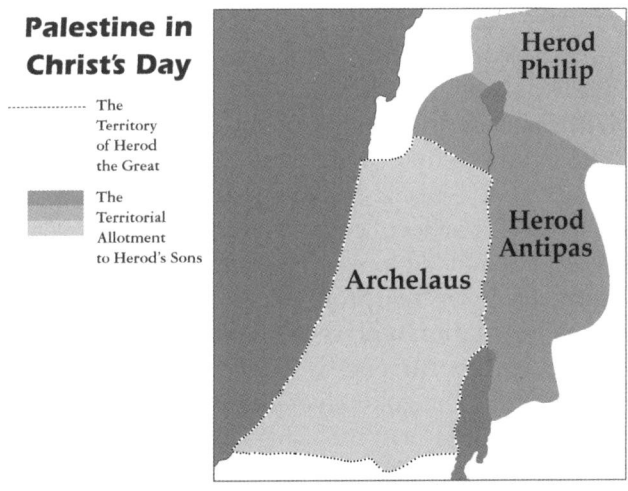

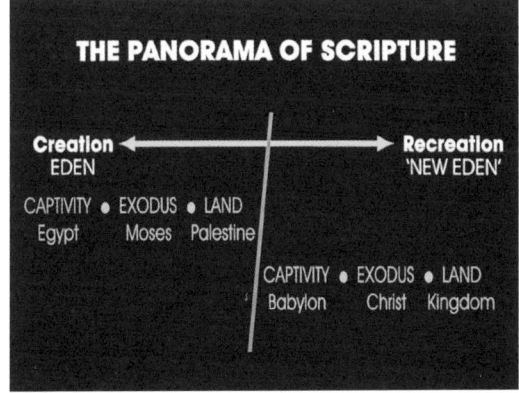

The return to Nazareth (vv. 19-23)

In a fourth dream, Joseph is informed that the child's nemesis was no longer a threat and that he should take his child and wife back to Israel. The location of return was not specified in the dream, but circumstances proved determinative.

Joseph must have expected Herod Antipas, one of Herod's sons, to rule in Judea, but Herod had changed his will. Archelaus, who was as horrible as his father, ruled in Judea until A.D. 6 when he was deposed and a series of Roman-appointed procurators replaced him, such as Pilate (A.D. 26–36), in succession for several decades.

Warned through a fifth dream, which seems to have validated his fear of Archelaus, Joseph brought his wife and son to his former village, Nazareth. Nazareth is not mentioned in the Old Testament, Josephus, the Talmud, or the Jewish Midrash. The village was a small (less than 480 people), unimportant place; Matthew seemingly is focusing on the general thrust of the Old Testament that Christ would come from obscurity and contempt (Isa. 53:3). If so, the citation contains the gist of several passages or a collective reflection; it is not a direct quotation. A clue may be found in that Matthew speaks of the source of the citing as 'the prophets' (a plural term). Also, he introduces the quotation with the words 'so that', and not with 'said', the only such occurrence in quotations in the gospel. As such, the quotation is a collective allusion to the teachings of the prophets as to the origins of Jesus. The point is that the promised One would come from obscurity.

R. T. France suggests an interesting perspective on the phrase, 'he would be called a Nazarene.'[4] To claim to be from such an obscure village as Nazareth would be to invite ridicule and disdain. 'Can anything good come out of Nazareth?' said Nathaniel (John 1:46). Perhaps Jesus was called a Nazarene because He too would experience rejection and disdain. In this line of thinking, 'Nazarene' would be used as a slang-word for a country bumpkin or backwoodsman, a slanderous connotation.

Others have argued that 'Nazarene' is not so much a geographic location (a resident of Nazareth). Though this seems a stretch, one might argue for multiple and simultaneous nuances as a description of a predicted person. There are two options in this line of thought. It may be an allusion to Isaiah 11:1

4. R. T. France, *The Gospel According to Matthew* (Grand Rapids, MI: William B. Eerdmans Publishing Co., 2007), pp. 94-95.

where the Messiah is described as 'a shoot (or branch, *netser*) who will spring from the stem of Jesse'. It could also be the English rendering of the Hebrew noun *Nazir* meaning one dedicated to God. The former would emphasize His obscure origins, the latter His moral character.

It is interesting that this chapter places Jesus, the New Israel, the 'true Joshua', on the same path as the experience of the ancient people of God. Like Abraham and Joseph, Jesus went from the land of promise into Egypt. As the 'New Moses', He was called out of Egypt to lead His people. As Matthew 1 presented an advance, a new chapter, in redemptive history by the One who would make all things new, this chapter calls forth for a new deliverer, a new Moses, having come out of Egypt.

The focus of chapter 1 is upon the legitimacy of Jesus as the fulfillment of promises made to Abraham and David; Jesus is the royal son who will bring blessings to the nations. In chapter 2, the theme appears to be opposition to Jesus' kingship. The established Herod was an illegitimate usurper to Israel's rulership who opposed the legitimate king of Israel. Opposition is a theme throughout the gospel. However, just as Jesus was sovereignly preserved as a helpless child and worshiped by foreigners, the gospel ends with His triumph and a call for His disciples to go to foreigners with a message of victory over death!

Between chapters 2 and 3 there is nearly a thirty-year gap in the narrative. Remember, the gospel writers did not purpose to present biographies; rather they wrote manuals of Christ's claims, providing evidence, and mentioning accomplishments with a view to their implications.

Applications

1. There are people you will meet who have knowledge in their heads, yet little grace in their hearts. Religionists, one would expect, should know spiritual things, but that is often not the case. Politicians are often unwise, selfish, and cruel. The rulers of this world are seldom friendly to the things of God. They, who are like Herod, are many; those like Josiah (2 Kings 22–23), few.

2. The magi are a striking example of faith, a profound contrast to others in this chapter. They came to a place they did not know and worshiped when they met Jesus. They possessed a paucity of information and great faith. It is not the strength of faith that is as important as the object of faith. How does this insight bring you comfort?

3. Jesus remains the greater divider of men and women. There are three responses to Him in this chapter: apathy with knowledge, fear with deception, and worship with gifts. Those responses are still with us when it comes to Him. Most are uninterested, others are aroused to hatred and fear, and still others recognize His worth. Where are you among these responses?

4. God protects His people from the tyrants of this world with His promises, His unexpected provisions, and His providential leadings. We are safe in the protective will of God even if the mightiest monarch should threaten us. Has this not been true in your experiences in life?

5. We should never think that an obscure life is an unimportant life. Jesus' years of public ministry were only three, yet He was on the earth some forty years. He was born in an obscure village and raised in a despised town, yet He is the greatest of the living. Small beginnings are no indication of small endings.

6. Matthew's message in this chapter is that Jesus is what Israel should have been, but failed to be. Spiritually, Jesus is the 'true Israel'. He replicated the nation's experience without the nation's failure. He is the promise to that nation, and to us, fulfilled. Do not miss who Jesus really is in the middle of so many events, stories, and reactions.

7. Matthew changed the way that the Hebrew Scriptures should be read. He believed that Jesus was the topic of the Old Testament. He sees Jesus; his contemporaries (and many today) do not. Perhaps this tells us that we should look more carefully for Jesus in the Old Testament and expect to see Him more often. Do you read the Old Testament looking for Jesus?

3. The Courier of the King (3:1-12)
The ministry of John (vv. 1-3)

The paragraph begins with the phrase, 'in those days,' suggestive of the importance and gravity of the beginning of John's ministry, the proclamation of the nearness of the kingdom in the person of the coming One.

Matthew does not provide the details of John's life and ministry that Luke does; his is simply an abbreviated account. John was one of the most famous men of his day in Palestine. He suddenly appears in the narrative as mysteriously as Elijah, and Jesus identified him as Elijah, the fulfillment of Malachi 4:5 (17:12-13) in appearance and message.

That John confined his ministry to the desert area north of the Dead Sea at the Jordan River (John 1:18; 3:23; 10:40) has significant overtones in that the Law was given in the wilderness. In the desert, Moses and David met God. The prophets frequently spoke of the wilderness as a place of new beginnings, a 'New Exodus' for the people of God. John's ministry in the wilderness would have suggested the Exodus to the Jews because the entrance into Canaan by the people of Israel was in the same general area. John is announcing a new exodus that was to culminate in Jesus, not in Canaan, not in an earthly kingdom, but in a heavenly one.

Herod Antipas ruled in the Galilee and the Transjordan areas, and John was arrested in his jurisdiction. Thus, John was baptizing on the east side of the Jordan River, and not in the jurisdiction of the procurators appointed by Rome. Further, when arrested, he most likely was incarcerated at Machaerus, a Herodian fortress in the Transjordan near the Dead Sea.

John preached a message of repentance, a change of mind and actions, because the kingdom was near in the presence of the king who was about to begin His public ministry. Matthew uses the phrase 'kingdom of heaven' while the other gospel writers use 'kingdom of God' (probably because Matthew's audience was primarily Jewish, and it would be offensive to use the word 'God' in this manner). The kingdom came with Jesus; it came more fully after His resurrection; it will come most fully at the end of this age. 'Kingdom' means a rule over a realm; that realm is the people who embrace Him. Entering the kingdom is the same as entering into life.

'Make his paths straight' is a metaphor using the image gathered from road construction to refer to repentance. In preparation for the arrival of dignitaries, roads were often improved; thus, the notion here is the coming of someone of importance. What is important is that John understood his role and connected it to prophetic fulfillment (Isa. 40:3).

The context of the quotation from the words of Isaiah is that of hope. The original referent was the return of the Babylonian exiles under Zerubbabel, yet that promised return was only a shadow of the one to come. Jesus is the foreshadowed One; but the return has not been fully realized, because all of God's people have not been gathered to Him. The fullest manifestation will be when Jesus reigns as king forever! Thus, the announcement of the return of the Babylonian captives was not the fullest meaning in the passage; it looks even beyond Jesus' first coming to His second, the final consummation and redemption of the 'captives'. A partial fulfillment of the passage was in the first coming of the king! In the Isaiah passage, the Coming One is God, so here is a significant claim by Matthew of the identity of Jesus.

The manner of John (v. 4)

John's dress suggests a poor man, accustomed to wilderness living, and one like the prophets. Like Elijah (2 Kings 1:8), John's dress was spartan and the comparison should not be missed. Both wore fabric of camel's hair that was girded by a leather belt. 'Elijah' had come in the personage of John!

His garb was as austere as his diet (honey and locusts), and he condemned physical and spiritual softness. Locust is the only insect that was kosher, though the particular variety cannot be identified. John was an ascetic, not a vegetarian. Because the biblical variety of locust is unknown, coupled with the fear of violating kosher, some claim that the reference to locust is to the green pods of the locust or carob tree, a form of chocolate.

The Meaning of Kingdom

It means a realm or rule

In Eternity Past: the realm over which God ruled: universal

In Genesis 1–2: the realm over which God ruled: all of creation

In Genesis 3: the realm was blighted by the intrusion of disobedience and judgment, and is not universal

In Genesis 4 to the incarnation of Christ: the realm embryonic and anticipated

In the incarnation: the ruler manifest, the realm partial

From Acts 2 to the coming of Christ: the realm of the rule expanding until Christ returns the Kingdom, the realm of the ruler's rule, universal once again

Not two in a garden of God's creation, but myriads of blood-bought people with God in their midst, the new heavens and a new earth (Rev. 21–22)

The popularity of John (vv. 5-6)

John appears to have been very popular; his following, according to Josephus, was so large that Herod Antipas thought it was the beginning of a popular uprising.[5] His was a ministry of preaching (more accurately, the term means 'to herald' or 'to announce'), with a view to repentance, a change of mind about the coming king evidenced by a change of conduct, signified by baptism. John is cast in the role of announcing something about to happen! Josephus makes it clear that it was understood that John's baptism was not a means of forgiveness, but a personal preparation for the coming of another.[6] This was not Jewish proselyte baptism, the initiation of non-Jews into Israel's faith, because the recipients were Jews. Jews practiced self-baptism; this

---

5. Josephus Flavius, *The History of the Jews*, 18.5.2. 'Now when [many] others came in crowds about him, for they were very greatly moved [or pleased] by hearing his words, Herod, who feared lest the great influence John had over the people might put it into his power and inclination to raise a rebellion, (for they seemed ready to do anything he should advise) thought it best, by putting him to death, to prevent any mischief he might cause, and not bring himself into difficulties, by sparing a man who might make him repent of it when it would be too late.'

6. ibid. 'Now some of the Jews thought that the destruction of Herod's army came from God, and that very justly, as a punishment of what he did against John, that was called the Baptist: for Herod slew him, who was a good man, and commanded the Jews to exercise virtue, both as to righteousness towards one another, and piety towards God, and so to come to baptism; for that the washing [with water] would be acceptable to him, if they made use of it, not in order to the putting away [or the remission] of some sins [only], but for the purification of the body; supposing still that the soul was thoroughly purified beforehand by righteousness.'

baptism was administered by the forerunner. The implication of John's message is the inadequacy of contemporary Judaism.

The condemnation by John (vv. 7-10)

In evaluating them, John singles out the Pharisees and Sadducees as a single entity (note 'the', a single article, also in 16:1, 6, 11, 12). The Sadducees were a high priestly religious sect that supposedly traced their ancestral origins to Zadok, the man appointed by David to the office of a priest (1 Kings 1:8; 2:35). They accepted only the Hebrew Scriptures, not the oral traditions developed by the perfectionistic and religiously zealous Pharisees. They tended to be aristocratic and pro-Roman in sympathies. The Pharisees were a religious sect within Judaism, and were the party most popular among the Jews; many were also scribes (sometimes designated as 'lawyers' since civil law deeply reflected religious law), interpreters of the Scriptures.

John's message is characterized by its hostility to the religious leadership of his day ('You brood of vipers!'), a group defined as poisonous in nature. Jesus uses the same terms to excoriate the leadership of the nation (12:34). This is a grave insult; vipers killed their own mothers! These will kill their own as well. This called for an investigation by the religious leadership, the Pharisees and Sadducees, two groups normally hostile to each other, here united by a common threat.

His message to them was that it is true fruit that shows the genuine, and not status or speech (v. 8). The genuineness of religious faith is not found merely in words or in one's status or knowledge or in one's popular acceptance (a message throughout the Holy Scriptures); the invisible is evidenced by the visible: as the 'root', so the fruit. The quest for behavior without an inner change of affections is the manifestation of falsehood. Jesus expounds on John's statement in His diatribe against 'the scribes and the Pharisees' in chapter 23.

Moreover, heritage does not indicate ownership (v. 9). John makes it clear that the dawning kingdom cannot be entered through ancestral connection. With rhetorical and literary flair, he argues that stones have a better chance of entering the kingdom than his audience. God is capable of raising up true children from the most unlikely of origins. The coming kingdom is entered by repentance, not heritage! This new age brings two things: blessing and judgment (vv. 8-10), the axe and the tree metaphor (an axe is normally not used to cut the root of a tree, but the trunk near ground level. The point of the metaphor is the certainty of judgment).

In stressing his verdict, John draws a simile from a fruit tree to establish his point (v. 10). As a fruitless tree faces judgment, so do those who refuse to change their evaluation of the coming One; figuratively speaking, they are like a fruitless tree!

The announcement of John (vv. 11-12)
By accepting that a greater One was coming, John understood his relationship to the coming One; John, in comparison to him, is the lowest of servants. The coming One would bring about a greater accomplishment and a greater separation than John could. His 'baptism by the Spirit' would indicate a new identity or alliance; those who repented, changed their minds about the coming One, evidenced by altered priorities, would experience, not judgment, but a 'fire' that truly purifies the inner being! 'Baptism' and 'fire' are closely related in meaning since one preposition connects them ('with'); both seem to hint at cleansing from the corruption of unbelief in preparation for the coming One.

Having employed the metaphors of fleeing snakes from a fire, trees cut down and burned, and a baptism in the Holy Spirit and fire, John adds a final one suggesting a sense of immediacy: the threshing floor (also involving fire or judgment). As threshing removes the grain from the chaff, so will the coming of Jesus; He will both gather (grain) and judge (burn chaff). Clearly, the judgment is upon the religious leadership and those who follow them in antithesis to the coming One. John, thus, saw the Messiah's ministry to be twofold: deliverance for those embracing His person and claims, and judgment for those who would not.

'Unquenchable fire' suggests interminable duration, not annihilation after some brief time of suffering, as some have argued. This also suggests eternal, conscious existence in death.

The Divine Approval of the King: His Identity with the Nation (3:13-17)

The initial appearance of Jesus in Matthew's narrative as an adult is in the context of John's ministry as a Galilean (v. 13). What is crucial to Matthew in the event is not the baptism but what follows, the divine affirmation of the person and message of Jesus. It seems that Matthew's point is that from the beginning of Jesus' ministry He possessed the approval of God; He was God's chosen instrument.

The coming of the King (v. 13)

The point of the baptism is to connect the ministries of John and Jesus; one will take over from the other, carrying it to another stage. The key phrase in this paragraph is 'to fulfill all righteousness' (the term meaning to fill with meaning or to complete [v. 15]). It appears that 'fulfill' also means the consummation of prophecy. By 'righteousness', Matthew implies several things: first, Christ identified with the nation in their need (He is 'true Israel'). Second, He defined in His person the meaning of righteousness so that in His baptism the ideal purpose of baptism by John was consummated (as heaven subsequently testifies). In His being baptized, the Messiah was being presented to the nation; He submitted to all the ordinances of God, and this is why He submitted to John's baptism (in a sense He was preparing for His ministry although having no need for repentance). This ritual was part of the inauguration of His public ministry. Third, He became one with the nation as the nation's redeemer ('numbered with the transgressors,' as in Isaiah 53:12).

John does not specifically refer to Jesus as the promised One, only one greater than himself (v. 11). Further, we are not told how John perceived his own inferior status. This may account for the inquiry of John about Jesus' identity later (11:3).

The hesitancy of John removed (vv. 14-15)

It is interesting that while John was not hesitant to administer the symbol of repentance in view of the spiritual void in the hearts of the nation's religious leaders (vv. 7-8), a view later shared by Jesus, here he is hesitant to baptize Jesus because of his own unworthiness and Jesus' superiority.

Jesus indicates to John that there is a purpose in His submission to baptism by John; it is to 'fulfill all righteousness', meaning that it was a fulfillment of God's will. By being baptized, Jesus affirmed His redemptive role through identifying with the people. He is one of them ('now'), but will soon be declared to be much more (vv. 16-17). He is the 'true Israel' manifest in every way; He is what the nation was meant to be, 'a light to the Gentiles,' as well as to the Jews. Therefore Jesus persuaded John to baptize Him.

The announcement and the descent (vv. 16-17)
The descent of the Spirit recalls the prophecies of Isaiah that God's Spirit would rest upon God's servant (Isa. 11:2; 42:1; 61:1). The Spirit's action would remind a Jewish reader of the Genesis account of creation (Gen. 1:2), the hovering Spirit assuming a bird-like action. A new step in the redemptive program of God is unfolding!

Rabbis expected a great outpouring of the Spirit at the beginning of the Messianic age. This is announced here and in Isaiah 61:1-2 (Jesus quoted from this passage in the synagogue in Nazareth, applying it to Himself [Luke 4:14-20]). As the dove announced safety from the Noahic judgment, so the dove-figure announced the One who will offer salvation from judgment. Such an allusion would suggest a new beginning.

Further, the dove is used in the Old Testament as a symbol of the nation of Israel (Hosea 7:11), suggestive of humility and servanthood. Israel failed in that capacity, but Jesus would not. He is all that the nation should have been.

The emphasis in this paragraph is not on the phenomena surrounding the Father's declaration, but what Jesus received. He received the approbation of His heavenly Father (v. 17). It is interesting that the Father was pleased with Him before He did any of His miracles or spoke any of His discourses in public. He had remained essentially silent for over thirty years! The voice from heaven announced the end of divine silence; God had sent His Son to speak! The kingdom is at hand.

'This is my Son' reflects Genesis 22:2 ('Your son, your only son'), Psalm 2:7, and Isaiah 42:1. The connection tells us that from the very beginning of His ministry Jesus was the suffering servant, that He is God, and that He is the representative of His people.

Applications

1. John the Baptist spoke openly and plainly about the coming One. The One has come in the person of God's Son. The era of anticipation that began with the devastations of Genesis 3 has ended and the era of fulfillment has dawned. Have you thought of the privilege of living on this side of the incarnation? Are you thrilled to let people know that the promised One has come?

2. We need people who sense the authority of God for what they say and do, a rootedness that comes from spending time in the Word of God, people with moral fortitude, and spiritual convictions, not popularity promoters. Perhaps, the quest to be liked and well received by people is not a virtue, particularly when it comes at the cost of clarity when the destiny of people is at stake. Do you find yourself a people pleaser when it comes to explaining the gospel?

3. If God takes delight in His Son, should not you and me? Is Jesus the joy of your life? Is meditation upon Him a great source of comfort to you? A key to a vital spiritual life is what we mentally find to be our preoccupations. Can there be a more wonderful thing to consciously think upon than God's Son?

4. Heaven is not gained by physical descent (v. 9); that was the error, among others, of first-century Judaism, and of many in our day. God does not have grandchildren, only children. Another's faith does not avail for those who have no faith. God can make 'stones' – people with stony, hard hearts – His own children. The famous, the well-heeled, the well-placed, are not privileged in God's mind. Does that not give you hope?

5. Heaven is not gained by works, yet no one is saved without them (v. 10). Works are the evidence of and not

the cause of the presence of divine grace in one's life. Works follow salvation; they do not cause it. If works are lacking, grace may be lacking as well. Profession of faith without characteristics of faith suggests lack of faith. Do you know people who sadly are like this?

6. Jesus pleased God before He began His ministry. This tells us that His character came before the external evidence of its excellence. The criterion for the approbation of another by God is conformity to His character; Jesus being very God was pleasing to God before He began His ministry. Not only is the title 'Son of God' a statement of the equality of Father and Son, the Father's declaration is as well. Do you take pleasure in Jesus as the Father does? Do you find great delight in Him?

7. God uses hard people to reach hard-hearted people. The emphasis in our culture upon inoffensiveness, gentility, and tolerance may be misplaced; gentleness may have its place, but it does not have every place. There is a time to be blunt. It requires skill to know when an approach is appropriate. John would be out of step with the postmodern culture of today. Perhaps we need a few like John in our churches. Truthfulness is powerful when combined with charity and care.

8. The message of impending judgment is part of the gospel message. To preach grace without justice trivializes grace. To preach justice without grace is to offer no hope. Jesus came to be a minister of life and death, life to those who believe and judgment to the unresponsive. He was serious in His teachings on both facets of His ministry. It is clear from our passage that Jesus came to announce the end of first-century Judaism, which was not the Judaism of the Old Testament Scriptures; it was a twisted, blind perversion.

4. The Moral Verification of the King (4:1-11)

The function of the temptation narrative is to demonstrate the moral qualification of Jesus as the promised One (it seems that chapters 1 to 4 of Matthew deal with the issue of Jesus' credentials). The key phrases in the passage are 'if you are the Son of God' (vv. 3, 6) and 'if you will fall down and worship me' (v. 9). These phrases link the baptismal narrative (3:17) with this one. Jesus is, indeed, the 'Son of God,' proven by divine decree and, here, by personal character!

If the baptismal site was near the northern end of the Dead Sea, it is reasonable that the 'wilderness' (v. 1) is a reference to the Judean area west of Jericho near the Wadi Kelt.

The approbation of God in Jesus' baptism led to His temptations; Satan tried to deflect Him from God's plan of glorification through suffering. Glory through suffering was God's will (v. 1). The same Spirit that attested His Sonship now leads Him into the desert to be tempted by the devil. The same word is translated 'tempt' and 'test'. Satan (the devil, the tempter) tempts or solicits to evil; God tests to reveal character. The motive for the former is destructive, while of the latter it is positive.

The context (vv. 1-2)

The reference to forty days and nights of fasting would remind Jews of the forty years in the wilderness, as do the quotations from Deuteronomy used by Jesus (Deut. 6:13, 16; 8:3). Israel failed morally and wandered aimlessly in the wilderness until a generation perished. Christ, in contrast, accomplished God's will. Christ is all that Israel was intended to be. He is again shown as identifying with His people, though superior to them. Jesus is the 'true Israel' figure who will lead the 'New Exodus'. He succeeded in the wilderness while Israel failed! Also, before the giving of the law in Sinai, Moses fasted for forty days (Exod. 34:28). The parallels are unmistakable.

The temptations were in three areas: desires of the flesh, pride of life, and lust of the eyes (see 1 John 2:16). Christ was tested in the realms of His attitude towards resources, reputation, and responsibility. Our Lord's answers seem to be as follows: trust God to provide in His time, trust God to protect you but do not be foolish, and trust God for spiritual needs.

Jesus rejects the temptations in each of the three instances by quoting Scripture, and in each case the quotations were out of the context of Israel's failure in the wilderness experience.

In each temptation Satan acknowledges that Jesus is the Son of God (the word 'if,' in some translations, should be rendered 'since' because it is grammatically a first-class condition, a statement of fact). The first temptation is answered by trust in God for His physical needs; the second, rooted in the first, is about assurance of God's protective mercies; and the third concerns His mission.

Parenthesis

Scholars have pondered the question of the legitimacy of the temptations since Jesus was without sin, being the Son of God (deity). If Jesus was tempted in all points like us ('... one who in every respect has been tempted as we are, yet without sin' [Heb. 4:15]), how can He be our great model for resistance to inappropriate solicitations? It would seem that a parallel of culpability and potentiality exists between Jesus' temptations and ours; otherwise, how could He be an example of non-necessity and compassionate identity with our struggles. Simply put, we fail; He did not. He is our model for resisting evil attitudes and consequent moral action. Jesus had no sin nature because He is the 'true second Adam' (Rom. 5:12-21). The blighted nature is an effect of Adam's fall in which Christ did not participate. Corruption of nature came after Adam's decision to distrust God and His goodness, which implies that the ability to sin was a potential for Adam before he actually did. Ability to do something is different from the actuation of the ability. Sinful actions are not in question for us; it is a clearly demonstrable fact. Jesus did not have a sinful capacity, but He did have capacity of choice without the negative consequence. He chose not to sin, so demonstrating that He alone is the 'true second Adam', being by His untainted holiness suitable to be our valid and acceptable substitute!

The first area of temptation: priorities and trust (vv. 3-4).

Here the temptation was to use His Sonship in a way inconsistent with His God-ordained mission. He was appointed to suffer, not indulge. Israel demanded bread in the wilderness and died there; Jesus denied Himself bread and lives forever! He quoted Deuteronomy 8:3. True bread is obedience to God's Word. Obedience to God's will takes precedence over immediate gratification! Jesus understood that hunger was God's will for

Him at that time and so He responded in obedience. Just as our Lord at the inception of His ministry embraced obedience to the will of God, preferring the pathway of trust, so at the very end, in the Garden of Gethsemane, He submitted to the will of God (Matt. 26:39, 42, 44). From the beginning to the cross our Lord demonstrated that there is only one way to triumph: through obedience!

It is interesting that Jesus' reply provides us with His view of the Hebrew Scriptures. They are the words of God; God is the author of them ('it is written'). As such, the words are absolutely reliable.

The second area of temptation: privileges and trust (vv. 5-6).
Again, the temptation was to use His Sonship in an inconsistent way. It was a test of His reliance on God's protection. Position did not lead to license, but to obedience. Once again Jesus quotes Scripture (Deut. 6:16). The event behind Jesus' comment is Exodus 17:1-7, the failure of Israel at Massah. Israel acted in unbelief there, Jesus in faith here.

It is interesting that in the second confrontation, unlike the first, Satan quotes Scripture to validate his claim; actually he misquoted it leaving out the phrase 'to guard you in all your ways' (Ps. 91:11b). Jesus did not doubt the truth of Psalm 91:11-12, the text the devil quoted, but his use of it. A text out of context is a pretext!

The devil quoted the verses correctly but misapplied them to support his plot. Jesus responded by quoting Deuteronomy 6:16. Scripture forbids putting God to the test; it is a lack of faith. The reference to testing alludes to Israel's failure in the wilderness (Exod. 17:1-7). Jesus, 'the true Israel', did not fail in His wilderness temptations. God found out what was in the nation's heart by the temptations – it was a rebellious heart. Jesus' heart was true to God; He was all Israel failed to be!

The third area of temptation: allegiance and trust (vv. 8-10).
Here the temptation was to receive authority and avoid the cross by worshiping God's adversary. Jesus is offered the kingdoms of the world, universal kingship, but apart from the will of God, glory without suffering. All three

temptations had to do with avoiding the cross and gaining glory without obedience. Jesus again quotes Scripture to rebuff Satan (Deut. 6:13).

A theme throughout the gospel is that Jesus obeyed while the nation consistently failed. Jesus is 'the true Israel'; He duplicated the experience of the nation, but He never failed. As Israel proved disobedient in the wilderness for forty years of testing (the source of the quotations of Jesus reveal that the wilderness experiences are His reference point), the 'true Israel' demonstrated moral integrity for forty days. Israel failed and a generation perished; Jesus triumphed, and a new generation will live forever!

> Both the nation and Jesus had a miraculous beginning.
> Both were taken to and brought out of Egypt.
> Both passed through water.
> Both were tested in the wilderness.

Now completely triumphant and the devil defeated (v. 10), angels come to serve the king. Angels fulfill the protective role the devil spoke of in the second temptation, in citing Psalm 91:11. Later Jesus will claim that He has legions of angels at His disposal (26:53).

Applications

1. The first message Jesus preached was the greatest need of mankind, the necessity of repentance. It is a universal message. It is how one comes to know the truths of God and the wonder of Jesus (we must abandon trust in ourselves) and how we are to live before Him daily. The key to knowing and walking with God is the renunciation of self. Have you learned that perfection belongs alone to God and repentance for brokenness to us?

2. Life is more than physical pleasures. While pleasures have a legitimate place in our daily experience, pleasures alone do not bring to us ultimate satisfaction unless they are connected with the service of others. Doing the will of God is fulfilling. Jesus found His ultimate

delight in obedience to His Father's will. Do you? Are you spending your days pursuing temporal pleasures?

3. Jesus realized that the will of God involved suffering. The road to glory is also the road of pain and sacrifice. There is no crown without it. He embraced the truth that pleasure deferred is the path to pleasures enjoyed. The Christian life involves pain, and it cannot be avoided. If you are seeking the crown of eternal life while avoiding the pains of genuine discipleship, you will in the least be a very disappointing disciple of the great king.

4. The devil knows who Jesus is, but he has no heart affection for Him. Knowledge without heartfelt attachment is not real knowledge. The heart and the head must act together. Do you know people who possess the verbage, but not the lifestyle? By their fruit you shall know them, argued Jesus, not by their talk. Such are children of the devil, perhaps.

2

The Proclamation of the King
(4:12–7:29)

This section details the beginning of the public ministry of Jesus, presenting His claims in the form of His words (chs. 5–7), the celebrated sermon on the mount, the first discourse in the book, followed by a series of nine miracles (chs. 8–9), mostly public in nature, though not exclusively. Jesus claims to possess the authority promised in the person of the Messiah and affirms the validity of His verbal claims by a demonstration of the works of the promised One – miracle healings and other demonstrations of authority over disease and nature. The emphasis in Matthew is not so much on the miracles themselves – these are stated without unnecessary elaboration – but on the implication of them. Here we have the claim that the promised One is Jesus accompanied by reaction from the religious leadership either in Galilee or Jerusalem. Interspersed throughout the section are instructions for the disciples in preparation for their sending in chapter 10 and beyond.

The Beginning of the Ministry of the King (4:12-17)
The context is given in verses 12 and 13. In verse 12, there is a clue for change. The incarceration of John, the function of the forerunner having been completed, was the signal for our Lord's commencement of public ministry that was inaugurated with His removal from Nazareth to Capernaum.

Jesus appeared on the scene in the context of the popular ministry of John the Baptizer; it marked the fulfillment of John's work as well as the prophecy of Isaiah 9:2 ('the people dwelling in darkness have seen a great light').

The significance of the relocation is seen in verses 14-16. Again, Matthew sees this as a fulfillment of prophecy found in Isaiah 9 (note the reference to 'Galilee of the Gentiles' in verse 15). Jesus began His ministry in a place despised by Judean Jews particularly. After the Assyrian destruction and deportation, the Israelite population was greatly reduced. Tragedy, with perspective, often ends in the realization of grace! This provides a hint that the Messiah's ministry would reach to the nations, to the world of the Gentiles.

The identification of Zebulun and Naphtali as 'beyond the Jordan' and 'on way to the sea (the Mediterranean)' seems odd geographically. The referent is to the major highway from the East (the Via Maris) and the perspective is from the East. Remember that the citation concerns the invasion of the Assyrians under Tiglath-pileser (2 Kings 15:29 and Isa. 9).

Matthew inserts an editorial comment that advances the narrative. The phrase, 'from that time,' is repeated in 16:21, marking out what some commentators suggest are the two major sections of the book. Here in 4:17, Jesus began His public ministry in the Galilee and in 16:21 He commenced His departure from Galilee for Matthew's only recorded visit to Jerusalem. Afterwards, He returned to the Galilee following the resurrection to meet the disciples.

The Call of the King's Disciples (4:18-22)

Matthew records the calling of five of Jesus' twelve disciples. There are four in this passage and one, Matthew, in chapter 9, though the full list occurs in chapter 10. In Judaism, disciples chose their rabbi; Christ chose His followers. It is interesting that from this point, Jesus does not operate alone until Gethsemane (26:56) when His disciples abandoned Him briefly.

Simon (who becomes Peter in 16:18), Andrew, James, and John were fishermen, two sets of brothers and, perhaps, related through marriage. Andrew was a follower of John the Baptist, though he left him to follow Jesus (John 1:40); he brought Peter to Jesus. James and John likely heard of Jesus through Andrew and Peter. Peter and Andrew probably lived in Capernaum, though they were originally from Bethsaida (the name means 'fish town' or 'the town of the fishermen' (John 1:44). Salome, the mother of James and John, is believed by some to have been the sister of the mother of Jesus. If so, Jesus was cousins with James and John. Andrew is a Greek name reflective of the mixed cultures in the Galilee. Of the four, three will form the most intimate circle of disciples (Peter, James, and John. See 17:1; 26:37). Is this a clue that discipleship is a small-group endeavor?

The reference to 'fishers of men' is probably an allusion to Jeremiah 16:16. There God sent 'fishermen' to gather His people from the exile. Jesus will use the disciples to deliver His people from a greater exile: the exile of divine, judicial condemnation.

The Confirmation of the King (4:23-25)

The Galilee comprised over 200 villages in Jesus' day, some quite large. The larger of them appear to have been Bethsaida, Capernaum, and Chorazim (ironically the three cities that Jesus cursed in 11:20-24).

Syria, to the north and east of the Galilee, was part of a large Roman province that included Palestine (Luke 2:2). Syria Palestina, the Roman designation for the area, was under the authority of the legate of Syria; Herod Antipas and Herod Philip ruled under their authority as rulers of a fourth of the territory, or a tetrarchy.

Decapolis means 'ten cities'. Nine of them were in the area ruled by Herod Philip, east and north of the Sea of Galilee. Only one was in the region governed by Herod Antipas, Scythopolis (today it is called Bethshean), south of the Sea of Galilee and west of the Jordan River. All were Gentile cities.

Jesus went about the Galilee healing people, caring for their physical and, ultimately, their spiritual needs. This is a manifestation of the sheer, unmerited mercies and grace of God. His justice demands judgment, but His grace brings mercy. Justice, mercy, and grace meet in the Lord Jesus. He became the object of divine justice for us on His cross and suffered so that God, the just God, could rightly and justly remain so, yet extend mercy and grace to us.

The maladies listed in verse 24 are subjects of His miracles subsequently. What is interesting is that demoniac possession is distinguished from epilepsy, giving evidence that in the first century people were acute enough in their observational skills to distinguish the two. While they may have the same outward characteristics at times (such as seizures), the origin is distinguished, the physical from the supernatural.

The Message of the King (5:1–7:29)

The sermon is the first of five lengthy discourses in Matthew, set apart by an introductory summary of Jesus' ministry (4:23-25). The sermon has several purposes. First, in it, Jesus explains the nature of the righteousness required for entrance into His kingdom, while, at the same time, it is a description of those already in His kingdom (5:20). Second, it is a polemic against the righteousness of the nation's religious leadership. Jesus makes it clear that Pharisaic piety will never qualify for entrance; in this case, the sermon is a confrontation of claims with the nation's respected and trusted religious leaders (5:20). Third, the sermon is a teaching tool designed to further the process of discipleship ('you are the salt of the earth' [5:13]). Commentators appear to prioritize one or another of these themes, but it seems that they are all operative. Jesus had the ability to address a variety of needs and audiences simultaneously.

The issue addressed in this discourse is life in the new community of God inaugurated in the coming and the promises of the Messianic figure. It is about the entrance requirements for His kingdom and conduct in it. Clearly, Pharisaic interpretation of the kingdom is erroneous in Jesus' view. He carefully distinguishes what Moses taught from that of the religious leadership of His day. Moses was right; they were wrong!

The setting of the sermon (5:1-2)

While Jesus gathered His disciples about Him (5:1), the crowds heard Him also (7:28). Perhaps Matthew is using the word 'disciple' simply for an interested learner, as is often the case in the gospels (John 6:66), or, here, maybe His disciples gathered nearest to Him while others listened from a distance. By assuming the posture of sitting, Jesus claimed to be a rabbinic teacher.

No specific mountain is envisioned here; the article 'the' does not suggest a well-known place. The NIV renders the phrase 'on a mountainside'. See 14:23; 15:29. It may simply mean the 'hills' or 'the mountain region'. Ascending a mountain would remind the people of Moses (Exod. 19:3; 24:8; 34:1-2); however, Moses ascended to receive revelation in stone; Jesus ascended to give revelation, writing it on our hearts. Jesus reveals truth as the 'new Moses' for His new people. Moses gave the ancient people the law; Jesus filled it with meaning!

What follows is a well-structured sermon containing an introduction, a three-point argument, and a conclusion (that is, an invitation). It has a central theme: to enter the kingdom of which Jesus speaks you must have righteousness greater than that of the Pharisees (5:20).

The Introduction (5:3-16)

The sermon begins with eight descriptions of those already in the kingdom. The first and last are in the present tense, the others are in the future tense. The eighth beatitude is repeated and personalized ('you'). The first six describe an inward state while the seventh and eighth a consequence of the state. Each beatitude has two parts: a condition that is blessed of God and a consequence or reason for the blessing from a human perspective.

Jesus describes those who are already in His kingdom (blessed, happy, favored, fortunate). Another phrase that may capture the concept of happy (the term indicating not so much an outward state of exuberance as an inward contentedness before God) is 'divine approval rests upon'. To hear these words would have been shocking. Another way to translate the words is as 'those are to be congratulated' because of God's mercy toward them in granting a repentant heart.

It seems that the initial four beatitudes emphasize dependence on God (poor, mourn, meek, and hunger) or personal, spiritual, inward qualities. Beatitudes 5 to 7 seem to emphasize outward consequences of the initial four (merciful, pure, peacemakers). The final beatitudes stress the consequences of a person's reception of the kingdom (i.e., persecution).

The character of those already in the King's kingdom (vv. 1-12)
The 'poor' (v. 3). 'Poor' suggests a sense of impoverishment; it is a condition that engenders humility rooted in the perception of helplessness. It is the recognition of spiritual bankruptcy

and utter dependency. It can be translated, 'How fortunate are those who know their need of God.' The 'fortunate' state rests in the fact that they are God's children.

The 'mourning' (v. 4)
'Mourn' suggests contriteness over personal sin and shortcomings. These initial beatitudes allude to the Messianic blessings of Isaiah 61:1-3. The reason for such a good thing as sorrow is that those who understand their circumstance possess the promise of divine comfort (I take mourning to be caused by a recognition of their spiritual state). The future tense of the verb after 'for' may indicate that comfort will finally come in the fullest manifestation of kingdom rule.

The 'meek' (v. 5)
'Meek' suggests gentleness and the self-control it engenders. 'Inherit' often means 'enter', as in entrance into the 'promised land'. Those who think highly of themselves, the religiously assertive, do not inhabit God's kingdom. Non-aggressiveness was respected neither in the Roman world nor presently in ours. However, the 'meek', and not the bullies, will inherit the earth, the divine kingdom.

The 'hungry' (v. 6)
'Hunger and thirst' suggest an inward desire, in this case for personal righteousness. The concept of personal righteousness in Matthew implies right moral conduct, living the way God expects of His children.

The 'merciful' (v.7)
'Merciful' embraces forgiveness for the guilty, as well as compassion for the needy. It means a generous attitude towards others, an unwillingness to take offense or gloat over the misdeeds of others.

The 'pure' (v. 8)
'Pure in heart' suggests a single-minded devotion to the things of God and moral purity. The issue is not outward appearances, but inward attitudes and motivation. Jesus' point becomes even more poignant when stated in the negative: 'Woe to the impure of heart, for they will never enter God's presence.'

The 'peacemakers' (v. 9)

'Peacemakers' suggests a spirit of reconciliation, the opposite of divisiveness, bitterness, and strife. Those who possess this characteristic possess the character of God and are thus 'sons of God'.

It has been estimated that in mankind's 4000 years of recorded history, there have been less than 300 years of peace. Between 1481 and World War II, Great Britain had endured seventy-eight military conflicts, France seventy-one, Spain sixty-four, Austria fifty-two, and Germany twenty-three.[1] The world has seen peacekeepers (remember Neville Chamberlain, prime minister of Great Britain in the 1930s), but there is only one real peacemaker!

'The persecuted' (vv. 10-12)

'The persecuted' is the only beatitude that is repeated, amplified, and personalized ('you'). The reward of the persecuted is the same as that of the 'poor'. The term, 'persecute', involves both physical and economic abuse. Notice that the persecution does not arise from mere human misdeeds, but 'because of me'. The blessing is not in the pain, but in the outcome.

Jesus notes three positive consequences of suffering for His sake: suffering for the Lord provides assurance that we are among the people of God; suffering causes us to focus on God with rejoicing that we are the people of God; and suffering brings solace in the fact that those who came before them received similar treatment. It is not unusual for kingdom-bound people. Criticism, insults and upbraiding are to be expected in a non-ideal world, a world that does not accept our values or priorities.

What is the reward that is 'great'? It would seem that the answer is heaven itself, eternal life, not some distinguishing status in this life or in the life to come. All of God's children will face persecution, though the degree may differ! All will receive the greatest crown of all: eternal life.

The influence of those already in the King's kingdom (vv. 13-16)

Here the emphasis is not on the character and experience of those in the divine kingdom, but upon the conduct of those

---

1. Billy Graham, *The Secret of Happiness*, p. 85. Quoted in Leon Morris, *The Gospel According to Matthew* (William B. Eerdmans Publishing Co.), pp. 100-101.

in it. It tells us what we are to be about in our Christian profession. Here is a description of what those who are God's children are to be and do. Each similitude contains an exhortation. Jesus does not call us to separate from the world around us, nor from its cares, but to live in it actively. We are not to live an escapist or monastic lifestyle!

Salt was a preservative, as well as a flavor-enhancing additive, in the ancient world. Roman soldiers were paid in salt. Hence the popular phrase, 'You are not worth your salt.' It gives savor to food, promotes preservation, and stimulates thirst (v. 13). Obviously, Jesus is using the concepts of salt and earth metaphorically. We are like salt in some way; 'earth' means where you live and the witness we reveal. It would seem that the hearers of these words would have interpreted the metaphor as preservation, promoting that which is good and wholesome in society.

Light is used metaphorically; it means visibility. Light dispels darkness so that people can see (vv. 14-16). It is about the good they do in their conduct toward others. This is not contradicted by Jesus' comment in 6:1 (the issue there is a poor motive for public behavior). 'Let' is a command, not an option. Light is not to be hidden. As a city in an open place is visible, a candle is not to be put under a basket but used to illumine space. The way to be light in a darkened world is through lives lived as an expression of obedience to God. Not by our words alone, but by our conduct towards others.

That Jesus refers to God as 'your Father' must have been shocking to those who heard Him. Jews thought of God as mighty, powerful, lofty, and holy, but not in personal and familiar terms.

Applications

1. The eight beatitudes are a portrait of the true Christian like the list of the fruit of the Spirit in Galatians 4. These two portions of Holy Scripture are succinct descriptions of the character of the child of God. All Christians possess the characteristics of the beatitudes though they have them in different portions relative to varying circumstances. If you find a person devoid

of these characteristics, you may be in the presence of one not in the kingdom. It is not in the abundance of these characteristics in one's life; it is the fact of their existence in our lives. We are not perfect people; we are forgiven and repentant people!

2. The approval of God rests on the dependent upon Him, not on those who are independent of Him. The Christian is one who has been humbled by God to see the impoverishment of his/her life apart from Him. Have you been brought to see your utter poverty and hopelessness before a holy God?

3. We are not immune from persecution; it is our lot if we would follow Christ. The road to the crown is the path of suffering. We should expect difficulties in life. Life in the kingdom is not a life without adversaries and enemies; however, there will come a day when persecution ends ('there is the kingdom of heaven'). Does this give perspective on your sufferings and difficulties today? They are not abnormalities; they are 'because of him'.

4. In fact, it is often in the context of persecution that the light most wonderfully shines for God and by our reactions and conduct a thirst is created for the Saviour. Persecution is not a goal; it is inevitable. We should embrace it when it comes as a means to share the wonder of how much change Jesus can bring into a human life. Do you see being rebuffed for your beliefs as an opportunity or an obstacle?

5. We are to create a thirst for the Saviour by the manner of living our lives. We cannot do this in a monastery or in a monastic retreat from the world, but by participation in it. You and I are called to be active in our communities for the Saviour. Does your life have a social dimension, or does it revolve around family, work, and church only? The issue is not to merely have connections outside the kingdom; it is to bring light into darkness.

6. We are to dispel the darkness of people's lives by our manner of living out the Christian life, by our joys,

contentment, sacrifices, and obedience that are not of this world. When neighbors or family members see you, do they see light or clouds?

7. The end of our efforts to witness for Christ in deed and word is that people might glorify God; that they might see that there is something more important than what we see and feel; that there is something greater to live for that brings meaning to our existence.

8. When you think of Jesus and His description of the eight beatitudes and two similitudes, there is remarkable congruity. Jesus was meek, a peacemaker, and persecuted; Jesus created thirst and dispelled darkness, the darkness in the human soul. However, the first two beatitudes reflect the life of our Lord but with a significant difference. Jesus was poor of spirit and did mourn, but it was not for His sin; it was for ours. He became identified with sin, took it upon Himself for us ('though rich he became impoverished for us'). He mourned for the devastation of sin, yet it was not in His own life but in ours. He wept over Jerusalem that killed the prophets and would not repent, but never was His lowliness only for Himself. It was also for us! Should we not worship Him?

The Argument: the Relationship of the King to the Law (5:17-20)

This section of the discourse, the body of it, is framed by the phrase 'the Law and the Prophets' (5:17; 7:12). Jesus begins, however, with an explanation of His relationship to the Law. He is not opposed to the Law, nor did He seek to abrogate it; He came to explain it correctly, to fill it with meaning, since He is the meaning personified. Since the 'Law and the Prophets' point to Christ, He is its fulfillment. He is the goal of the Hebrew Scriptures.

While such a highly respected commentator as R. T. France argues that the major theme of the Sermon on the Mount focuses on the instruction of the disciples,[2] it seems that

---

2. R. T. France, *The Gospel of Matthew* (Grand Rapids, MI: William B. Eerdmans Publishing Co., 2007), p. 153.

Jesus is mounting a very strong argument that the religious leaders of the day, the Pharisees particularly, were completely wrong in their approach to the Scriptures; they have severely distorted its teachings. While instruction is involved, the theme is that the Pharisees are not worthy guides to kingdom entrance. The theme of the message is found in 5:20 ('... unless your righteousness exceeds that of the scribes and Pharisees, you shall never enter the kingdom of heaven') with the body of the sermon a defense and demonstration of the thesis (the sub-thesis is this: if you are blind to the teachings of the Scriptures, how can you enter the kingdom the Scriptures delineate?). The sermon ends with an explanation of the manner of entrance that, again, has anti-Pharisaic tones.

Jesus begins the sermon proper by answering a question that would have been in the mind of His hearers (v. 17). What is His relationship to the Law of Moses and the interpreters of it? Is the approach of the Pharisees the correct way into the kingdom? Is His message the same or antithetical?

This paragraph is important because Jesus makes clear His relationship to the Old Testament Scriptures. He is not opposed to Moses in any way; in fact, He came to recover Moses, as well as the prophets, from Pharisaic distortions.

The term 'fulfill' has three nuances. First, it can mean to obey what the Scriptures demand (Jesus certainly did that). Second, it has the idea of filling with its proper interpretative meaning. This would seem to be what Jesus is doing in the remainder of the chapter. Third, it can mean to bring to completion. In a sense the Hebrew Scriptures were a pointer, a volume that anticipates the coming of the promised One. That One came in the person of Jesus, thus completing its role of anticipation.

Until the end of the age ('until heaven and earth pass away') the Old Testament is valid and enduring (v. 18); however, it must be interpreted properly (Jesus asserts that the religious leadership did not do so!). The smallest letter in the Hebrew alphabet is the 'iota' (the 'yod', a letter resembling an apostrophe, the smallest stroke in making a letter), and the 'dot' is the 'tittle' (the difference between the letters P and R). Jesus is using those letters metaphorically to make a point; the Law in its intensions and purposes will be actualized.

He is making the claim that He does not stand in opposition to the teachings of Moses (by implication Jesus is saying the Pharisees misinterpret Moses and are an obstacle to entering the kingdom).

Most likely, the 'commandments' (v. 19) refer to the 'Law and the Prophets'. We ('whoever') are to obey them as they point to Christ, their fulfillment. It appears that in the kingdom, as it is now manifest, rank is determined by conformity to the person anticipated in the Hebrew Scriptures. Since the Law pointed forward to Jesus and His teachings, it is properly obeyed by conforming to His Word, interpreting them properly as He is about to illustrate.

That stated, the phrase 'least in the kingdom' might imply that some, like the Pharisees, are 'in the kingdom of heaven'. This seems to present a contradiction because Jesus' point in the sermon is that they not only prevent people from entering it, but they will not enter themselves (7:23; 25:12, 41-46). Perhaps a less confusing way to interpret this verse is that Jesus is making a statement about the seriousness of keeping the Law, a point made in the previous verses, and not who will and who will not enter the kingdom (though a Pharisee who is devoted to Pharisaic teaching from the heart will not). He is saying to His hearers that disparaging the Law is a serious matter for those who embrace the true kingdom. Thus, Matthew might be anticipating a Gentile-Christian reaction to Jewish believers who follow the Law or the hesitancy of Jewish believers to see Gentile believers as their equal in the kingdom. It seems that Jesus' statement, 'least of these commands,' is rhetorical, paralleling 'least in the kingdom'.

Jesus' evaluation of Pharisaic righteousness is telling (v. 20). If one is only cleansed outwardly, one will never enter God's kingdom. This sermon is an assertion that Pharisaic righteousness is inadequate and distorted.

Jesus, the Law, and Pharisaic Interpretation (5:21-47)

Jesus begins by explaining that the Pharisees had distorted the truest meaning of the Law (see also 23:3-8); they were simply ignorant of Moses. The recurring phrase is 'You have heard it said ... but I say to you.' He uses six examples to make His point. The six are divided into sets of three, divided by 'again' (v. 33). The first three deal with issues of the heart or attitudes (murder, adultery, divorce), things that spring from the heart. The second set seems to be actions (truth-telling, non-retaliation, love). Jesus' criticism of Pharisaic interpretation of the Hebrew Scripture is that they emphasized outward issues, not issues of the heart or inward concerns and attitudes.

The Law, Jesus, and murder (5:21-26)
Jesus cites Scripture, defines it correctly, and states a remedy for its violation. In God's kingdom, there is no place for hatred. Malicious anger is so heinous that it must be dealt with immediately. The reference is to hatred that is the root of murder, prohibited in the sixth commandment (Exod. 20:13).

The law against murder goes much further than the physical destruction of life; it involves desecration of character. It consists of malicious anger, contempt – 'raca', meaning fool or knucklehead is an attack on a person's intellectual capacities and public spiteful criticism (an affront to a person's moral character). The first has the potential of landing one in court, the second before Israel's high court (the Sanhedrin), and the third severe judgment.

There is a shift in verses 23-26 to the second person singular from the second person plural in the previous verses indicating that Jesus is stating two personal correctives to the exhibition of anger. We are to seek immediate restitution; inharmonious relationships demand rapid remediation.

The gravity of the consequence of violent hatred ('hell of fire') seems not to be read literally since actions are not causes (the origin of every violation of the law being in the heart with outward evidence of it [15:18]). It seems that Jesus is describing the seriousness of Pharisaic error by starkly stating a shocking consequence, as He does in 5:30 and 18:8 (see also 23:23).

There seems to be hyperbole in Jesus' instruction about worship (vv. 23-24). If a Galilean was in Jerusalem worshiping, and there remembers that they have offended someone, unless he resides in the city, he/she would have to make a lengthy trek home and then return. The point is the violation's seriousness and its incongruity with one's claim to be in the act of worshiping God.

In the context of a legal breach (vv. 25-26), the emphasis as in the previous remedies, is to make amends; here the emphasis is not only do it, but do it quickly. Matters such as these only get worse with procrastination.

The Law, Jesus, and adultery (5:27-30)

Adultery is the theft of another's most intimate possession in the covenant of marriage; it is about sexual coveting, a violation of the seventh and tenth commandments (Exod. 20:14, 17; Deut. 5:18, 21). This sin, like all sins, begins in the imagination. The issue is not mere sexual attraction, but the desire, even planning, for a sexual encounter with another's wife. From an inner sense of desire comes an outward action.

According to Jesus, the desire of sexual conquest ('looks at a woman with lustful intent') is the act consummated whether or not the thought leads to action; it is adultery (v. 28). The remedy is radical action (vv. 29-30). Clearly, Jesus is using hyperbolic language because He has made the point that desire is rooted in motives issuing from the heart, not the actions of hand or eye; our hands and eyes may be involved in an action, but they are not the root of the action (15:10-20). The remedy is so bizarre that it suggests the ludicrousness of saying that my sin is not 'my' personal responsibility. Neither the eye nor the hand (perception or instrument) is the cause of adultery; it is personal desire or coveting a pleasurable object that God prohibits. Marriage is a sacred covenant between a man and a woman that must not be violated!

Since the seriousness of the offence calls for a serious remedy, a solution not to be taken literally but metaphorically as argued above, the reference to 'hell' (the word here is Gehenna, the city dump where refuse was burned in the Valley of Hinnom outside the ancient city of Jerusalem) is most likely a metaphor for the serious negative consequences of disobedience in this regard.

The Law, Jesus, adultery, and divorce (5:31-32)

The reference is to the seventh commandment (Exod. 20:14), though Jesus' statement concerning it is from Deuteronomy

24:1, 3. The preface, 'it was also said,' connects divorce and adultery in that both are rooted in lust, one often leading to the other. Divorce is wrong because it generates adultery. When marital unfaithfulness occurs (the term covers a variety of sexual perversions), divorce is then implicitly permitted. The implication is that a person legitimately divorced is free to remarry. If the cause for the divorce is invalid, any later marital union is considered adultery! Adultery becomes a legitimate basis for remarriage for the innocent party. It is important to see that the portion of Scripture that Jesus quotes (Deut. 24:1-4) assumes the validity of divorce.

As in the case of Joseph with Mary, the grounds of divorce were established by Mary's pregnancy, so the only issue was a private or public repudiation (1:18. See also comments at 19:3-12). To treat a wife in this fashion, when adultery had not happened, was to treat her as adulterous and the husband becomes adulterous should he remarry. The point of Jesus' teaching is that it corrects the misuse of Deuteronomy 24:1-4. While Deuteronomy 24 is not invalidated, its contemporary misuse in Judaism is curbed.

Among the Jews of Jesus' day divorce was a simple procedure of placing in the hand of a wife before witnesses a document dissolving the marriage, releasing the male from any claim or obligation to be a husband. There were two views among Israel's leadership on the issue, a liberal and a moderate school. The liberal approach, the School of Hillel, argued for divorce based on a variety of causes at the discretion of the husband with no recourse by the wife; it simply was activated by a declaration of dismissal. The moderate School of Shammai argued that divorce was permitted but only on the grounds of sexual infidelity.

Jesus is more conservative than either Jewish school in His opinion, restricting the grounds of divorce to adultery, and placing guilt on a male that dismisses his wife for any lesser cause. Simply put, the severance of the marriage contract is wrong because it leads to adultery, except where marital unfaithfulness is involved. In Jewish culture a dismissed wife had no choice but to seek a second marriage, or hopefully find relief in returning to her parents' home, because she would have no proper protection or means of livelihood otherwise.

The point of the teaching is that divorce is wrong *unless* the cause is the breaking of the marriage covenant because of adultery. In the case of remarriage by the innocent party, the guilt emanating from the second marriage, the cause of the divorce, falls upon the guilty party. While divorce might happen in a world where promises are not kept, it is not God's ideal at all. The right of remarriage was to protect the innocent and provide for the offended one.

The Law, Jesus, and deceptive speech (5:33-37)

The word 'again' (v. 33) suggests that with the next three topics Jesus continued His direct attack on the Pharisees' misuse of Scripture with a slight shift of method. Matthew uses the re-occurring literary unit of threes and so cites three additional examples of Pharisaic misconstruing of Holy Scripture. One difference in those issues is that they are derived from the general moral code, and not the citing of a specific commandment among the ten (though the statement on the 'exception' to the permanency of the marriage covenant is not from the Decalogue, although the cause is found there: adultery).

Jesus begins with deceptive speech (perhaps an allusion to the ninth commandment concerning false testimony [Exod. 20:16], oaths that are uttered with no intent of keeping them). Deceptive oaths are a poor substitute for truth and integrity. According to the Pharisees, some oaths, sworn by heaven and earth, or by Jerusalem, were not binding although oaths towards Jerusalem would be. Simply put, God demands truthfulness.

The prohibition against oaths cannot be universalized because God makes oaths in Scripture, not because He ever lies, but in order to strengthen surety for us (Heb. 6:17: '... he guaranteed it with an oath') by invoking His divine character. This text is about deceptive speech; it also can be found in Jesus' comments in 23:16-22.

Jesus does not cite the Decalogue in verse 33, as the quotation here is found in Deuteronomy 23:21, 23, and Leviticus 19:12. The point of the comment is that the name of God, reflecting His holy character, must not be sullied by misappropriation.

The Jews employed deceptive speech in the manner of oaths (vv. 34-36). As long as the name of God was not involved in the oath, it was not considered binding. Jesus' point is that whenever an oath is invoked, whether it be by heaven, earth, Jerusalem, or one's head, God is involved because He is the creator of all those things. Though the name of God may not be technically used, it is hair-splitting!

I must repeat, it is important to note that swearing an oath is not a violation of Scripture; the act is not wrong, but the motive may be. The proof of the point is that God invokes oaths to substantiate the veracity of His claims. 'By myself, I have sworn, declares the Lord ....' (Gen. 22:16; quoted in Heb. 6:13).

All our answers and pledges should be clear and completely reliable; there is to be no refuge in the use of double innuendos (v. 37).

The Law, Jesus, and vengeance (5:38-42)

The Law provided for the extension of justice to curb violation (v. 38), but it prohibited excess punishment that was exercised in vengeance (Exod. 21:23-25; Lev. 24:19-21, the famous 'eye for an eye, tooth for a tooth' passages). The purpose of such legislation was to limit retaliation. Mosaic legislation limited punishment to the size of the injustice, not beyond it.

What is the correct interpretation? Jesus gives three examples (vv. 39-42). The three illustrations, and a concluding clarifying statement, make the point that vendettas for wrong are not permissible for Jesus' followers. Further, retaliation is out of the question; kindness and generosity should take its place (5:11-12). The three examples illustrate serious violations of dignity and rights, with the consequent proper demeanor to violent insults, the violation of personal rights, and unsanctioned demands. The use of the second person singular pronoun, 'you,' indicates that the instructions are addressed to each of His hearers. What are the instructions?

(1) Do not respond to insults in kind (v. 39). There is hyperbole here as above in the recommendation that mutilation is the answer to lust (v. 30). The point is that

we are not to seek vengeance. (2) Rights do not limit duty (v. 40). A coat was an inalienable possession according to the Law (Exod. 22:25-26; Deut. 24:13), but the rule does not limit privilege. Again, there is hyperbole here; no Jew at this time would go home wearing only a loincloth! (3) Duty does not limit obligation (v. 41). While citizens were required to carry a Roman soldier's baggage for a mile, a rule should not limit the expression of obedience. Here is a case that we should submit to forced labor at times and go beyond the requirements at others. (4) Be motivated by generosity in helping others (v. 42). This does not mean we should impoverish ourselves because we give to everyone who requests. See Proverbs 11:17; 22:26. Jesus' point is that among His disciples self-interest or legal limits should not be the rule!

The Law, Jesus, and discrimination (5:43-47)
The command to love your neighbor is found in Leviticus 19:18. The Bible does not instruct us to hate our enemies (v. 43). The point is that a disciple's love should be without discrimination. The reason for this is that such actions reveal the character of our Father who does not discriminate (v. 45) and that such behavior is the lot of those despised, such as the tax-gatherers (vv. 46-47). To love an enemy is an oxymoron; enemies are to be hated seems a natural truism. We are to look at another standard than that of the world.

In verse 43, Jesus quotes from Leviticus 19:18, perhaps in the way that the Jews of the day read it. They deleted 'your neighbor as yourself' and added 'hate your enemy', a phrase not in the text. He then correctly interprets the command: love is to be manifested universally, not merely for convenience, personal advantage, or limited to friends (v. 44).

What reasons are there for His application? First, there is the universal love that God expresses (v. 45). God's kindness and mercy is not limited to the compliant but extends to the ungrateful and unrighteous and is displayed in God's provisions of sunshine and rain, so necessary in an agrarian culture, universally. Second, His disciples have a greater motivation (v. 46). The manifestation of kindness is a natural human response even for the most despised in Jewish culture, among them being tax collectors for an oppressive government. Third, there is a common-sense universal principle (v. 47). Common gratitude expressed by grateful people, such as a 'thank you' or a greeting, is what the Gentiles did. By redefining neighbor, the Jewish people merely conducted themselves in a manner similar to how those they despised responded to kindness.

The conclusion: the demand for perfection (5:48)
The 'therefore' implies a conclusion; it ends the first major point in the body of the discourse. This is the first time in the Bible that God is referred to as absolutely perfect in the totality of His person. Jesus appears to be saying that the intent of the Law was to point to Himself, the end, the fullness of it. Believers should strive toward the law's intent, which is the manifestation of love (22:37-40). 'As' is comparative not absolute; we are to strive to embrace the same meaning of the Law as God's intent for it, we who are children of the kingdom. 'Perfect' can also have the sense of mature, suggesting moral blamelessness.

It is interesting that the verb could be in the future tense ('you shall be'), though most commentators take it as a command ('you therefore must be'). Taking it in the latter sense reflects its connection to Leviticus 19:2 and Deuteronomy 7:6. However, it seems that we can take it as a promise reflecting our ultimate destiny as well as a command reflective of the allusions to the Old Testament passages.

Applications

1. Jesus gives us a clue about how to read the Hebrew Scriptures. They point to Him; He is the meaning of them in that they were shadows that anticipated several things about Him: that He is the grand deliverer, that He would deliver through suffering, and that He would reign victoriously. To read the Hebrew Scriptures correctly is to ask, 'What do they tell me of Jesus?' In relationship to this chapter, 'How should I conduct my life as a child of the kingdom?' Jesus is the end of the Hebrew Scriptures as well as the model of obedience to them.

2. To enter Christ's kingdom, righteousness is required, a righteousness that is far more than external conformity to God's law; it requires motives that create actions that reach to the inner depth of our fallen being. Jesus' standards are impossible to meet because they are conformity to His character, which is perfection. This tells us that we need a divine substitute, one to take our place, someone to stand in the place of our sin and act as our righteousness. Jesus is our righteousness. Is He yours?

3. The standards for a follower of Christ, proper conduct or kingdom righteousness, are not like the standards of the world. The world accepts moral conformity without any movement of the heart; the world operates by the law of threat. God's standards are only expressed outwardly, but in God's family morals begin with right heart attitudes. Do you find solace in outward conformity more than conformity of affections to the will of God? The world punishes actions, not attitudes. This tells me that when it comes to discipleship there has to be a lot of repentance daily.

4. God prohibits all degrees of anger towards others by calling it murder. It is not uncommon for Christians to entertain animosity towards acquaintances and relatives. Is there someone in your life who has offended you, but you have not forgiven her/him? Do you carry anger, perhaps legitimately so, in your heart? Has someone hurt you and you find it hard to let go of the hurt? The consequences are self-destructive; they can damage family relationships.

5. The most sacred earthly relationship is that of marriage, the consenting of a couple to share their lives exclusively with each other. One of the great scourges today is the dissolution of that bond. For the Christian, marriage cannot be broken except when it has been broken by sexual promiscuity, because sexual union is the outward sign of commitment to oneness. We must teach our children the sacredness of marriage. While we live

in a less than perfect world, we must neither teach nor imbibe the standards of our culture if they stand in antithesis to the Bible.

6. We live in a culture where deception is rampant, from the advertising industry to political offices. 'Truth is found in the fine print,' a saying goes, meaning that purposeful, misleading use of words abounds. For the Christian, the use of deceptive speech is forbidden. We are to speak the truth plainly so as to be clearly understood, no deceptive speech. Is that true of how you talk to your mate, to your children, in the workplace, at church? Do you keep your promises?

7. Those living in Christ's kingdom should not go around demanding their just rights all the time. In fact, being a Christian, receiving undeserved kindness from God, should lead us to be willing to give up our rights for the sake of others even when it is not justifiable. Our society is factitiously tribal with people demanding minority rights; we fill the courts seeking adjudication for wrongs done to us. For the Christian, we do not have to act that way. With a kingdom perspective on life, we can give up our rights rather than demand them with retaliation.

8. We are to love our enemies returning kindness for harshness, gentleness for hurt. Jesus will later say that the essence of the commandments can be summarized in the word love – love for God and love for others. Are there people that you simply do not love? Are there people that you do not love for justifiable reasons? Does that make an unloving spirit valid? Loving one another leads to freedom and joy, its absence leads to narrowness and bitterness.

Jesus' Repudiation of Pharisaic Religious Practices (6:1-18)

Not only did the Pharisees misinterpret the Law of God, they also distorted the application of it in their religious practices. A distortion of God's Word always leads to perverted religious practices. Jesus picks three religious practices or devotional exercises highly esteemed in Judaism to make His point: the manner of giving (vv. 2-4), of praying (vv. 5-7), and of fasting (vv. 16-18).

Jesus first states what the Pharisees do, their motives and reward, and then what His followers should do and their reward. There are several reoccurring words or phrases in the section: 'hypocrite', 'reward', 'secret', and 'seen of men'.

Verse 1 presents a general principle relative to religious practice. While religion must be outwardly manifested, it should be without ostentation or showmanship. If executed for the applause and recognition of the observer, the recognition is the measure of the reward. When we manifest our religious commitments, it should be for God, not to be seen necessarily of people, certainly not to impress them of our piety.

An application – the manner of giving (6:2-4)

The behavior to avoid is mentioned in verse 2. 'Sound no trumpet' may refer to the horn-shaped receptacles for donations in the temple, in which tossed coins causing an echoing effect. The great failure of the Pharisees was that they loved men's praise; they were self-centered. We have no record of a literal blowing of an instrument to announce giving in Jewish history. It may be that Jesus is speaking figuratively, saying, 'When you give, do not announce it.'

The behavior to embrace is described in verse 3. The 'hand' is not a thinking mechanism; it is a doing mechanism. Clearly, as in 5:29-30, it is figurative speech. 'Secret' is a figure of speech for non-showmanship. Giving is to be done for the Lord, not for the praise of men. Planned giving is wise; that is not the issue here.

A promise of reward is stated in verse 4. It is a wonderful promise; the most important person in the world knows when we serve Him.

An application – the manner of praying (6:5-15)

The wrong motive and the wrong reward are stated in verse 5 and the correct behavior and the promise of a divine reward are stated in verse 6. Regarding the manner of praying, the language is once more figurative; it's not necessary to have a private room set aside for prayer and only to pray there. The issue is the avoidance of public exhibitions.

Instructions on prayer are given in verses 7-15. Regarding how not to pray, the point is neither repetition nor length of prayers (v. 7); we are not to babble. 'Now I lay me down to sleep'; 'Dear Lord Jesus, be thou our guest and let this food to us be blessed'; or 'God is great, God is good ...' are fine prayers! It is about earnestness and focus. Jesus also highlights a powerful rejoinder for praying in such ways (v. 8). This is rather wonderful; we are to pray in a certain manner because God is aware of our needs before we approach Him.

Parenthesis

If God knows our needs and prayer does not inform God [it is not about information], why pray? Prayer is a mystery beyond human conception in how it works. If God knows before we ask and the answer is part of His eternal determination, why pray? [1] God commands us to talk to Him. [2] It is a means of joining with the Lord in the outworking of His will. [3] It is a means of expressing our devotion as well as our needs to God. It is a manner of releasing our concerns to God and trusting Him to answer as He pleases. [4] It is a means of glorifying God in that it raises our awareness of His answers, with the result that we praise Him more for the answers. [5] God has willed to accomplish His will through our participation in His will. [6] In trusting that God tells the truth, prayer is a means of obtaining what we would not otherwise obtain.

The way to pray (6:9-15)

This is a wonderful model ('like this,' v. 9) or structure for our prayer life. The 'you' is plural indicating that this is a corporate prayer. There are six requests, three concerning God's interests and three of personal interest. The prayer presumes a relationship (v. 9) and reminds us that God is with us and above us. The first things to pray about are God's honor, kingdom, and purpose. Interestingly, there is no thanksgiving offered to God, or intercession for others in the family and for the world. Further, the features of the instructions are its simplicity, conciseness, clarity, and comprehensiveness.

That God be reverenced as holy (v. 9): This is a clear statement that while the kingdom began to emerge in Jesus, it was not fully manifested, but it will come (there are stages in its visible manifestation, culminating in the eternal state). The prayer is that God's rule be consummated.

That God's saving rule be extended (v. 10a): The request is that God's rule be consummated for His glory, not so much for our benefit.

That God's will be done on earth (v. 10b): The essence of this petition is an amplification of the two previous requests, that in Jesus' kingdom now His will be obeyed and His kingship accepted.

The remaining three requests have to do with the corporate, personal needs of those who embrace kingdom affiliation and ideals. These three requests are interconnected, unlike the previous ones, by the 'and' in verses 12 and 13.

That our needs be met (v. 11): The request is for daily needs reminding the hearer of the provision of manna in the wilderness. The issue is our needs on a daily basis (remember the birds [6:26]), not indefinite future needs.

That our sins be forgiven (v. 12): This is the only petition singled out for comment at the end of the prayer, the point being that forgiveness is a reciprocal principle (vv. 14-15). The assumption is that sin puts people at distance from God, as well as others.

The term used for sin is 'debts' and it applies to those who have wronged us ('debtors'). It is most likely to be taken figuratively for wrongs done in general, not merely the failure to return what has been borrowed. It means any obligation. Forgiving others of wrongs done to us is an obligation because we have been forgiven a much larger 'debt'.

That we be delivered from temptation (v. 13): The point is that we are to pray for deliverance from the solicitations of the evil one, of actions contrary to the character of God, a reality modeled by our Lord through His temptations by the devil (4:1-11).

An additional clarification (vv. 14-15): These verses are an expansion of the issue of forgiveness, further nuancing the implication of verse 12. Since the point of the verse is that we should forgive those who wrong us and that an unwillingness to forgive is sin on our part, God's forgiveness of us should result in our forgiveness of others. Forgiveness by God results in a forgiving spirit. Thus, these verses state the reason that we should not withhold forgiveness from others. To not forgive the infractions of others is evidence that we have not been forgiven of God ('will' is future, indicating the final judgment). Unwillingness to forgive may suggest an unrepentant heart!

An Application – the manner of fasting (6:16-18)
Fasting in the Old Testament was commanded only on the Day of Atonement, but during the exile regular fasts were instituted. Fasting was not a required practice, but it was engaged in on certain occasions, and individuals could fast voluntarily. It is not that the disciples presently were fasting; it is that they will fast in the future (9:15).

Within the broader context of the sermon, Jesus is speaking of the proper actions of the church as a collective body, rather than private actions. Fasting is a means of focusing on the things of the Lord by suspending normal routines. It seems that the context is calamity, mourning, loss, or specific moments in the life of the church (such as times of significant spiritual endeavors [e.g. missionary work], threats, and persecution). It is to be accompanied with prayer. It does not necessarily imply abstinence from food or drink; but to indulge only sparingly.

As in the two previous examples, the issue is not the activity, but the motive for it ('seen by others'). While fasting is not prohibited, it must not be practiced in such a way as to impress others. It is to be done with a degree of privacy and the person fasting has the comfort of knowing that God understands and cares for His people.

Jesus' Repudiation of Pharisaic Personal Practices (6:19–7:6)

Ignorance of God's Word always leads to perverted religious (6:1-18) and personal practices. Jesus selects three moral practices of the Pharisees: their attitude towards material things and hoarding (6:19-24), their lack of trusting God for the necessities of life (6:25-34), and their critical judgmentalism (7:1-6) to illustrate His point. A reoccurring phrase in the section that introduces each of the three errant behaviors is the negative 'do not' (6:19, 25; 7:1).

The instruction for the disciples suggests that those who follow Jesus will not be among the affluent generally, that concerns other than material things should consume them, and they should be unstintingly generous.

Relative to materialism and hoarding (6:19-24)

First, the principle is stated negatively (v. 19). Wealth in the first century was in clothing or possessions, all subject to moth, mice ('rust' means to eat), and thievery. 'Break through' suggests that robbers literally dug through mud and stone walls to enter places. Remember, there were no banks in the first century or safe deposit boxes. The issue is not prudence in financial planning for the unexpected exigencies on life; it is about the motive for wealth accumulation as captured in the phrase 'for yourselves'.

Then Jesus explains the principle positively (v. 20). Wealth of any amount is a blessing from God, but it is to be used for God's glory in service to others; every privilege is a call to service, not self-aggrandizement. He further explains the principle in verse 21. The quest for physical comfort, if misplaced, has the tragic potential of distorting our true values because what we most prize becomes our focus. The problem with placing our confidence in the security of material accumulation is that it can confuse the temporal for the eternal, the impermanent for the permanent. When one treasures the temporal over the eternal, their priorities stand in stark contrast to Jesus' statement, 'You shall love the Lord your God with all your heart ...' (22:37).

Jesus uses an illustration of this principle in verses 22-23. In this metaphor, the eye is equivalent to the heart. If a person is singularly focused (eye/heart), things are fine; if the focus is divided, there will be confusion and distortion, blindness. God and materialism are each portrayed as slave-owners, not employers (v. 24). A person may work for two employers but cannot be a slave of two masters. Slavery involves single-eyed devotion. Thus, devotion to God and prioritizing materialism at the same time is simply antithetical; actually, it is impossible!

Relative to worry (6:25-34)

'Therefore' indicates an implication drawn from the previous paragraph. Ownership by a good master should eliminate fear and worry; a good master is obligated to provide for his servants. The root of anxiety in such matters is unbelief.

This passage does not forbid wise financial planning for the exigencies of life. It denounces fretting. This outlook is argued from eight viewpoints:

First, from the provision of life (v. 25). This is an argument from the lesser to the greater. If God gives life, He can surely sustain it as well.

Second, from the worth of birds (v. 26). Again, here is an argument from the lesser to the greater. If God provides for the wren, He will care for us, His people.

Third, from the fact of human inability (v. 27). Here the argument is the foolishness of worry based on its potential for gain. It can neither get us an additional day of life nor an inch of additional height.

Fourth, from the care of flowers (vv. 28-30). Even as birds do not store up for the future, flowers are not exercised about their maintenance. Yet, they are robed more beautifully than Solomon. Though elegant in beauty they were used to light fires. Here is another argument for the greater because of the provision of the lesser.

Fifth, from the conduct of unbelievers (vv. 31-32a). Those without a sovereign Lord, one who is committed to them by a unilateral covenant, should worry. We should not act like them; we have a caring master!

Sixth, from divine knowledge (v. 32b). The all-powerful God, who loves us with infinite compassion, is also omniscient. He is aware of our needs, and He lacks no want of power to meet them.

Seventh, from God's directive (v. 33). The way to put an end to worry is to focus on things far more significant, sure, and enduring. What could be greater than the person, purposes, and pleasures of God in the choices we make!

Eighth, from a day's sufficiency (v. 34). Fretting over the cares of tomorrow only multiplies the things that disturb us today. It affects no positive benefits to our well-being or to the goal of trusting God in everything.

Relative to judgmentalism (7:1-6)

The issue here is unjust and critical attitudes of censoriousness, not the employment of wisdom and discretion. Jesus turns from a negative attitude of one's own life-experience to our attitude towards others. The structure of the passage consists of negative instruction (v. 1), a reason for the warning (v. 2), the origins of a critical spirit (vv. 3-5), and a balancing perspective (v. 6).

The issue with a critical spirit, or fault finding, is that it can be a boomerang if unjustly employed. The point is unjust criticism, not criticism *per se*. Using a commercial metaphor, what 'often comes around goes around'; verse 2 reminds me of the biblical story of Adoni-bezek who in conquering seventy kings cut off their big toes and thumbs. After suffering the same fate, he said, 'As I have done, so has God repaid me' (Judg. 1:7b).

Jesus uses an illustration to make His point (vv. 3-5). The speck-and-beam picture notes the inappropriateness of criticism. He seems to be indicating that what bothers a person may be a mirror image of a greater personal problem in themselves.

Though we are to love our enemies (5:43-47) and avoid a critical spirit, there is a balance to keep (v. 6). We must be discerning. Dogs may become vicious and unruly animals, prone to rip and tear with their teeth, when presented with a piece of meat we might consider choice. Precious pearls would have no value for pigs, and they simply walk over them. Criticism is not always wrong; it simply must be valid and offered in a proper manner with the proper motive. The principle is that of wisdom and discernment.

Applications

1. While the expression of religion is often done in public, it must never be done to impress people. Faith is first a matter of inward affection and consequently of outward manifestation; it is neither first nor foremost an outward show. More importantly, in the context of our passage, the issue is the motive for outward pious exercises; it should never be to impress people. Do you find yourself proud of your religious piety? Do you give in order for people to notice? Do you pray publicly to gain an audience?

2. Prayer is an act of worship. What is important in prayer is the object, not the duration, posture, or profundity. Prayer is not a time to transfer information, as if God is unaware of what we know; it is a time to express intimacy with and dependence on God. Do you view prayer as an act of submission and adoration?

3. Prayer should have several components, though they vary in number, based upon urgency and circumstance. Prayer is foremostly a form of adoration and dependence. We come to God, recognizing His worth, to lay our petitions before Him with the knowledge that He is the source of our longings and needs. Is prayer for you more or less a give-me session? It is worth meditating on the lines of this prayer, the six petitions, as a way for us to structure our praying. Is prayer a daily component in your spiritual life? It is how we respond to God, think about Him, and worship Him.

4. Fasting does not have the prominence in the Holy Scriptures that prayer seems to have. Perhaps this is because it is a personal, private exercise often in times of great grief and exigency. It would seem that when the pains of life inordinately descend upon us, it is the occasion to forego the joys of life to concentrate on prayer and meditation. Before important decisions must be made, fasting is appropriate. Fasting is a form of worship, like giving and prayer, but it should not be announced. It is a private form of devotion. There are no instructions to fast regularly in the Bible, but it is a way to periodically focus on God. Have you expressed your devotion to God in this manner?

5. Living in a very materialistic, prosperity-oriented culture has its dangers. We are a culture of much, but the possessing and maintaining of material status consumes us. Sadly, our value is determined by the wealth we generate, the health we possess, and good looks. There are grave dangers in it for us individually, our families, our churches, and our society. The inordinate pursuit of wealth accumulation has caused

disruption and division. How has wealth been a detriment in the life of your family or your home? Has money created unity and love in your family, or has it brought separation and isolation?

6. Giving is an important component of worship for the disciple of Jesus. It is an expression of trust in God's provision and the recognition that life is more than material things. When we give, the focus should not be on the gift but the One who made it possible. Do you regularly give to the Lord's work? Do you see giving as an act of worship and delight?

7. Worry is one of the most prevalent sins of believers; it is the evidence of a lack of trust in God. Of all the things Jesus could have spoken about, He began with wealth accumulation and then worry; the two are often interconnected. Worry, a manifestation of fear that unpleasantness will overtake us, should not dominate us. Our focus should be elsewhere; it should be on the kindness and generosity of God. You can only concentrate on one thing at a time. What do you fill your mind with, fretting or trust? Does God not care for the birds? Does God not provide flowers with inordinate beauty? Can you trust Him? Can you think of any reasons not to do so? If you cannot find legitimate reasons to do so, why do you continue to worry? If you are willing to leave a storm-tossed life, you have to decide who your master is. To have a mind set on heaven and a mind set on earth is impossible.

8. The key to relief from worry is a change of focus from personal concerns to the things of the kingdom, to the things about being a disciple. Being preoccupied with the things of God mitigates against concern for ourselves. Remember in the prayer in this passage Jesus instructed us that, of the six petitions, three concern the things of God and those things should be held as first priority. Our first concern should be the honor of His name, the recognition of His character, and His kingdom purposes. If we 'seek first the kingdom', we

need not worry and fret because we have the promise of God that He will provide for us. Are you putting Him first? Could your failure to do so be a cause of discontent and friction in your life and social relationships?

An invitation (7:7-11)

In verse 7, there is a triple imperative; clearly the point is to emphasize the urgency and importance of action. The tone of the sermon shifts from instruction to invitation, from an appeal to information to a call for a decision. The reoccurring words are 'ask', 'seek', 'knock', and 'give' ('give' is used five times in verses 7-11). The commands in this verse are present tense indicating the need for ongoing action or persistence.

In verse 8, the opening 'for' gives a reason for asking; there is a wonderful promise that God has given! God will hear the request of the penitent. Reasons for asking are provided in verses 9-11. First, the kindness of fathers is stated (vv. 9-10). Here is an illustration that argues for the potency of God's promise to receive a person who asks for entrance into the kingdom based on the analogy of a father's answer to a child's request. Second, the greater kindness of God is mentioned (v. 11). If earthly fathers, being evil, act kindly to the object of their affection, how much more will our holy Father who infinitely loves us? God loves us far more than any earthly parent so we should expect good outcomes when requesting His help. In a parallel account, the 'gift' is designated as the Holy Spirit (Luke 11:13), suggesting the topic is entrance into the kingdom, eternal life, which is the gift of the Spirit to us.

Conclusion (7:12)

This verse is difficult to place contextually in an outline. The 'so' indicates an implication, but the content seems incongruous with verses 7-11, the gist of the paragraph being that we are to turn to our heavenly Father.

If this verse is a conclusion to verses 7-11, being about the treatment of others, it perhaps has a connection to 6:14-15. The treatment of others (such as in forgiving wrongs done to us by others being a sign of a change in our hearts because of Jesus and being in His kingdom) is not how we enter the kingdom; it is evidence that we are in the kingdom. Here, then, Jesus would be saying that love is the evidence of being in the kingdom, which is the intent of the Hebrew Scriptures, the Law and the Prophets (22:37-40).

The verse may be a summary of the sermon and a synopsis of the intent of the Hebrew Scriptures. The reference to 'Law and the Prophets' ties the verse to 5:17 (a phrase repeated at the beginning and end of the sermon). Taken in this way, the verse may function as a summary of the entire sermon.

Though the 'Golden Rule' was common among the rabbis of the Hillel school, they stated it in the negative ('What is hateful to you, do not do to others'). Only Jesus states it positively. The negative suggests the implementation of justice. The way Jesus stated it implies the need for grace, forgiveness, and mercy.

A choice: two gates (7:13-23)

The way of life is described as two roads; the validity of the road is determined by the destination to which it brings the traveler. The road is to be chosen by the traveler; again, the stress is on response. Jesus urged His hearers to enter the gate of discipleship on the road of persecution (5:10-12) that ends in heaven. The broad gate is attractive, the way of cultural and religious affirmation by the nation's leadership, but its end is tragic. Jesus is clearly asserting that there is only one way into His kingdom and that there is a literal hell, contrary to the thinking of even some postmodern religious leaders.

First, there is the fact of two gates (vv. 13-14). The point of the metaphor of the two gates is that there are only two choices people can make in life, heaven or hell. One is more temporally attractive than the other, but the less attractive is ultimately preferable. The narrow road, the road entered through Jesus, is not the most obvious or attractive way to go.

Second, there is the difficulty in finding the right gate (vv. 15-23). The reason that the broad gate is so alluring is that false teachers and deceivers abound. Specifically, the referent is to the teachings of the Pharisees and scribes in Jesus' day, but we have our own plethora of false messages and messengers.

The fact of false teachers (v. 15a) reminds me of the story of the false prophet Micaiah ben Imah and the 400 prophets of Baal, who in opposing the judgmental message of Jeremiah, prophesized peace, but only destruction came (1 Kings 22:5-28).

The false teachers are deceptive; they come disguised (v. 15b). How can they be detected? Jesus tells how they can be recognized (vv. 16-20). It seems that He is speaking of the religious leadership (see also 23:2-7). What they say is true, but they do not bear the fruit of their teaching.

In verse 16a, He states the principle: trees and bushes produce what is consistent with their character. False teachers produce false fruit; they lead followers down the wrong path. The metaphor of grapes/figs and thorns/bushes (v. 16b) reminds us that bushes produce after their kind. From a grape bush comes grapes or fruit; a thorn bush does not produce grapes but thorns. The metaphor of the trees (vv. 17-20) is lengthier. The emphasis here is on the quality of the fruit rather than the kind. The good fruit of teaching, when embraced, puts one on the narrow path and the destiny, as evidenced by fruit, is the kingdom. As the root, so the fruit, suggesting that the teachings of the nation's leadership were corrupt and consequently their instruction was invalid. It places a person on an attractive road, but it leads to destruction.

The fate of false professors is described in verses 21-23. These verses are as shocking as they are graphic and arresting. To make claims of affiliation without entering through the 'narrow gate' is without validity. To suggest allegiance to Jesus on the basis of being acquainted with miraculous powers, without entering the 'narrow gate', will only lead to terrifying consequences ('I never knew you' [v. 23]).

A final exhortation, involving two foundations, is given in verses 24-27. This brief section is amazing on several scores. First, you have a wonderful declaration of who Jesus is; He is Lord. As Lord, He alone will make all final judgments and all of them will be just! Second, 'know' does not mean a factual awareness; it means an affectionate heart relationship. The leadership, and many in the crowds, knew about Him, but few actually knew Him. Third, 'enter the kingdom' means to become a follower, a disciple of Jesus. Fourth, 'on that day' refers to the final judgment.

The function of the illustration of wisdom expressed in building an edifice on a secure foundation and the foolishness of building the structure of life on weakness is a wonderful invitation by Jesus to heed His words. Works do not redeem us; however, they do reveal whether or not we are redeemed! Works are an effect or consequence, not a cause of belief in Jesus. The 'foolish man' is one who constructed his building on the errors of the scribes and Pharisees. In the great judgment they will suffer a 'collapse' as well as those who follow their errors.

The Authority of Jesus Recognized (7:28-29)

The brief comment about the impression that the message had upon the hearers, that of amazement, closes the narration of Jesus' discourse. It parallels the opening verses (5:1-2) of the sermon. This indicates that chapters 5–7 are a single literary unit of our Lord's teaching. The crowds perceived that Jesus did not teach as the scribes, validating their words by citing secondary sources; He spoke on His own authority though He had no formal training. He cited Scripture but assumed the role of its interpreter; He did not quote any secondary sources. Clearly, He has authority to do what the scribes do not!

Applications

1. We are often sensitive to the weaknesses of others because we share in them ourselves. Spiteful criticism is an art form in our culture; sadly, it is often found in the Christian culture. While criticism can be constructive, when it is employed to justify ourselves and condemn others in so doing, it should have no place among us. What we often find disturbing in others are characteristics we detect readily because we see them in ourselves. Do you find yourself negatively judging other's actions because you think you know that it springs from an evil selfish motive? There is a danger in doing this; it can come back to haunt you.

2. It is wonderful that the greatest gift, the gift of life, is simply for the asking. It does not require a college education; it does not matter whether or not you are

well connected in society; who your parents were is of no consequence; financial security is not an issue. The best things in life come without cost, have you noticed? A walk with your best friend, a fresh cup of coffee with the one you cherish most, the availability of a painted sunset or a majestic sunrise are for everyone. So is the gift of life. O! There is a cost, but it has been paid. It is now free. Have you taken God's free gift?

3. The way to heaven is a narrow way. It is through Christ alone. Our culture values tolerance, the equal value of all opinions, but that has nothing of resemblance to the message of the Saviour. There is only one way to God and that is through the provision of Jesus Christ. Many voices may seem attractive, but they will prove gravely disappointing. Are you on the narrow path that brings with it temporal restrictions because you are a follower of Jesus or are you on the broad path that offers temporal pleasures, but eternal failure?

4. The reason there is so much confusion over religious issues is that there are many hucksters peddling error in the guise of truth. When you listen to religious broadcasts can you spot wolves dressed in attractive attire? Do you hear error from the pulpits of our land? Truth does not come from wolves in sheep's clothing. The antidote to gullibility is knowledge of the true shepherd. Are you regularly reading the Word of God? What shepherd are you listening to these days?

5. The difficulty of spotting false teachers is that their words are often pleasant, and their appeal is attractive. You can only know the quality of a teacher by the fruit that comes from his/her work. 'As the root, so the fruit,' is the litmus test of truthfulness. The actions of a person often tell us more than his/her words. Is their message in conformity to that of Jesus? If not, they are false teachers.

6. Knowledge of the Lord does not make a person a Christian. Clearly in our passage false teachers profess to be followers of Jesus and are capable of miracle-working.

The fact of spiritual words or benevolent deeds does not make one a saint. You can have God in your mouth, while empty of Him in the heart. The most important question in life is not, 'Have you met Jesus?' It is, 'Has He met you?' Though a person may know about Him, redemption does not occur essentially in the mental faculties. It occurs in the heart, in the affections. False teachers speak of Him, but they have no love for Him. Their love is greed of place and cultural values.

7. Sand is a good foundation as long as there are no storms. When battering storms come to the shore of your life, sand is not stable enough to keep you erect. What you need is to stand on something that is impervious to storms, a rock. Jesus is that rock. All other foundations will prove inadequate, not in the good days and years of our lives, but when the storms come. The greatest of these storms will be the final judgment. Do you want to stand before God on a porous foundation of religious error or on the truth, the rock, Christ Jesus? What foundation are you building your life upon these days?

8. Do not miss Jesus' invitation. Now is the day to ask, seek, and knock. Are you willing to do that? Jesus will not ask you about significant accomplishments, pedigree, or your benevolences; He will ask you if you were willing to come to Him, to enter the narrow gate. Are you willing to become a follower of Jesus? The choice is yours, but there will come a time when that choice will no longer be yours to make. Are you willing to embrace the love of God revealed in the person and work of Jesus for you?

3

The Miracles of the King
(8:1–9:34)

While Matthew records twenty of the thirty-five specific miracles performed by Christ (there are several general summaries of multiple miracles as well [4:23; 8:16; 9:35; 14:34-36; 15:29-31]), these two chapters contain ten of them (one is a double miracle). Nine of the ten miracles deal with a person's healing, the exception being the stilling of the storm. The miracles appear in groups of three (three groups of three miracles) with narrative, instructional information between the units. Miracles witness to His person (that He is the Messiah). The teaching material after the miracle draws forth the implications for those who grasp His claims with a believing heart (discipleship). The two are intertwined!

The miracles are important for three reasons: first, they substantiate Jesus' claims that His actions are fulfillment of prophecy, that He is the promised One; second, they demonstrate that His teachings are opposed to the tenets of the Judaism of His day, such as the source of defilement; and third, they forced the religious leadership to render a verdict about Him. Is He the true messiah-figure or is He a fake?

If the Sermon on the Mount evidenced our Lord's authority to teach truth, correcting scribal distortions, these miracles demonstrate His power and the heavenly authority of His instruction.

Three Miracles of Healing (8:1-17)

The leper (vv. 1-4)

Leprosy, a tragic disfiguring disease, was thought to be a skin ailment in that day; the only treatment was quarantine. Lepers were separated from the community and required to call out 'unclean, unclean' (Lev. 13:45) to anyone who came near them. To touch such a one was to become defiled (interestingly, every defiled person Jesus touched was made clean). Verse 4 is important: the religious leaders (the text says, 'the priest') were to be informed that one was healed of this disease because it was a claim of the Messiah's presence (Lev. 14:8-10). This would demand that the leadership evaluate the claim of the 'New Moses' (Deut. 18:15; Matt. 12). The journey from the Galilee to Jerusalem took several days and the cleansing ritual eight; the priests in Jerusalem must have been shocked.

The geographical location of this miracle-healing seems to have taken place between the location of the conclusion of Jesus' sermon on entering the kingdom and His entrance into Capernaum (vv. 1, 8), suggesting their proximity. Matthew mentions the leper's request, the action of Jesus, and the instruction of Jesus. Interestingly, the text does not say the leper was healed; it says that he was cleansed. There was no known cure for the disease. The cleansing of a leper was a miracle on a par with the raising of the dead, an evidence of the Messiah's presence!

As in the case of the other two miracles in this unit, the effect was immediate. The leper was cleansed; the centurion's servant and Peter's mother-in-law were healed immediately as well. The leper came in faith believing that Jesus could heal him if willing; the servant was healed because of another's faith; and Peter's mother-in-law was healed without the evidence of faith.

The centurion's servant (vv. 5-13)

The centurion, a commander of 100 soldiers, was likely an auxiliary officer in the employ of Herod Antipas (so technically in the service of Rome); his servant was a slave; both were Gentiles. Soldiers were not permitted to have legal families during their twenty years of military service. The servant was likely the only 'real' family the centurion had. Luke tells us that this centurion was very kind to the Jews and even built a synagogue in Capernaum for them (Luke 7:4-5). This is the first recorded miracle in Capernaum though several will follow in this section.

Matthew mentions the centurion's request, the Lord's reply, and the centurion's respect for Jesus. It is interesting that the centurion says, 'Lord, I am not worthy ...' to have Jesus enter his home (v. 8). John the Baptist also said that he was neither worthy to baptize Him nor even carry His shoes ('I am not worthy ....' [3:11]).

The centurion's understanding of the circumstances is insightful. The fact of a racial/religious barrier, the common hostility to the Roman occupation particularly in the Galilee, the recognition that Jesus was a person of authority (as was the centurion) so that He issues orders, and they are obeyed (implying with Jesus physical illness is not a problem for such an authoritarian to subdue) is remarkable.

As in the healing of the daughter of a Canaanite woman (15:21-28), Jesus comments on the centurion's faith. In both instances, they were Gentiles ('... with no one in Israel have I found such faith' [v.10]).

Jesus then comments that many Gentiles will join Abraham in the kingdom, but many of Abraham's own descendants will not (vv. 11-12). Jesus uses 'the sons of the kingdom' to mean Israelites who believe that they are the objects of God's mercy because of mere ethnicity. Since Jesus makes it clear that such 'sons' face judgment, the phrase is clearly being used as a figure of speech for lost people. Here is a hint, also found in the visit of the wise men (2:1-11), that the Messiah's kingdom would embrace Gentiles.

There are two miracles in Matthew, both Gentile healings, from a distance (the other is the healing of the daughter of the Canaanite woman, 15:21-28). In this case Jesus showed no reluctance, though the centurion did; the faith of both was commended. It is not that Jews are excluded from the Messiah's kingdom; it is that Gentiles are welcomed into the new community.

An important insight of the relationship of faith to healing is found in verse 13. The 'as' seemingly does not suggest that the healing here was due to the depth of his faith (he grasped the fact that Jesus was a man of great authority), but 'because' (a better rendering of the term than 'as') he expressed faith. It is not because of the greatness of our faith that God acts on our behalf, but because of the object of our faith. Whereas the leper understood that Jesus could cleanse him ('if you will' [v. 2]), the centurion emphasized his unworthiness of Jesus' favor. It is not our merit that is the cause of divine mercy; it is Jesus' willingness to heal!

Peter's mother-in-law (vv. 14-15)

The healing of Peter's mother-in-law, again in Capernaum, is unique in that it is the only personal miracle performed without a request for it. Fever was considered a disease in that day, not a symptom. Jesus' touch healed the defiled; it did not defile the healer! Two miracles occur here; she was immediately healed, as was the centurion's servant, and immediately restored to full strength.

Three inferences may be drawn from this miracle: first, Peter was married at this time, having a mother-in-law; second, Jesus may have resided with Peter at his home in Capernaum (if not, certainly nearby); and third, Peter's mother-in-law immediately became a disciple of the Lord (the verb is used in that manner [serve, servant] and the pronoun 'him', not 'them', suggests attachment).

In verses 16 and 17, there is a summary of numerous miracles. The comment that it was in the same 'evening' that Jesus healed so many suggests that it was at the end of a Sabbath day (Mark 1:21); people began to stir. In Mark's gospel the healing of a demoniac in the synagogue, the healing of Peter's mother-in-law, and this array of miracles, occurred on the same day in Capernaum.

In that day, sickness was understood to be caused by sin (John 9:1-3), thus the citation of Isaiah 53:4 (v. 17), though it is unusual to connect this citation to illness rather than moral evil. Since all healing comes from God, and physical healing is a portent of a greater healing (9:6), Matthew seems to connect the two (the visible as evidence of the invisible). There is healing in the atonement from the effects of sin as a shadowed fulfillment of the anticipated final victory over sin and death in the resurrection. Miracles are immediate in effect. However, only in the fullest manifestation of the kingdom of God will the atonement's complete purpose be accomplished; only then will all be healed of all illnesses and death.

Another way to view the use of Isaiah 53:4 here, since physical liabilities may not be the subject, is to note that Jesus had performed three miracles that involved contact with uncleanness which incurred ritual defilement. Matthew may have cited the verse to simply indicate that Jesus was willing to 'become unclean' in order to heal us. Jesus became sin for us that we might be forgiven and spiritually healed! In a very real sense, there is healing in the atonement, though final physical healing awaits our final redemption!

An Interlude: The Instruction of the Disciples (8:18-22)

The point of this interlude is that of the necessity of wholeheartedness in following Jesus. Jesus sought to separate from the increasing crowds by leaving the scene (going from Capernaum to the eastern shore of the lake beyond the Jordan, a Gentile area controlled by Herod Phillip – Jews would likely not desire to go there). Two men indicate that they want to follow Him, but have immediate needs and concerns that prevent them.

Jesus first focuses on the implications of an itinerant lifestyle. To those seeking material security, Jesus states that one should not wait for it as a prerequisite for following Him, as He Himself does not have it (the only other time the gospel uses the word 'lay' [v. 20] is for Jesus reclining His head on the cross). The second case deals with the priority of family over discipleship. Possibly, the individual's father has died, and the man is asking for a year to wait for the secondary burial, when the bones were placed in a crypt. Or it could mean that he is asking to become a disciple at some indeterminable future date after his family obligations are fulfilled. Either explanation is possible. Jesus' response seems to be a breach of the fifth commandment concerning honoring of parents, though he did advocate obedience to them elsewhere. Is this not a case of conflicting absolutes in the context of greater and lesser ultimate authorities? Could it be that Jesus answers the inquiry in this way to reveal the lack of commitment on the man's part? Could a similar situation account for Jesus' comments to the Canaanite mother (14:26) and the rich young inquirer (19:17-22)?

A scribe and the cost of discipleship (vv. 18-20)

Jesus' point is that true discipleship involves deprivation and suffering, even as He is the great example of obedience to the will of God. Another lens might be that He is addressing the desire for recognition. A 'scribe' was not merely a copyist of sacred writings but an interpreter as well. Scholars are generally agreed that the designation 'Son of Man' is rooted in Daniel 7:13 and has Messianic connotations (this was Jesus' most frequent title for Himself, not by any gospel writer of Him). The point is that true Christ-following demands true righteousness that comes through real faith, and not through mere external, religious behavioral patterns.

A son and the cost of discipleship (vv. 21-23)

It is interesting at this point (v. 21) that Matthew speaks of this man as 'another of the disciples'. This suggests that the term 'disciple' did not always entail the level of commitment that it later implies; it means here an uncommitted, willing learner, as it does in John 6:66. The scribe seemed eager to follow Jesus, but he was unaware of the costs involved. The evidence of his ignorance of true discipleship was made clear by the fact that he laid down conditions. Jesus indicated that a true disciple cannot decide when obedience can be temporally laid aside!

Though it is the most frequently used title by the Lord of Himself, this is the first occurrence of 'Son of Man' in the book. In Daniel 7:13-14, 'one like a Son of Man' is enthroned by God to rule in heaven over the nations. Here, however, the Son of Man shared in the insecurities of earthly existence. In neither of the two interchanges are we told the response of the inquirers.

Miracles are a disclosure of Christ's person and claims; they demand a decision! They are also invitations to faith and discipleship so that the instruction at this point makes sense. This indicates that the miracles Matthew placed here have a purpose beyond making a statement about Jesus' identity; they demand a response on our part. They demand that He be followed! Remember that Matthew's purpose for writing was more than to present the claims and evidence that Jesus is the fulfillment of the expectation of the prophets; it was to stir his readers to pursue God's interests.

Three Miracles of Quieting (8:23–9:8)

In the second trilogy of miracles, the first occurs on the lake, the second in Gentile territory on the eastern side of the Sea of Galilee, and the third after returning to Capernaum. The first emphasizes Jesus' power over nature, the second over evil forces, and the third over sin. The emphasis does not appear to be upon the miracles themselves, for they are passed over quickly by Jesus, but upon the lessons involved in each case. In the first miracle, there are faithless disciples; in the second, there are disappointed farmers and two healed men; and in the third, there is an external healing, but the focus is upon Jesus' claim to have the power to forgive sin.

The stilling of the storm (vv. 23-27)

This is the first of two miracles that occurred on the Sea of Galilee (cf. 14:22-33). In this one Jesus is with His disciples but He is asleep; in chapter 14, they are alone in the storm. Here, Jesus did not chide the disciples for waking Him with their pleas for help, but for their fears. It is interesting that Jesus deals with the disciples before He deals with the storm. There seems to be two parts in this event: the sudden ending of the storm and the immediate calming of the sea (normally a body of water continues to have evidence of a storm even with its passing).

The particular circumstances are described in verse 24; the cry of the disciples is recorded in verse 25; and the answer by Jesus in verse 26. His power over wind and waves would remind the reader of the control of Jehovah in the Hebrew Scriptures (Pss. 104:7; 107:23-32; Jonah 1–2). By this miracle Jesus is claiming to be Jehovah, the true LORD. The disciples are on a learning-curve as to the person that called them to become His followers ('What sort of man is this, that even the winds and sea obey him?').

The healing of the Gadarene demoniacs (vv. 28-34)

This healing occurred in a predominately Gentile area on the east side of the Sea of Galilee; Jews did not keep swine. What is interesting in the account is that Matthew does not focus on the deliverance of the two demon-possessed men, but the reaction of the citizens of the nearby city. Again, the incident is used to reveal Jesus' claims about Himself and to instruct the disciples.

The village of Gadara is inland from the sea and located north of the Yarmuck River (the northern border between Israel and Jordan today), but their lands must have reached down to the sea. It was a Gentile region. According to Mark and Luke the miracle took place at Gerasa near the shore of the lake (today's Kursi). Matthew may be referring to the province, while Mark and Luke specify a nearby town (ancient manuscripts offer variant readings).

The circumstance is described in verse 28 and is followed by the query of the indwelling demons (v. 29). The demons know who Jesus is, but they remained demons because they lacked heart affection for Him. Often when demons are cast out in the gospel accounts, they express rage; this is likely why they asked permission to enter the swine and destroy them (vv. 30-31). Further, the demons are aware that they face divine judgment. (There are two types of fallen angels, minions of Satan. Some fallen beings have been confined from further activities and wait judgment for their actions [Jude 1:6]; others operate in the world as Satan's agents to oppose the extension of the kingdom of God and God's people [Rev. 16:14].)

In granting the request of the demons (v. 32), He revealed His authority over demons and their habits, as well as revealing the nature of the Gentiles who, in this case, loved business more than human health and wellness. These people may have preferred pigs to Jesus! The notion that Gentiles will also reject Him seems to be a lesson here (vv. 33-34). It may have been that the people feared Jesus as much as they did the demoniacs, seeing the devastation that He could bring to them, as with what happened to the swine.

Applications

1. The miracles of Jesus were performed, in part, to verify the claim that He is the promised deliverer, that a new age was about to dawn. Though Jesus clearly had compassion and concern for the physical plight

of people, His miracles were performed to focus on Himself as the promised One, not upon the objects of the healing. The miracles point us to the miracle worker. Do the miracles in this passage bring you comfort? Has He stilled the storms that rage in your life? Is your life storm-tossed now? Remember there is someone in the 'boat' with you. Turn to Him.

2. In the healing of the social outcast, the leper, there is a wonderfully comforting line. When asked by the leper if Jesus was willing to cure him, the reply was, 'I am willing; be cleansed' (8:2). Jesus is not only able; He is willing to cleanse those whose lives are broken. Jesus cares and has the power to effect healing. Has He done that for you? Are you willing to take your brokenness to Him?

3. I find in the leper's conversation with Jesus a wonderful approach to our requests of Him. We should never doubt the power and authority of God to help us ('you can' [v. 2]). However, we should simultaneously realize that God acts according to His will ('if you will' [v. 2]). It is not our asking that determines the answer; it is the divine will. If God does not give us our request, we must realize that it was not outside His power to do so, though it may not be His will to do so. That seems very comforting to me.

4. Jesus is pleased and perhaps amazed when we trust in Him. The centurion recognized what others often did not. The Lord was a man of power and authority who gives commands, and they are accomplished. Perception led to trust and respect. He recognized Jesus' Jewishness and thought to respect that relative to entering a Gentile's house. Jesus rightly marveled at this man's faith. When Jesus sees your life, is He amazed at your faith or at the lack of it? When is your faith the weakest? When is it strong?

5. To truly follow Jesus is to make Him a greater priority in your life than even family or physical comforts. Jesus is not saying that family is unimportant; that would

contradict His teaching later in the book. He is saying that discipleship involves degrees of commitment that transcend other communities such as family ties. He expects and demands no conditional discipleship; it should be total, not partial. For Jesus, to be a disciple, a follower, is the same as being a Christian. Discipleship is not optional; it is not a preferred status within the community of God. To be a Christian is the same as being a disciple. Are you a disciple?

6. When Jesus is near to us, and He always is, there is no need to fear. Even when storms come that cause us to despair, and Jesus appears to be unaware, such a perception is simply untrue and invalid. Sometimes the reason He does not respond is that He has a lesson for us to learn. Trust is not about the cessation of storms in our lives; it is about a person we can rely upon in any and all circumstances.

7. There are people in our world more concerned with keeping the sources of creaturely comfort than they are with the surpassing comforts of Christ's presence. Have you met people like the people of Gadarene who are more concerned for their own lives than they are for the enormous tragedy of others? Further, can you imagine having Jesus in our presence and be more concerned about pigs? Have you ever had instances when you valued the temporal over the eternal? Have you ever had times when you wished Jesus would just go away?

8. Miracles do not cause faith; Christianity is not true because of the wonders Jesus performed. Wonders point to Jesus and demand of us a decision. Will we accept Him or reject Him? This is why Matthew put miracles in a succinct manner but emphasized the response to them. Can you list times when Jesus has stepped into your life and done wonders? Did you respond with a greater realization of His person and deeper faith?

9. '… O you of little faith?' (8:26) is something that Jesus does not commend. This is said of those who had been with Him for some time observing His miracles and

hearing Him preach. However, a Gentile soldier of an army of occupation possessed such faith and trust in Jesus that He felt compelled to comment on it. Here was a man that had no direct experience with Jesus, but his hearing about Him generated trust in Him. You and I have been with Him; we have experienced His power and mercy. Would Jesus criticize the quality of your faith when difficulties come? What practical steps are you taking to increase your faith and trust in Him?

The healing of the paralytic (9:1-8)

Having returned to Capernaum, Jesus was once more confronted with a request for healing. This miracle is important for several reasons: First, this is the first time that Jesus talks of His ability to forgive sins, though we have the statement in 1:21 to that effect. Second, the rising tide of criticism from the religious leadership manifests itself in certain scribes being there. These leaders appear to be Galileans, not leaders from Jerusalem (15:1). Perhaps the cleansed leper alerted them to Jesus' claims (8:1-4), though Jesus had made negative comments about the nation's religious leadership in 5:20 and 7:29. Third, spiritual healing is impossible to prove, so Jesus linked it with something very obvious. Fourth, the claim to forgive sin is a claim to deity. Fifth, the reaction of the masses is enough to bring the nation to a crisis (cf. 27:18). Sixth, the passage is Christological; it has nothing to do with the disciples. Jesus claims to forgive sin on His own authority. Only God can forgive sin, though it is easier to make the claim when there is no immediate external confirmation as in a healing.

The outline of the incident is (1) the circumstance (vv. 1-2a), (2) the declaration of Jesus (v. 2b), the response of some scribes (v. 3), the response of Jesus (vv. 4-6a), the command of Jesus (v. 6b), the miracle of healing (v. 7a), and the response of the witness (v. 7b).

Since Jesus connected the walking with forgiveness, was the man's physical problem of paralysis a result of judgment? Such is not stated in this or any parallel account of the healing. Faith brought the healing, the faith most likely being that of the paralytic and his friends ('their faith'). The healing itself seems incidental to Jesus' claim to forgive sin, a claim judged to be blasphemous (v. 3).

Again, the title 'Son of Man' (v. 6), Jesus' most common appellation, is used by Him. It is derived from Daniel 7:13-14 and indicates that He shares God's sovereignty and dominion over the people of the world. It is the authority of heaven that accounts for the miracles He performed.

An Interlude: Matthew's Call and a Question (9:9-17)

In the previous interlude, after a series of miracles, Jesus applied the implications of them to the demanding nature of discipleship (8:18-22). Here He examples the cost of discipleship in the call of Matthew. Jesus called a social outcast, a tax collector, to Himself.

Matthew's encounter with Jesus (vv. 9-13)

The call of Matthew has been previously noted (cf. Introduction). Matthew, like the other four disciples called by Jesus in the gospel (4:18-22), immediately followed Him. Capernaum, the site of this incident, was a commercial center. Matthew, in the hire of Herod Antipas, collected toll or custom taxes on the transportation of goods at this point on the Via Maris, the highway to the sea. Capernaum was the initial major city located in the jurisdiction of Herod Antipas when traveling from the northeast.

The reaction of Matthew is described in verse 10. His joyful response to Jesus' call was to arrange a dinner party ('were reclining with Jesus and his disciples') for his friends, social outcasts like himself, and invite Jesus to it (v. 10). Jesus ate with sinners, not because they were particularly open to Him, but because they were sinners having need of Him.

The criticism of the Pharisees is mentioned in verses 11-13. Their reaction, which is for the first time regarded as opposing Jesus, indicates the rising tide of animosity they felt towards Him (see 10:25; 12:24, 27). Jesus answers them here in two ways. First, He explains His action by quoting a saying that physicians are called to help the sick (v. 12). Second, He cites Hosea 6:6, equating the Pharisees of His day with those who opposed the prophets in ancient Israel, because they have placed ritualistic conformity over care and compassion (v. 13).

Clearly, they and He were on a collision course! According to Jesus, the Pharisees aligned with the apostates of ancient Israel. According to the Pharisees, Jesus is empowered by 'the prince of demons' (v. 34).

The question of John's disciples (vv. 14-17)

Some of the disciples of John the Baptist came to Jesus with a question about fasting that reveals them to be more aligned with the Pharisees than with Jesus on the issue. The only day of prescribed fasting in the Law was the Day of Atonement, though pious Jews fasted on Monday and Thursday in Jesus' day.

Jesus is seen fasting only once in Matthew, relative to His temptations recorded in chapter 4. Though He states the fact that His disciples will fast later (see Acts 9:9; 13:3; 14:23; 27:9), it will only occur after the 'groom' has departed; He does not give a commandment for them to fast. He makes the point of the inappropriateness of fasting while He is present with two illustrations. Jesus is, in effect, rejecting contemporary Judaism; His way is not to amend contemporary Judaism, but to explain something entirely different. He affirms Old Testament Judaism (5:17), but not Pharisaic Judaism.

In addition to scribes and Pharisees, John's disciples came to Him with a question (v. 14). Clearly, Jesus aligns with neither the religious leadership nor John's followers. The Pharisees and John's disciples fast; Jesus' disciples did not. The question may have arisen from the feast in Matthew's home in the previous paragraph.

Jesus' answer is that fasting is not consistent with celebration (v. 15). He likens His presence with the disciples to a joyful wedding feast. The absence of the bridegroom will lead to a time of fasting. This is the first hint to the disciples that there will be a time that Jesus will not be with them. The use of the verb 'taken away' (the verb being passive) suggests a violent departure. The first hint of His death is connected to Pharisaic opposition that emerged at this time.

The point of the illustrations used by Jesus – the new-cloth-on-old garments and new-wine-in-old-skins (vv. 16-17) – is that He did not come to patch up or reform first-century Judaism. Cloth not pre-washed makes for failed patching, actually making matters worse; new wine in old wine skins has the same failed effect – fermentation bursts them, so creating waste. Jesus' teaching is incompatible with that of the Pharisees! The new teaching and the old teaching are antithetical!

Three Miracles of Personal Healing (9:18-34)

Matthew ends the section with three miracles, one of them a double healing episode and one involving two people. In this series of miracles, Jesus conquers death and incurable diseases (issues of uncleanness, blindness, and deafness). An important insight is the developing theme of the acceptance and rejection of His claims. The crowds marveled and saw the connection between His miracles and Messiahship (v. 33); the leadership recognized the supernatural origin of His works, but they assigned the origin of them to the evil minions of the devil (v. 34).

Two healings, a young girl, and a woman (vv. 18-26)

The story of Jairus' daughter is told in verses 18-19 and 23-26. This healing of this twelve-year-old (Mark 5:42) is interesting because it was performed in Capernaum and the father was a synagogue official. Touching the deceased was defiling, so Jesus' action is again a commentary on His relationship to official Judaism. Further, the father's request that He come to his daughter's aid suggests that he had a deep perception of the uniqueness of Jesus or that he was desperately overcome with grief, perhaps both. The synagogue was built with the generous support of the Roman centurion (Luke 7:5) whose slave Jesus healed (Matt. 8:5-13). There is no recorded conversation with Jairus; Jesus simply moved toward his home.

With burial the same day as death, Jesus enters the home with the burial ritual in progress, including the presence of hired mourners. The resurrection of Jairus' daughter is arguably the greatest miracle Jesus performed up to this time (two more such miracles will follow, the son of a widow [Luke 7] and Lazarus [John 11], though neither are recorded by Matthew). These miracles link Jesus to Israel's greatest prophets, Elijah and Elisha (1 Kings 17:20-24; 2 Kings 4:17-37).

In the midst of going to Jairus' house (Jesus never entered the home of a Gentile to our knowledge), a woman with severe cervical bleeding, having suffered twelve years with it, touched him (ironically, Jairus' daughter was the same age as the length of her suffering) and she was healed by contacting the tassels of his shirt-like outer garment (tassels were worn to remind the Jew of the commandments, Num. 15:37-38). Again, being touched by a person with a blood issue was thought to cause defilement. Jesus will explain the cause of defilement later (15:19).

Jesus frequently asks questions as teaching devices, not for self-understanding. He wanted the woman to know that it was not some kind of magic that caused her healing, such as touching a holy man, but a divine intervention; further, He desired to make the healing public knowledge. It is faith (v. 22) that brings healing if God wills it to be so, not magic! This is the only recorded time that Jesus calls a woman 'daughter'. Blomberg has an insightful comment at this point: 'Praiseworthy faith does not doubt God's ability to act, but it does not presume to know how he will choose to act.'[1]

The healing of two blind men (vv. 27-31)
With the healing of the two blind men by His touch, there is a phrase that is repeated in substance from the previous miracle, the growing 'fame' of Jesus (v. 31, 'report' v. 26). The rising popularity of Jesus demanded a verdict from the leadership. This miracle occurs indoors, away from the crowds, perhaps to lessen the excitement about Jesus' claims. For the first time in the book, Jesus is called the Son of David, the Messiah, by a person other that the writer of the book (see 1:1), this having clear Messianic implications. The title is found six additional times in the book (12:23; 15:22; 20:30, 31; 21:9, 15).

This is the only time in Matthew's gospel that faith is required of the recipient as a condition for healing (remember, a blind person cannot see what is happening; he/she can only believe what they hear). The object of faith is not that they would be healed, but that Jesus can heal them; it is faith in a person (Jesus does not indicate the amount of faith these men had, but the fact of it). Though they had faith through what they had heard about Jesus, they did not consequently obey

---

1. Craig Blomberg, *Matthew*, p. 161.

His instructions for silence (perhaps out of their enthusiasm). As a pattern demonstrated elsewhere in the narrative, Jesus often sought to prevent a premature confrontation (Matt. 14:22; John 6:14-15) over the validity of His claims until Jerusalem! Interestingly, there are no recorded miracles of sight-restoration in the Old Testament, nor in the New Testament after the gospels, but in Jesus' ministry this is the most frequent miracle.

The healing of a mute demoniac (vv. 32-34)

In the healing of the mute demoniac, there is no reference to faith, although the man had some degree of hope in the miracle-worker or of a healing touch. Of importance to the developing theme of rejection is that here the Pharisees render a verdict about Jesus for the first time in the book (v. 34), though the charge of demonic powers is repeated in 12:24. The Pharisees did not question Jesus' power to heal; they questioned the source of the authority to do so. Here is another hint, this time from the religious leadership, that hostility is reaching a breaking point. The descriptive brevity of the healing, the briefness of its description, places the emphasis on the reaction to the miracle more than the miracle itself.

Applications

1. The call of Matthew illustrates the fact that the worst of society are not out of Jesus' reach. A person's past, no matter how sordid, or his present circumstances, does not put him or her outside the mercy of God. God chose four fishermen to be with Him, not the highest on the social scale, and a marginalized political turncoat. There is hope for any and every one if Jesus comes our way and calls us. Has He called you to be a follower?

2. The reaction of Matthew to Jesus' call, gathering him into a new community, is also instructive. Suddenly he is filled with delight and joy. What a picture of the consequence of knowing Jesus. Matthew had wealth and position among the politically dominant, but

lacked a warm heart born of acceptance by another. The change is a picture of redemption, Christian faith and discipleship (three equivalent concepts for new life in Jesus). Further, Matthew expressed his joy in a party and invited his former colleagues to meet Jesus. Redemption is such a wonderful experience that we want others to share it. Joy within and concern for others are marks of true discipleship. Are they true of you?

3. It is wise to come to Jesus when our loved ones are in need. Jairus realized that Jesus was the answer to his grief. In faith he brought his need to Jesus. When tragedy strikes in your family, do your instinctively turn to Jesus for solace? Though Jesus may not choose to bring physical healing, His presence and power is our comfort. Do you know that?

4. Strong faith is often found in strange places. The two blind men 'saw' more clearly than those with sight, and a deaf person heard. The woman with the twelve-year health issue knew where to go. The point of these miracles is not in the healing but in the recognition of the healer. Not that He has the power to do so only, but that the one who does so is the Son of David, the Messiah, the Son of Man, and the Son of God. The point is the person, not the miracle!

5. In the story of the calling of Matthew, he followed Jesus (v. 9). In the Jairus story, Jesus followed him (v. 19). The first episode about Jairus' daughter expresses authority and power as the sovereign Lord; the second, about the woman, the compassion and condescension of the same powerful and sovereign Lord. You and I have a Lord who is worthy of following because of who He is. However, His compassion towards us in order to serve us makes our service of Him a delight. 'What a wonderful Saviour is Jesus our Lord,' goes an old hymn.

6. There are several kinds of laughter, I suppose. The laughter of ridicule is the harshest upon us emotionally, joy the most delightful. The laughter of the mourners in Jairus' home was that of scorn; the laughter of

Sarah was that of shock, perhaps unbelief (Gen. 18:12). People ridicule what they find strange to their social experience, even as they did on that day. The laughter of unbelief when one hears the truth is sad. When you read the great events and sayings in the Bible, is your response that of joy or disbelief or even scorn? Do you laugh in faithlessness at the power of God because it seems strange?

7. What a wonderful faith statement was made by the woman with the issue of blood. 'If only I touch his garment, I will get well' (v. 21). The answer to life's dilemmas is a divine touch. The lady was quite correct and insightful. Where do we find this divine touch? It comes from intimacy with the risen Jesus through prayer and the ingestion of His Word through the witness of the Spirit of God taking the Bible and making it come alive in our hearts. Do you believe what this woman had no trouble believing?

8. The miracles in this chapter are an argument from the lesser to the greater. If Jesus can help the blind, cast out demons from the dumb (a double miracle in this case), and raise the dead, He can forgive sin (9:56). Do you value divine healing of the heart more than the healing of the body? Do you rejoice more that you are known by the greatest person in the world rather than that you have health? Is the physical a greater source of joy to you than the spiritual?

4

The Instruction of the King
to the Disciples
(9:35–11:1)

This section contains Jesus' second major discourse in the book. The first was to the disciples, as well as the crowds, and the theme was a general description of life in His kingdom and His view of contemporary Judaism (chs. 5–7). Here the message is to His disciples only and it contains instructions for service; obviously, the disciples had matured somewhat through contact with Jesus. The content of the discourse is the immediate issues of ministry, but some of that content is ageless instruction. Jesus is also preparing His church for centuries of service. The mission here is a limited one; the disciples are in training.

The theme of increased hostility to Jesus' claims connects this section to chapters 11 and 12. His words (chs. 5–7) and His works or miracles (chs. 8–9) have brought a crisis. The people were seeing Jesus' increasing Messianic claims; the leadership is forced to respond. They are on a collision course that will bring Jesus to Calvary.

The Context of the Discourse (9:35–10:4)
These verses give us the context for Jesus' instructions that follow. The reason for sending out the twelve is Jesus' compassion for the multitudes who are without a true shepherd.

The prefatory statement (v. 35)

Prior to each of the five discourses in the book, Matthew inserts a summary statement of Jesus' ministry and concludes with a similar statement. This seems clearly the case when one compares 4:23-24 with the statement here; thus, you have a literary device, repetition, that frames a major section (chs. 5–9), Jesus' words and works. This verse is also part of a framing technique that is completed in 11:1.

The compassion of Christ for the multitudes (vv. 36-37)

The word translated 'compassion' suggests movement from one's inner being, deep within oneself. Outside the parables, it is used only six times of Jesus' reactions. It is the same word used of Jesus' attitude in the cleansing of the leper (Mark 1:41, a parallel to the account found in Matthew 8:1-4).

Matthew describes the compassion of Jesus for the crowds as connected to His perception of their spiritual plight: exhaustion, oppression, and lack of direction. He sees (the tense of the verb indicates a present, ongoing condition) a people striving, expending energy, but accomplishing little. Sheep are defenseless animals and unable to forage on their own; they require guidance for food and protection. Goats do well on their own; sheep do not (interesting is it not that helpless sheep are depicted as His while goats that can make it on their own are not His metaphorically!). They are a people surrounded by failed leadership, as sheep without the comfort and care of a shepherd.

Jesus also employed a second metaphor, an agricultural image. He does so not to emphasize the plight of the people, but the enormity of the task of reaching them in light of the paucity of workers. The potential for a harvest is great, but workers few. The words 'send out' are better translated 'thrust out'; it suggests a state of urgency. We would say that people need a circumstance to see a need and respond!

The request of Christ for the multitudes (v. 38)

Ironically, Jesus does not command the disciples to go into the 'harvest' of Israel, but to pray.

The empowerment of the disciples to go to the multitudes (10:1)
Authority to do the works of the Messiah is granted to the twelve,
works of exorcism and physical healing. This is the first time in
the book that the twelve are presented as a group. Perhaps Jesus
chose twelve to suggest the twelve tribes; whereas old Israel
failed in its mission, 'New Israel' through 'True Israel' will not.

The naming of the apostles to go to the multitudes (10:2-4)
This is the only mention of the twelve with the designation 'the
apostles' (basically meaning 'sent ones') in Matthew. The twelve
were a recognized group before, but this appears to be another
step in the development of these men for special privilege. It is
also the only time they are sent exclusively to Israel.

In every list of the disciples, Peter is the first named and
Judas Iscariot is last. Peter is clearly the leader among the
apostles; he was the one who was most prominent in the early
chapters of Acts, a time when the church was predominately
Jewish in constituency. Most of the twelve left little mark
on the history of the church; perhaps they were simply not
outstanding men. Jesus does not choose many superstars; the
ordinary is mixed with the unusual!

Of the twelve, Andrew and Philip had been followers of
John; Peter is the extrovert of the group; Peter, Andrew, James,
and John were fishermen together; Bartholomew is likely
Nathaniel; we know nothing of the later work of Thomas,
Matthew, James the son of Alphaeus, Thaddeus (called Judas,
not Iscariot), or Simon the Zealot, though tradition has sought
to fill in some gaps. Within this band of men was a pro-Roman
tax-gatherer and an extreme Jewish patriot (unless 'Zealot' is
used to describe his religious zeal)! Three were from Bethsaida
(Peter, Andrew, and Philip [west of the Jordan under the rule
of Herod Philip] and may account for their Greek names being
reflective of a greater Hellenistic cultural influence. Another
was from Cana of Galilee (Nathaniel). Only Judas Iscariot was
from Judea of the twelve. They are arranged in pairs of six each
('and'). Peter is the first *among* them, but not placed *over* them.

The content of the discourse (10:5–11:1)
It is evident here and elsewhere (vv. 24-25) that Jesus was
willing to discuss widely separated events within the

same framework. Some of this discourse has immediate application to the mission at hand (v. 5), some applies to the post-Pentecost mission found in Acts and the epistles (v. 18), and some is timeless (v. 23). At least it is applicable until the Son of Man is fully reigning over all the peoples of the earth! This matter of incorporating the near and distant together gives His words a timelessness, though it is sometimes difficult for the interpreter to know Jesus' reference point. The emphasis in the section is upon instruction for a mission, not the mission itself since it is not mentioned.

The instructions for their mission (vv. 5-15)

Their audience is described in verses 5-6. The geographical limitations (neither to Gentiles [north and east] nor Samaritans [south]) suggest that this first mission was restricted to the Galilee. Jesus enjoyed greater popularity there than in Judea where the religious leadership opposed Him. This is the only reference to Samaritans in Matthew.

Their message is stated in verse 7. The disciples went out as emissaries of Jesus, having His authority and announcing His message. The message was the same that John announced (3:1-2) and Jesus proclaimed (4:17), a message of repentance with a view to the coming of the kingdom.

Their confirmation is seen in verse 8. The tenses of the verbs change from present, suggesting ongoing action, to a tense normally translated as past. The authority and ability to serve has been granted to them ('you received') from the Lord; it is a gift and privilege. As they received ability to serve freely, they were to serve freely. While we have subsequent data that the apostles exercised the gifts of various healings and demonic deliverances, we do not have a record of their raising the dead.

In verses 9-10 the issue of their provisions is dealt with. The disciples were to travel unencumbered, avoiding any hint of a profit motive. D. A. Carson has a wonderful comment at this point: 'The church does not *pay* its ministers; rather, it provides them with resources so that they are able to serve freely.'[1] The

---

1. This comment by D. A. Carson is quoted by Blomberg, *Matthew*, pp. 171-72.

emphasis here is upon simplicity, austerity, and the urgency of the mission. It is not so much that Jesus desires His servants to suffer from lack; it is that He wants them to remain dependent and, most likely, to grow in faith and trust. They are to receive no remuneration for the miracles they effect; frugality is to characterize their demeanor in the work (for example, only have the shoes they wear), though they can accept lodging, drink, and food.

It is clear from verses 11-15 that the disciples are to encounter appreciation as well as rejection and hostility from their endeavors. The image of shaking off dust, since Jews often did this in returning from Gentile territories, being unclean through contact with the dust of their ground, suggests that hostile Jews are to be treated like Gentiles. This is confirmed by verse 15.

In the Sodom/Gomorrah judgment (Gen. 19), the Sodomites acted with social incivility to guests. The rejection of the message of the kingdom will incur greater judgment because of the greater person they reject.

Verse 15, along with 12:47-48, is used by some commentators, such as Blomberg,[2] to suggest degrees of punishment for disobedience. It would seem that this has very little textual warrant. While punishment should fit the crime and the heinousness of sin may vary as it relates to people, all sin is ultimately against God. Since God is infinite, all sin is infinite travesty and must be punished with infinite judgment. I take such statements as we have here, and elsewhere, to be literary figures of speech suggesting severity.

The difficulties in their mission are mentioned in verses 16-23. The apostles are to anticipate difficulties from three kinds of 'wolves': religious wolves, political wolves, and familial wolves. It is interesting that the circumstances detailed in verses 17-23 happened during the post-resurrection ministry of the disciples, not before. Verses 24-42 appear to focus on both the immediate present and the future as well, though the emphasis seems to be more upon their future ministry. Here is an example of the overlapping or the compressing of time that is clearly evident in the

---

2. Blomberg, *Matthew*, p. 173.

Olivet Discourse (chs. 24–25). Jesus at times combines the near and the far without distinguishing the two.

Jesus made it clear, using a metaphor in this case, that He was sending His disciples into danger (v. 16). Sheep are defenceless animals and wolves are carnivorous predators. Living among 'wolves' demands that they act wisely and faithfully (a dove is characterized by loyalty and gentleness). We must use our heads, knowing the danger 'wolves' pose, but also be focused upon and remain faithful to the Lord.

The reference to governors, kings, and Gentiles (vv. 17-18) seems to project the instruction beyond Jesus' immediate context (v. 5), as does the reference 'until the Son of Man comes' (v. 23). However, the term used for 'courts' means the Sanhedrin or local councils; here Jewish resistance is in view. At this time Galilee had neither a governor nor a king. Herod Antipas, a tetrarch and puppet monarch, ruled the area. Jesus seems to be referring to events that will happen in mixed Jew and Gentile areas. This sounds like the early chapters of the Book of Acts.

In the crises that the disciples will face, they are promised strength to fulfill their task 'by the Spirit of your Father speaking in you' (vv. 19-20). This seems to be a fulfillment of 3:11, that Jesus would baptize or empower His people with the Holy Spirit for service.

When speaking of the disciples, it is interesting that Jesus refers to the Spirit as of 'your Father', but when He refers to His relationship to the Father, He uses the word 'my'. This suggests the intimacy and identity of a close relationship between them.

To use verse 20 as a basis to justify shoddy preparation is simply to miss the context and create a pretext. The subject is trust in very difficult circumstances; it is no warrant to justify dereliction in preparation for public addresses.

The response of opponents is expanded in verses 21-22. The penalty for following Jesus was previously predicted to be flogging (v. 17). Here it is death. The term 'betray' is the word used of Judas' action later on. The tragedy is so severe that it strikes at the root of family unity, the basic unit of society. This indicates the fulfillment of Jesus' words implying circumstances beyond preaching in the Galilee since there is no record of their martyrdom until later (James met death under Herod Agrippa I in the A.D. 40s, later Peter and Paul at Rome in the 60s). Jesus validates this by an allusion to Micah 7:6, a text that speaks of the chaos with the breaking up of the social order. The preaching of the disciples will bring social disruption with serious consequences.

Persistence is required (v. 23). The title 'Son of Man', Jesus' most used self-designation, is a reference to Daniel 7:13-14. In Daniel, a person is brought before God's throne in heaven and granted lordship over all the peoples of the world. The phrase, 'the coming of the Son of Man,' suggests his vindication and sovereign rule. The phrase, 'before the Son of Man comes' (v. 23), appears to be one of those lines that has multiple references. In a sense, it can refer to the judgment that befell the nation in the Roman suppression of A.D. 70, so making sense of the comment that the task on which the disciples are about to embark will be incomplete at our Lord's 'coming'. While the phrase can be taken as a reference to the final coming in eschatological judgment, it seems difficult to understand how the task will then be incomplete. It may be best to refer the statement to the advent of the 'now-but-not-yet' aspect of the kingdom that Jesus instructed His disciples to include in their prayers (6:10), the vindication and enthronement of the Son of Man (Acts 1–2). This verse may account for the impression within the early church that the Lord would return within their era (see also John 21:22-23).

The reason for their rejection in the mission is given in verses 24-25. The cause of the disciples' mistreatment is their master; a student can expect no better fare than his/ her mentor. A disciple is always a learner and, as such, not superior to his teacher. While a slave can share in the glories of his/her master, he/she is never more than a humble member in the household, never rising to a position of authority.

The term 'Beelzebul' is difficult to precisely understand. It is used in 2 Kings 1:2, 3, 6, 16 for a pagan deity. The Jews used the term in a derogatory sense. Thus, the Jews took a negative term and applied it to evil people. Used in this fashion, it suggests that the Pharisees interpreted Jesus as being evil. If Jesus' enemies saw Him as evil, being demonical, they will see His followers in the same light.

The consolation in their mission is described in verses 26-33. 'So have no fear,' a command, occurs three times in this section; the disciples are assured that they will be treated as the master and that He knows them intimately. Warnings of peril and encouragement of His presence are blended. What a beautifully comforting passage!

God will vindicate His people (vv. 26-27). Because the disciples received their message from the Lord, it was not of human invention. God is behind our message and that message should be published broadly and publicly. We need not fear failure in the enterprise. Judgment in the final day is two-edged; it will be punishment for the wicked and vindication for God's children. In the sense of vindication, it will be a great day for them.

God will preserve His people (v. 28). We are not to fear men because the worst they can do does not match what God can do. The possibility of death was raised in verse 21; here it is made explicit. We are beyond destruction by those who only have access to the body. We are never told to fear Satan!

The reference to 'hell' in this passage (v. 28) is a direct rebuttal of those who believe that the soul of mankind is not immortal. The body can suffer destruction, but the soul cannot. There is existence beyond the demise of the physical body! The preservation of life is only a short-term advantage; far more important is obedience to God for that issue has eternal significance.

God cares for His people (vv. 29-31). Danger is juxtaposed against trust in our heavenly Father, the God who is all-powerful and also all-caring. God's sovereignty extends to the smallest details, even to brown birds, so we should have confidence that He superintends larger matters. Here is an argument from the lesser to the greater. Nothing is beyond His knowledge and control!

God will honor those who follow Him (vv. 32-33). The 'I' is emphatic in this sentence meaning that we have here a promise based on the character and integrity of the promise giver. He will not forget those who follow after Him ('everyone' [v. 32] 'whoever' [v. 33])! However, those who deny Him on earth face dire consequences.

Nevertheless, a remembrance is needed (vv. 34-42). A corrective is stated in verses 34-36. While Jesus is the 'prince of peace', His ministry will bring violence and disruption as a consequence. Jesus came to bring peace to the earth, but until the kingdom is fully manifest there will be no peace on the earth. 'I came' suggests that this was Jesus' purpose in coming and it should characterize our ministries as well. Interestingly, Jesus is asserting that He existed before He came! Here is a clear statement of His deity.

If one result of Jesus' ministry is hinted as family disruption (v. 21), it is made explicit here as Jesus quotes Micah 7:6. Jesus is not saying that such will always be the case, but in prophetic announcements there are often no qualifications. Such are stated in 'black and white' terms. Jesus is indicating that following Him can lead to temporal heartbreak!

Therefore, devotion is necessary (vv. 37-39). The issue of 'love' (v. 37) is an issue of priorities. We are to love our families (Eph. 6:1-4; 1 Tim. 5:8); Jesus is only speaking in 'black-white' prophetic terms to make a point. To make the point of the extreme sacrifice necessary in following Him, Jesus raises the metaphor of crucifixion. To suffer such a death is the ultimate shame in a family; it is a subhuman death. Taking up a cross suggests a call to the highest of sacrifices.

The section ends with a promise in the form of two statements. To lose one's life is to gain it if lost in the service of the king; to gain it in life is to lose it ultimately if used in the service of selfish ends. Those who live a life characterized by empty pursuits will end empty handed!

A reward will be issued (vv. 40-42). This section is composed of three sayings suggesting Jesus' high estimation of the disciples and their mission; the disciples are an extension of Jesus. The grace extended to a disciple is in the acceptance by others of Jesus and the One who sent Him (v. 40). Disciples are Jesus' representatives. As Jesus, so his disciples; they are prophets; they speak with the same authority (v. 41).

Jesus will remember them (v. 42). The phrase 'little ones' will be more fully explained in 18:6-14 where Jesus uses it as a metaphor for all those who are disciples, members of His community. See also 25:40, 45. All disciples of Jesus are 'little ones'. The content of His statement is about the smallest of gifts given by the most insignificant of people. The 'insignificant ones' are His followers; those who stand in authority with the prophets, who speak the Word of God with the authority of God upon them. It seems to suggest those who are without earthly strength.

Blomberg has an interesting observation about Jesus' reference to 'prophets', 'a righteous man,' and 'little ones'.[3] He speculates that it indicates people of varying authority and influence, the prophet being a public leader in the assembly, the righteous being the spiritually mature, and the little ones being the lowest of influence (the unobtrusive, the average, and the insignificant). However, status is not the ground of reward; it is faithfulness relative to circumstance, privilege, and capacity.

The *conclusion* of the address is given in 11:1. This verse follows the Matthean pattern of a summary proceeding and following a discourse (4:23; 7:28-29; 9:35), though in the two previous cases the summary is more replete.

It seems clear in the previous two chapters that Jesus' instruction (9:35–10:42) was to prepare them to go with Him, not to go alone. In 12:1 the disciples are with the Lord and there is nothing in chapter 11 to suggest otherwise. The only time the disciples operated without Jesus they were a failure (17:16). It is only after the resurrection that the disciples go without Him. However, He did not leave them alone as the promise in the final verse of the book makes clear (28:20, 'I am with you always ...'). Jesus never leaves us alone!

Applications

1. When you think of the men that Jesus chose to be with Him, the diversity is striking. Lowly fishermen, a pro-Herodian tax accessor/collector, and a religious/political Zealot. Peter was impetuous, acting before thinking, yet often insightful and failing at crucial moments; Andrew was contemplative and more people-observant; Thomas had difficulty learning about faith and trust. Jesus could mold each of them. The lesson is that He can make

---

3. Blomberg, *Matthew*, p. 182.

disciples out of all kinds of different personalities. Are you not glad that is the case? There are no prerequisites except a willingness to follow. All you have to be is willing. Are you willing to follow?

2. The rejection of Christ through rejection of His messengers has dire consequences. To refuse infinite generosity is an infinite travesty of divine mercy and, therefore, worthy of just wrath. As the cities rejected the Saviour's words and works (Bethsaida, Chorazin, and Capernaum [11:21-24]), they were left without hope. This experience should bring tears to our eyes as it did to Jesus (23:37-39). While it is painful for us when we encounter persons who have no interest in the gospel, it will be far more painful for them should their hardness of heart continue. While we should expect rejection, it is never easy.

3. God's servants should expect rebuff, sometimes from family members. Struggles, pain, and hardship are not foreign from the experience of disciples. Rejection of the Saviour is a ground for the justice of divine wrath in the last day. You and I will leave behind us blessing and cursing. Blessing for those who believe and receive the divine gospel, judgment for those who do not. God clearly has not promised us unmitigated success. Sobering, is it not?

4. When you share the gospel-claims of Jesus with people, expect to be challenged. While only a few are called before politically powerful people, we will all face confrontation. Jesus did not shrink from it when the opportunity was right, and neither should we. Sometimes you have to step out of your retiring demeanor and 'tell it like it is'.

5. It is wise to fear God more than mankind. Opponents can threaten the body which is our temporal tent; they have no control over our immaterial being. How often do we fear people more than God? This realization should help us with the common abnormality of fearing people, their reactions and ridicule. Do you live in the

fear of people or the fear of the Lord? We fear people because of the threat of the damage they could cause to our psyche or body; we should fear God because of His great kindness and mercy with a holy, compelling awe. Is that true of you?

6. God has a complete knowledge of His children, even the hairs of their heads. This minute knowledge is actually a figure of speech, a metaphor (though I know that He actually does), suggestive of His great love, care, and interest towards us. He cares for us far more than for the smallest sparrow, though His care for the sparrow should remind us of His greater love for us. He did not give His Son for sparrows, and He did not spare His Son for us. Do you regularly take the time to think about how much God loves and cares for you? Is there any place for justifiable fear for your life and safety?

7. That Jesus did not send the disciples out alone after the instructions of this chapter (He was going with them) brings out two very important truths. First, Jesus will not send us into circumstances that He has not prepared us to endure. He is a wise teacher, combining instruction with example before execution by the disciples. Second, that Jesus went with them is a great comfort. You and I are never alone in the service of the King. He said, 'I will be with you always ...' (28:20). He is with you today though He is the resurrected Lord of heaven! The clue is found in verse 20, the ministry of the Spirit of God in 'you'. The promise of God's presence is through the gift of the indwelling Holy Spirit. Does that not excite you? Does that not encourage you?

The Rejection of Jesus: The King
(11:2–27:66)

5

The Responses to and Rejection
of the King
(11:2–12:50)

The formal response of the leadership of the nation came as the disciples took a more active part in the proclamation of the message of the kingdom. What we have in these two chapters are reactions culminating in the declaration of the religious leadership in Jerusalem that credits Jesus' claims and verifications to the power of the devil. The hint of discredit by the religious leadership in 9:34 becomes increasingly clear in this section (12:14). Again, something about John introduces a new direction for Jesus in the book; this time the theme is not announcement, but rejection.

The Inquiry of John (11:2-19)

John's request (vv. 2-6)

There are various views of what precipitated the inquiry of John (personal doubt, the depressing effect of imprisonment [4:12], a declining level of patience). However, it may be that John was simply puzzled. Could Jesus be simply a forerunner like himself? John, in the least, seems unsure; there were differences in John's conduct of ministry and that of Jesus (9:14-17). Perhaps those differences and an immediate expectation of the Messiah's reign proved disconcerting. John was a prophet announcing the coming One, but he lived before the inauguration of Jesus' kingdom and the new community of faith.

A possible clue to John's inquiry may be found in the phrase 'what you hear and see' (v. 4). John was incarcerated at the inception of Jesus' public ministry (4:13). Reports had come to him of the ministry and claims of the One he had baptized with a view to the advent of the kingdom (discourses, miracles, and expanding popularity). Yet, the promised kingdom had not come. The parallels between John and Elijah, his prototype (11:14), are of interest since both were powerful preachers who became demoralized (1 Kings 19:4).

Jesus replies with a summary of His ministry in the language of Isaiah 35:5-7 and 61:1. The first of these promised a return from Israel's captivity with a listing of signs that would accompany its fulfillment (in quoting this text the immediate, shadowed prediction has to do with the return from the Babylonian Captivity, yet it is fulfilled in Jesus' coming, as indicated in Jesus' identity with it [the now-but-not-yet], and its completeness in the eternal kingdom). The second is clearly predictive of the ministry of the Messiah.

Jesus cites six types of miracles presented in couplets. He is saying to the disciples of John that they should look at the evidence and answer their own question (of the blind man healed in 9:27-31, there are no recorded miracles of this type in the Old Testament; clearly, something new has come about); so also of the lame walking (9:2-8, the paralytic), lepers cleansed (8:1-4), the deaf hearing (9:32-33), the dead raised (9:18-26, also Jairus' daughter) when the gospel is preached.

In the prophetic passages from Isaiah that Jesus cites, the cleansing of lepers and raising the dead are not mentioned. Jesus' ministry evidentially exceeds that envisioned by the great prophet.

The section ends (v. 6) with a beatitude-like statement to encourage John. The word for 'offended' is one from which we get the word 'scandal'. God's approval rests upon those not embarrassed over Jesus!

Jesus' evaluation of John (vv. 7-19)

The tables have been turned. Jesus now witnesses about the man who had witnessed of Him (clearly, John was not embarrassed by Jesus). Jesus must have received John's messengers in a public setting because His reply is public. Here is Jesus' view of John: John is 'Elijah' (there are multiple fulfillments in prophetic announcements). He is least in the kingdom, because he announced only its coming fuller manifestation, the Old Testament era being the age of shadows. John announced a new era, the age of fullness or light, but did not enter it. As John's disciples leave to make their report to John, Jesus turns to the crowd to publicly speak of His forerunner (v. 7).

Jesus begins with four questions drawing the crowd into the conversation (vv. 7-9). 'A reed shaken by the wind' is a metaphor for a person who accommodates his message to the desire of the crowd, a person who seeks affirmation and vacillates. Perhaps they were attracted to a person of rhetorical grace; however, that type is found in palaces, not in the wilderness. They came to hear a prophet, and that John was!

Jesus confirms His view of John as being identified as Elijah by quoting Malachi 3:1, the fulfillment of prophecy. John's ministry was eschatological in importance; it was he who announced the end of an era. It is interesting that God would send a messenger to prepare for the Messiah; Jesus applies its fulfillment to Himself. Clearly, Jesus is claiming to be the Messiah. John's role was to prepare for Jesus; he should look for no other to come!

There has been 'no one greater' born of a woman because He announced the end of the era of anticipation, the fulfillment of prophecy, and the nearness of a new era, a monumental turning-point in all of redemptive history, the fulcrum of the new era of hope. John is 'least' because he only announced the era; he did not enter it (that is, the new community inaugurated by Jesus' resurrection and enthronement). John's greatness seems to be rooted in two realities: his proximity to the king and the kingdom, and that he is the fulfillment of Malachi 3:1, the king's announcer. His greatness was to be found in his privilege!

'The one least who is in the kingdom is greater ...' does not mean a person was outside of God's blessing for having not entered the kingdom, but simply that they were not in the new era (this would include all the Old Testament prophets). Simply put, John climaxed the pre-Christian era, the era of revelation! 'Greatness and least-ness' must refer to the benefits of participation in the earthly aspects of the kingdom, not rewards in heaven, the final and fullest manifestation of the kingdom. Jesus' point seems to be that any degree of participation in the now-and-not-yet kingdom is better than anything in the old era (the literary form is rhetorical. In this instance, it is a comparison between two eras. In a sense, the form functions the same as a parable to make a single point and little more).

'The kingdom of heaven has suffered violence' is difficult to understand. It is most likely a metaphor for the controversy that was rising about Jesus' ministry, the negative repercussions mentioned in chapter 10. With that understanding, Jesus was speaking of the religious leadership of His day who rose in opposition to Him ('suffered violence' would then be translated 'suffering violent attack'). It could also be a reference to the Zealots of Jesus' day who adopted a militant approach to ridding the country of Roman oppression, though this is less likely considering the context.

Jesus states that the primary function of the Hebrew Scriptures was to point to Him (v. 13). Not only the prophets (the proclaimers), but the Law and the Prophets (the Scriptures) prophesied of the dawn of a new era. The whole of the Old Testament is to be viewed as preparatory for the coming of the Messiah!

Jesus makes it unambiguously evident that John was 'Elijah' (Mal. 4:5-6; Matt. 17:12). Quite clearly John was not Elijah in a literal sense (this John specifically denied [John 1:21]). John fulfilled the great prophet's role.

Jesus' conclusion is that He and John were both rejected because of their manner of life, though for opposite reasons. John was ascetic, but accused of demonism; Jesus dined with the marginal and was accused of excess. Jesus uses a village metaphor to express the fickleness of the crowds' reception of Himself and John (vv. 16-17). 'Played the flute' suggests the gaiety of a wedding feast, also a dirge at a funeral (it seems to be a metaphor for the unwillingness to cooperate in the games). Jesus is accused of not being stately and austere ('you did not mourn'); John seemed joyless and did not participate in the joys of life ('you did not dance'). He was conceived as a stern, meandering maniac. The word 'children' can mean grown men (John 21:5); often Jesus uses terms with multiple meanings. The crowd, 'this generation,' simply misinterpreted both men.

John's austerity led to a misinterpretation (inspired by evil forces) and Jesus' social dealings with poor habits (keeping company with extortionists) resulting in ceremonial uncleanness – these specific charges are made here for the first time in the book (vv. 18-19). Jesus' reply is that validity is determined by outcomes, not appearances, and outcomes by motives.

Condemnation of the Unrepentant Cities (11:20-24)

Jesus condemned three cities where many of His miracles were performed; all lie in ruins today. This was not because of open opposition to Him in those places, but their lack of repentance. Jesus lived in one of them, Capernaum; three disciples came from Bethsaida (Andrew, Peter, and Philip) where Jesus healed a blind man (Mark 8:22-26); and Matthew (likely James and John also) lived in Capernaum where Peter later resided (8:14) with his mother-in-law. Is this why we have the calling of only five disciples (Philip excluded)? Chorazin is only mentioned here in the Bible and there is no record of any miracles performed there; but this is a clue that much is not recorded of Jesus' wide ministry in the Galilee (4:23; 9:35; 11:1; John 21:25). The initial enthusiasm and interest for Jesus apparently waned with the passing of time.

Had the same number of miracles been performed in Tyre and Sidon, large Phoenician cities, or even in notoriously wicked Sodom, they would have repented. Perhaps even more telling is that Sodom was in ruins, but Tyre and Sidon had not been destroyed as yet. Jesus' language seems more like John's than generally His own. Miracles were not performed in Tyre and Sidon indicating that Jesus was selective in His calling of people to Himself in verifying His claims; He did not aim at the most fruitful potential harvest. Apparently, God does not owe revelation to everyone or anyone! Tyre, an island city off the Mediterranean coast, once known for its commerce, was often denounced for its wickedness by the prophets (Isa. 23; Ezek. 26; Amos 1:9-10), Sodom as well (Matt. 10:15; 2 Pet. 2:6; Jude 7).

'Repent' or repentance does not mean merely a change of mind; it means a change in priorities, of motives, that result in a change of behavior.

A Concluding Insight and Invitation (11:25-30)

Before returning to the motif of confrontation, hostility, and rejection, Jesus focuses on the true community of God, 'little children' (see 10:42, 12:49). Clearly in this passage 'little children' are members of His new community through faith in Him as the Messiah; the term is used non-literally of God's people. Recorded here is Jesus' first prayer in the gospel. It seems that Jesus employed conversational prayer at this point rather that a more formal and private conversation.

The prayer has two parts: Jesus expressed thankfulness to the Father (vv. 25-26), and His relationship to the Father (v. 27), concluding by turning to the crowds inviting them to come to Him (vv. 28-30). Jesus invited the crowds to come into His kingdom in the discourse on the mountain as well (chs. 5–7).

Verses 25 and 26 explain the reason the cities in which Jesus performed significant miracles did not accept His claims. It is to be found in the Father's selectivity in a passage that echoes John 17:9. The Father, says Jesus, has revealed Himself, not to the wise, but to the simple of faith and trust. To personally address God as 'Father' would be shocking to a Jewish audience in the sense that for a person to call Him Father was unprecedented (it was used in a collective sense only before this citing; the prayer of Matthew 6:9 contained a corporate address to 'our Father'). He is not only Jesus' Father, the One to whom He submitted in the procurement of the wonder of redemption, He is 'Lord of heaven and earth', the intimate and all-powerful God! God's determination is a ground of our confidence and comfort. He does as He pleases, but always with righteousness, love, and justice combined.

In verse 27 is found a wonderful description of the relationship of the Father and Jesus; it is an intimate relationship; only the Father knows the Son, and the reverse. Here is a clear claim to the Son's deity and the exclusiveness of His message. Their knowledge and mutual relationship are equal, both divine!

Jesus concluded by calling the people to Himself (vv. 28-30); it is a universal invitation, the claims of His personhood applied. Unlike wisdom literature that invites a sharing in a wise person's insights, Jesus claims to be wisdom itself. Wisdom is in His person; it is who He is! 'Labor' suggests weariness, a burden too difficult to endure.

An animal yoke is a metaphor, something heavy or a burden such as social and political oppression in the Hebrew Scriptures; here it suggests the demands of the law as imposed by the Pharisees (12:1-4; 23:4). It is something of a hindrance, something restrictive and unwelcomed. 'The yoke' (in the New Testament it means submission to authority of some kind) of Jesus is a personal one; it is meant to make burdens lighter; it is about discipleship (actually a benevolent slavery). Both in the law and in Jesus, the yoke is about learning ('learn from me'). Jesus replaces the yoke with another of a new kind.

Applications

1. God uses all kinds of personality types in His service. John was a rough and tumble sort that spoke with conviction, even harshness at times. Jesus thought very highly of this prophet, though in a qualified sense he was 'least' in God's community. We all have roles to fulfill, and they are not the same. Jesus does not expect uniformity in abilities, strengths, or performance. The common factor is devotion and commitment in the service of the King. That seems to be comforting to me. I do not have the callings and gifts of others; I have a unique calling and fitness for the task of service. And so do you. Imagine that the smallest in the kingdom is more privileged than John because privilege is determined by proximity to Jesus. Nearness to Jesus is our greatest privilege.

2. It is interesting to think about the fact that sometimes no matter what we do we will be misunderstood by someone. In life, the expectancies of people will

prove impossible and disappointing. If we curb our exuberance, we will be criticized for not enjoying life; if we are sober minded, we will be credited with being a killjoy. If we live separate from sinners, we will be accused of incivility and social awkwardness; but if we socialize with sinners, we will be accused of acting like them. Since you simply cannot please all the people, we must live with our focus on the Lord and accept non-acceptance.

3. Jesus' words on condemnation are sobering. It tells us that special privilege with a proper response has grave implications. Are you similar to the cities of the Galilee that had so many divine favors, but never repented? All that spurn the mercies of God bring judgment justifiably upon themselves. The cities that Jesus mentioned are silent witnesses today, being now in ruins, of the seriousness of rejecting grace when it is extended. That is clearly true of unbelievers, but in a limited sense it is true for those in the community of the faithful, certainly not a final judgment, but loss of the experience of blessing and privilege. Do you know this to be true?

4. When I read of such rejection of grace, such light of gospel privilege, I cannot but think of the peril of my city, my nation. As a nation we have been blessed beyond compare with a rich religious heritage, yet the past is no guarantee of a tomorrow. Our nation will eventually join the graveyard of nations that perished from the face of the earth. Does that make you cry out for our people? Do you cry to God for our waywardness? Do you care?

5. If Jesus were interested in large numbers and great responses, He would have called the people of Sodom, Tyre, and Sidon, but they were not His people. God selects the citizens of His community, and He is not in a popularity contest. This tells me several things: first, numbers may not be where true significance is to be found; second, God is searching for His people in the crowds though they are not the crowds; and third, God's group is a special community. We can rejoice

that He has revealed Himself to us. This is called grace! Grace, to be grace, is not based on merit or reward.

6. The call of Jesus to follow Him is a sincere, universal invitation. Anyone who desires to follow may do so. Jesus placed the responsibility for faith on personal willingness (v. 14), not on inability and incapacity. Because people are unwilling, the issue of ability is mute. They are unable because they simply do not see any value in coming to Jesus. Their unwillingness is the ground of judgment, not inability. We are to cry for mercy, 'Lord, help my unbelief.' We will never put together God's selectivity of His citizens and universality of His call; we believe both. Some things are beyond the smallness of the human mind to put together, but our ignorance does not limit the truth. Are you not glad?

7. How can the call to be a follower of Jesus be described as 'easy' and 'light' when it is accompanied with rejection, ridicule, even martyrdom? It is because our 'yoke' is to become a student of the Lord. He is so great that it lessens any pain or sorrow that may be involved. If delight is a matter of what we supremely value, then any adversity for Him is simply not our focus. Further, Jesus carries our burdens and the delight of knowing Him makes service joyful and meaningful. Have you found that to be true? Life is a matter of focus and priority. Is that true in your experience or do you take your eyes off your proper delight for lesser things?

The Condemnation of the King (12:1-50)

This chapter is a pivotal section in the book; here the religious leadership makes their official pronouncement concerning the claims of Jesus; they reject Him and plot His demise (v. 14). Opposition had been mounting (9:3, 11, 14, 34; 10:25; 11:19), but here it reaches a climax. This will bring a change in Jesus' ministry, turning increasingly to private instruction, the preparation of His disciples for His death, signified by His departure from the Galilee to Jerusalem (in Matthew His only appearance in the city). In this section Matthew cites five instances that evidence growing opposition; in each there is a negative encounter followed by a positive reply by Jesus (this should remind the reader of the method, a statement followed by a correction, that Jesus employed in chapter 5 concerning the Pharisaic interpretation of the law).

The Law, Judaism, and the conflict with Christ (vv. 1-14)

It is interesting that Jesus, after having spoken about rest, immediately took up the issue of the Sabbath, the Pharisees having made the day more of a burden than a blessing. According to the rabbis, thirty-nine specific activities were prohibited. To preserve the intent of the Sabbath, the Pharisees invented laws designed to prevent its violation (fence laws). Jesus challenges Pharisaic authority to make and impose such laws and argues that they had violated the intent of the Law in doing so.

The Sabbath was sacred in Israel and Jews often refused to engage in self-defense on that day. In the Maccabean Revolt (168 B.C.), the Syrians massacred hundreds because they would not resist.[1] The same occurred in the Roman vassalage of Palestine under Pompey in the 60s B.C.[2]

The initial two sources of conflict concern Sabbath observance. The first was eating on the Sabbath (vv. 1-8). According to Deuteronomy 23:25, the poor and strangers could casually eat grain (wheat or barley) growing in the margins of the fields (cf. Ruth 2:2-3). According to the Pharisees, they could not do this on the Sabbath (food had to be prepared before

---

1. I Maccabees 2: 32-38. 'Many pursued them, and overtook them; they encamped opposite them and prepared for battle against them on the sabbath day. They [the pursuers] said to them, "Enough of this! Come out and do what the king commands, and you will live." But they said, "We will not come out, nor will we do what the king commands and so profane the sabbath day." Then the enemy quickly attacked them. But they did not answer them or hurl a stone at them or block up their hiding places, for they said, "Let us all die in our innocence; heaven and earth testify for us that you are killing us unjustly. So they attacked them on the sabbath, and they died, with their wives and children and livestock, to the number of a thousand persons."'

2. Josephus Flavius, *The Wars of the Jews*, 14.4.2. Knowing that the Jews would not resist war preparations on the sabbath, Pompey prepared that day for breaching the walls. '... and the enemy then fell upon them and cut the throats of those that were in the temple; yet could not those that offered the sacrifices be compelled to run away, neither by the fear they were in of their own lives, nor by the number that were already slain, as thinking it better to suffer whatever came upon them, at their very altars, than to omit anything that their laws required of them.'

the Sabbath). They created rules that made it prohibitive on the Sabbath. Where this event happened had to be less than a Sabbath day's journey from a town since Jesus is not accused in that regard and the Pharisees are in a field; however, the disciples do casually glean. The accusation is that the disciples had violated the Sabbath by reaping grain, hence working.

Jesus' defense is not so much the urgency of need, but His own authority (vv. 3-8). He appealed to several Old Testament passages to construct His argument, Daniel 7 being the clincher! He cites two examples of sanctioned conduct on the Sabbath as well as a principle. It is interesting to note that when Jesus spoke to the Pharisees He said, 'Have you not read?' When He spoke to the crowds, He said, 'Have you not heard?' (5:21, 27). The crowds were unlearned, trusting their learned leadership.

It is likely that David's taking the consecrated bread from the tabernacle (1 Sam. 21:1-6), which was then at Nob, occurred on the Sabbath because the bread was fresh. Jesus' point is that David did not violate the Law in eating. In so doing, He questioned the Pharisees' use of the Scriptures, stating as His authority the example of David, Israel's greatest king. Human need takes precedence over Sabbath restrictions and Jesus had the authority to make that judgment!

Jesus' second argument would have carried greater weight than the previous one, being only an example of conduct, because the work of priests on the Sabbath was commanded by God; they worked! By implication, the priests who labored in the tabernacle broke the Sabbath weekly (Num. 28:9-10; Lev. 24:5-8). If the priests labor on the Sabbath without guilt, Jesus, the fulfillment of temple imagery, can also. The Law points to Jesus! The Pharisees did not really know the sacred Scriptures they claimed to teach.

Jesus' verdict is that Pharisaic Judaism missed the intent of the Law, which was compassion. He was challenging the authority of the Pharisees to determine the meaning of the Law. For the second time, He quotes from Hosea 6:6, which He previously cited in 9:13. The Sabbath is about Jesus, the compassionate One.

'Son of Man' is a title derived from Daniel 7:13-14. By taking this title, Jesus is asserting authority over all people;

He is the authority when it comes to Sabbath observance, He is the greatest of mankind and one entitled to exercise all authority. He is the determiner of the meaning of the Sabbath as its 'Lord'.

The second source of conflict was a Sabbath healing (vv. 9-14). Jesus' view of the Sabbath is applied in the case of it, although it was a set-up by his opponents! The Pharisees had arranged to have a cripple in the synagogue knowing that Jesus might incriminate Himself by healing him on the Sabbath. They were looking for grounds to discredit Jesus. Jesus' point is that when good has occasion to be done, the day of the week is inconsequential.

It was not uncommon in Jesus' day that the situation that He mentioned, remediation of a dangerous situation, was acceptable practice, so He assumed that there would be no objection; people were allowed to help on the Sabbath (though a paralyzed arm is not a threat to life). Also, this is the third time in the book that Jesus builds an argument on the relative value of animals (6:26; 10:31), a lesser-to-greater argument. The Jewish attitude towards animals contradicted their interpretation of the Law for people.

Since little is made of the circumstances of the miracle, the attendant dialogue, the emphasis is on the healing itself. That is the point of contention. Since the healing was verbal only, there was no work involved. Jesus only gave a command.

The verdict concerning Jesus had been determined; the Pharisees had had enough of the Galilean, and they plotted His demise. The contradiction in the Pharisees is clear in that they professed Sabbath observance, but missed the point of mercy by plotting Jesus' death on the Sabbath.

The reaction of Christ to the verdict (vv. 15-21)
Jesus understood that the reaction of the leadership was a fulfillment of prophecy, seeing in His ministry Isaiah's prediction of the deliverer (42:1-4). So having heard the verdict of the Pharisees, He withdrew, but still heals many (v. 15), warning His followers not to preach Him any longer (v. 16). The point seems to be that Jesus needed to diffuse His mounting popularity, an action He did frequently by exiting the scene. He wants confrontation with the national religious

leadership on His own terms, not prematurely, in Jerusalem and not in the Galilee.

Matthew quotes Isaiah 42:1-4 (the longest quotation in the book), to show that what had happened to Jesus was a fulfillment of prophecy. Note the stress on Gentiles (vv. 18-21)! This is a wonderful description of the promised One! The true Messiah/deliverer is one characterized by humility and mercy, not militant triumphalism.

In verse 18, we can see (1) God's view of Jesus: love and delight; (2) God's gift to Jesus: the enablement of the Spirit; and (3) God's appointment of Jesus: to preach. In verse 19, we see His demeanor: deeds of love and mercy done in humility (He has just withdrawn from controversy). His character is seen in verse 20: the appearance of weakness, defeat and insignificance, yet He is victorious (reeds, growing in abundance in marshy areas, were used, for example, as measuring rods or pens; fragile, they were easily broken and often discarded). A lamp wick when burned down only smolders, giving no light. It may appear that Jesus is extinguishable, but He will shine brightly, never failing. The outcome is stated in verse 21: the nations will be blessed (see verse 18d).

The final verdict and Jesus' response (vv. 22-37)

After a brief respite, the controversy is resumed. These Pharisees seem to be local, not from Jerusalem. They accepted the reality of Jesus' miracles, but they questioned the origin of His power to do them. Suggesting that Jesus performed His miracles by evil powers is an affront to His credibility and authority. Jesus says that in this world there are two kingdoms that strongly oppose each other. He is not of the kingdom the Pharisees suppose!

Parenthesis:

The classic statement of the two-kingdom or two-cities theory was stated by Augustine in the fifth century. In this world there are two kingdom or realms of rule: the Kingdom of Man (the seed of serpent) and the Kingdom of God (the seed of the woman); one under the headship of Satan and the other under the rule of God. These are simultaneous and conflictive but will be separated at the end of time in the great, final judgment. The Kingdom of God will triumph!

That this section is significant is suggested by its lengthy treatment by Matthew.

The context is the healing of a blind, speechless demoniac (v. 22). Again, the lack of detail about the healing itself places the emphasis on the implications of the healing, the confrontation. The hopeless condition of this man (blind, mute, and demon-possessed) reminds the readers of a similar healing in 9:32-34; the people marveled while the leadership embraced the demonic explanation of Jesus' power to do so. However, here the situation is much more polarized.

The crowds ask a question in verse 23. This is the first time in Matthew's account that the crowds acknowledged the Messianic implications of Jesus. They are awakening to the conclusion that John the Baptist should have drawn (11:2-6).

While the crowds were thinking that Jesus may be the promised One, the Pharisees had come to an opposing conclusion (v. 24). They must act quickly before the crowds embrace Him. Here is the official verdict of the leadership concerning Jesus; He is demon-possessed. There have been hints of this attitude previously (9:34; 10:25), but this time the ruler of the demons is named, and his power attributed to Jesus, Beelzebul ('the lord of the house'), Satan. Jesus, they say, is the devil incarnate!

In His defense (vv. 25-37), Jesus first uses an argument from common sense (vv. 25-26). If Jesus casts out demons by the authority of the devil, the devil would be working against himself. Demons do not act contrary to their self-interest. If this were the case, there would be hopeless division among them (demons only act in conformity to their natures!).

Jesus also asks a question (v. 27). If the devil alone is the authority behind exorcisms, how would they explain the fact of those performed by the Pharisees? Since humans cannot overcome demons in their own power, and demons do not work against themselves, his work must be from another source like 'your sons', said Jesus.

Jesus simply states that the power behind His performances is the Spirit of God (v. 28). The defeat of the devil in casting off his authority is evidence that the kingdom has been inaugurated. Satan will be banished when the kingdom is fully realized! The demons were being defeated by the coming of the kingdom of God in the person of Jesus.

The purpose of exorcisms is stated in verses 29-30. Jesus' point is that His miracles were not evidence of the devil's power in Him, but of His defeat of the devil. The proof that the kingdom is here is that the devil is being defeated. Using imagery from Isaiah 49:24-25, Jesus is saying that He has defeated the 'strong man'. The image of 'scatters' makes the same point as 'binding the strong man'; Jesus was defeating the powers of evil.

A tragic consequence of the rejection of Jesus' authority is detailed in verses 31-37.

His first point is that to sin against the Holy Spirit is blasphemy and unforgivable. '… in this age or in the age to come' is a Jewish idiom for this life or the next (vv. 31-32). The unpardonable sin is the rejection of the true power behind Christ's miracles, the immediate issue. To assign miracles to Satan, not the Holy Spirit, is to reject the One who draws to Christ. There is no hope if the Spirit is repudiated.

Parenthesis:

The unpardonable sin has often been a source of discomfort, even disquieting fear, for the Lord's people. Can a saint do such an awful thing that it is unforgivable? My answer is 'NO' for the following reasons.

(1) The context of the passage is our Lord's repudiation of the Pharisees for attributing the origin of His power and the validity of His claims to the devil. This passage is about Israel's national leadership, 'a brood of vipers' (3:7), a people whose righteousness is not sufficient to enter the kingdom (5:20).

(2) The unforgivable sin is in attributing Christ's claims to demonic origin; no believer thinks Christ is demonically inspired. Indisputably, all Christians believe that Christ's origin is heavenly and that He performed miracles through the Spirit (certainly not through the devil, the one He defeated in His temptations [4:1-11] and at the cross).

(3) The sin in this passage is such that it cannot and will not be forgiven. Can a believer do something to forfeit his/her

sainthood? Can God change His mind about the status of a person that His Son died to redeem? 'Who can bring a charge against God's elect (Rom. 8:33)?' 'Who shall separate us from the love of Christ (Rom. 8:35)?'

(4) Salvation is not contingent upon our faithfulness; it is rooted in the faithfulness of God to His own Son who purchased us! Would God reject His own Son whom He raised from the dead, verifying the accomplishment of redemption for us? God cannot reject His Son, or the children of His Son.

(5) The emphasis on fruit (vv. 33, 35) does not suggest a single act, but a habitual action. The habitual action of the leadership was to produce bad fruit (to reject Him). The only single act for which we are condemned is the first sin of Adam, our representative. However, the great second Adam, Jesus Christ, paid the penalty due to justice (i.e., death) for us.

(6) The real change in a believer's life occurs in the heart (v. 34). The 'heart' of the leadership never changed their evaluation of Jesus, and the evidence was their rejection of the Messiah.

(7) In thinking lowly of Christ, the leadership rejected both Christ and the Spirit, the heavenly origin of His power. The Spirit's task is to point to Christ (v. 33); Christ's task was to reveal the Father; and the Father's task is to declare it. If the Spirit is rejected, there is no pointing to Christ or beyond Him to the Father. This is simply not a description of the believer. We love the Father and the Son!

(8) Think of how many of your sins Jesus died for on the cross. How many of your sins were future when Christ died for you nearly two millennia ago? All of our sins were in the future and Christ died for all of them (Romans 8:1; Heb. 8:12-13). If Christ died for all our sins, the debt having been paid, no sin can separate us from God.

(9) Think of the great comfort in this passage. Jesus says that every sin will be forgiven ('… a word against the Son of Man will be forgiven' [v. 32]) except the one you and I will never commit! All others will be forgiven! That means all of your sins, unless Jesus is wrong! The verb tense is future, perfect, passive. God says that He has assured these things to be true.

The evidence of condemnation is the fruit revealed in them (vv. 33-37). The outward reveals the inward (vv. 33-35).

The tree metaphor is simply that actions reveal more about the nature of things than words, fruit more than leaves (see 7:1-20). The nature of the heart is revealed by outward actions (see 15:18-20). Whenever Jesus uses 'brood of vipers', the Pharisees are in view (23:33), as with John the Baptist (3:7). Consequences have a cause. 'As the root, so the fruit' is Jesus' point. Deeds reveal the quality of the inner person, the quality of the heart.

Since the outward reveals the inward, Jesus' point is that words are not idle (vv. 36-37); they reveal what is in the heart. The negative connotation of the words must be contextually qualified; that is, how they are to be interpreted. The issue is not words, even light talk; it is the quality of the content expressed in words. A wholesome lifestyle reveals a healthy heart; a poor one reveals an empty heart.

The demand for further proof and Jesus' response (vv. 38-45)

The Pharisees ask for an immediate verdict from heaven in the form of a miracle, a sign, evidence (v. 38). Jesus refuses, but predicts His resurrection as the sign. Even in the Old Testament, a sign miracle may or may not authenticate a prophet's office.

The 'sign of the prophet Jonah' (vv. 39-40) means the sign that Jonah himself was to the Ninevites. His ashen appearance from the acids in the great fish made him appear to fish worshipers to be alive from the dead! Just as Jonah was miraculously released from death ('the belly of Sheol' [Jonah 2:2], 'You brought up my life from the pit' [2:6]), so would Jesus be. Jonah's death, however, was not literal; Jesus' was! One, however, prefigures the other, according to Jesus. 'Three days and three nights' means no more than three days or a combination of three days. The latter was our Lord's case as He was buried late Friday and rose to life early Sunday (v. 40).

In verses 41-42, the gravity of their rejection of Jesus is illustrated from two Old Testament incidents involving Gentiles (the people of Nineveh and a queen) responding to two Jewish figures (Jonah and Solomon). It is an argument from the lesser to the greater. Gentiles responded but the Jewish leadership will not, though a greater than Jonah and Solomon is in their midst. The Queen of Sheba (an area on the Arabian Peninsula, then considered the end of the world) accepted the wisdom of Solomon (1 Kings 10:1-10), but the leaders would not recognize one greater than Solomon. She went to great lengths to hear Solomon, but the leadership refused to hear the words of his greater Son.

The point of the brief paragraph is that those who listen to Jesus cannot be neutral; if they refuse to embrace Him, it will lead to disaster (vv. 43-45). Jesus concluded with an illustration of the acts of demons that reminds us of the Gadarene story. He seems to be saying that a less than sincere repentance only makes matters worse. The rejection by the nation's leadership, 'this evil generation,' will prove to be disastrous (the destruction of the temple in A.D. 70). See 24:1-35.

An interlude: Jesus and His family (vv. 46-50)

Jesus' immediate family appears not to have understood Him. Clearly His brothers did not believe in Him (John 7:5) and they tried on one occasion to seize Him because they thought He was mentally unstable (Mark 3:20-21). The theme in this chapter is the rejection of Jesus, first by the religious leadership and here by His family.

Jesus here is not so much demeaning family loyalty as He is arguing for a higher loyalty to God. The paragraph is not about His mother and siblings (they disappear from the narrative so they only function as the occasion of Jesus' comments); it is about Jesus' new family. Those who are Jesus' disciples are His family; they have entered a new community.

Jesus often speaks in symbolical terms that can be understood in a variety of ways. The leadership of Israel should have welcomed Him, but they refused to do His will, so He announces a new family, one greater than earthly families. This family is not entered by blood ties, but through Jesus' blood sacrifice!

Applications

1. Sabbath is a symbol of rest. In the Hebrew Scriptures it pointed to Christ and the spiritual rest He would bring to His people. Sabbath was not abolished in Christ; it was fulfilled in Christ. He is our rest. It is a day to celebrate His triumph! Sadly, we have an illustration

that, contrary to the religious leaders, Jesus' yoke is easy. The Pharisees made Sabbath a burden instead of a celebration. Is there a sense that we have twisted the intent of the Sabbath by not treating it as special? Do you use the day to worship, rest, and enjoy the family or is your afternoon and evening full of chores?

2. The Sabbath is a day of a different focus, away from wage-earning and other professional cares of securing the necessities for life and family. However, it is not a day to avoid pleasure or merely sit quietly. It is not unlawful to do the necessary on the Sabbath or make a special day for the family, but the focus should be around the Lord in the process. Sabbath was made for us to enjoy. It is a day for family. Do you use it that way? It is a day for worship and religious instruction. Is that true in your family's life? It is a day to look forward to as a family. Do you?

3. One of the amazing things in this chapter, as well as throughout Matthew, is the grasp the writer has of the Hebrew Scriptures, particularly as he understands that they speak or predict the coming and identification of the Lord. While we know the stories of the Bible, can we use it to point people to the Saviour? One thing is unmistakable; Matthew believed that the Old Testament was about a person, the coming of the great redeemer. Can you take the Old Testament and show people the claims and person of Jesus?

4. While you and I prize the miraculous as verification of religious claims, they prove neither the godliness of the performer nor the source behind them. Others than Jesus performed miracles. They are not alone proof of anything; it requires faith in the performer. The religious leadership lacked that and easily found an alternate explanation. Is it more likely that Jesus was a deceiver than a truthful person sent from heaven? The quality of His life, His morals and demeanor, were congruent with His actions. When words and morals match actions, you have the litmus test of a person's claims. Trust without proof is gullibility; trust without

a lifestyle is dangerous. You and I should have no fear or uncertainty when it comes to trusting Jesus. Is there anyone as trustworthy as He? Is your faith proportionate to His character?

5. Christians are incapable of doing something so bad that God changes His mind about any one of them and rescinds His commitment. The unpardonable sin is the error of claiming that Jesus was a deceiver and a charlatan. Further, an unpardonable sin is reflected in constancy of character, not momentary lapse. It is about actions without remorse. More importantly, it is a rejection of the Spirit of God as the divine power behind the actions of claiming that Jesus was a deceiver and charlatan. Further, an unpardonable sin is one of constancy of character, not momentary lapse. It is an attitude without remorse. Jesus is now enthroned; His redemptive and incarnational work is done. Now He is exalted in the heavenly kingdom. His labor of care and maintenance is through the Spirit to us; He is absent for a while. You and I do not have to ever fear stepping outside the boundary. Think of what Peter did; he denied and cursed the Lord. Jesus never stopped loving and caring for him.

6. The rejection of the person and claims of Jesus are the most serious issue in this life and determinative of what all of us will hear in the Last Judgment. While the embrace of the uniqueness of Jesus, His deity and truth claims, are culturally unpopular and even considered audacious, bigoted, narrow, and socially intolerant, it does not mean that it is untrue. To believe contrary to Jesus' truth claims is utter foolishness and eternally destructive. This suggests that we should be zealous to tell people about the Lord. Who knows, God may use your words to grant a supernatural hearing for the person with whom you are talking. Would that not be great?

7. It is absolutely amazing that Jesus would call us His family. Jesus came to create a new family on the earth that someday will fill it, a new community. As amazing as it is, Jesus considers believers to be His

family members; such are His children, with the earthly family a beautiful picture of it. The best of our family life on earth is a picture of it, but only a frail one at best. It is worth meditating on the fact that you and I are part of a new family. Family membership entails great privileges and duties; facts to enjoy and duties as a consequence. You did not choose your parents and you did not choose your new family; it was the gift of God. Are you a responsible family member?

6

The Consequence of Rejecting
the King's Teaching
(13:1-52)

While Jesus often taught in synagogues, here He
speaks elsewhere. More importantly, He now speaks
in concealed speech (parables). The eight parables here
are divided into two groups of four each: the initial four
were given to the multitudes, the last four to the disciples.
Two of the parables are interpreted, both for the disciples
privately. The first four parables picture the opposition
that will come in the extension of the kingdom; the private
four parables emphasize the triumph of the kingdom in the
midst of adversaries. These parables describe the extension
of the kingdom and what His followers can expect until the
final judgment.

Matthew uses the word 'parable' in twenty-eight of the
thirty-three occurrences of the term in the New Testament.
It can cover a variety of literary forms: proverbs, maxims,
similes, fables, allegories, comparisons, riddles, taunts, and
stories. A parable is an illustration set beside a point to
explain it. Parables have appeared in 7:24-27; 9:15-17; and
11:16-19. The phrase, 'Kingdom of Heaven,' appears here in
seven of the parables, the exception being the Parable of the
Soils. The parables here seem to have been given on one
occasion (v. 53). This passage is considered the third major
discourse in the book.

Another way of thinking about these parables is to label them this way:

The Sower and the Seed:	Responses to the gospel
The Wheat and Tares:	Mixed peoples in the now-not-yet kingdom
The Mustard Seed:	Great growth of the kingdom
The Leaven and Loaf:	Great growth of the kingdom
The Hidden Treasure:	Preciousness of the gospel
The Pearl of Great Price:	Preciousness of the gospel
The Dragnet:	Mixed peoples in the kingdom and judgment
The Householder:	Uniqueness of things in the kingdom

Two of the parables are interpreted by Jesus, but only to the disciples, as well as the reason for speaking in veiled speech. This fits Jesus' shift to speaking in such a manner, as well as His rejection by the nation's leadership. That is, He spoke in this manner to conceal as well as to reveal. Two of the parables indicate that before the final, consummated form of the kingdom, there will be a mixture of the peoples until the final judgment (wheat and tares [#2], dragnet [#7]); two parables emphasize the great values that the kingdom represents (treasure [#5] and pearl [#6]); and two suggest the spectacular growth of the kingdom (mustard seed [#3] and leaven [#4]). The first parable suggests the types of responses to the gospel and the last the blend of new and old in the message of the kingdom.

Parables to the multitudes (vv. 1-33)

The setting is mentioned in verses 1-2. His first parable, about the sower and effects of the seed, concerns responses to the proclamation of the kingdom (vv. 3-23). The story is straightforward (vv. 1-9). A farmer scatters seed in his field and a variety of things happen to it. Some fall on paths and are devoured by birds (v. 4); some fall among rocks and growth is retarded due to poor root support, only to wither

(vv. 5-6); some fall among weeds and are choked (v. 7); and some fall on good soil and multiply bountifully (vv. 8- 9). The character of the soil determined the crop.

The reason for parables is given in verses 10-17 in response to an inquiry of the disciples. Since Jesus began His parabolic teaching speaking to the crowd (v. 2), the disciples must have been with Him. Jesus left the crowds after the fourth parable and the disciples followed Him. However, in the confines of the boat a short distance from the shore and the crowd, the disciples seem confused and asked a private question. Why is He speaking indirectly to the people by employing a story to convey His teaching?

The purpose of parables is to reveal truth to those whom God wills to reveal it and hide it from those whom He does not want to understand it. Parables are instruction for those who know the 'secrets of the kingdom'; allegiance to Jesus is a prerequisite for understanding. God has revealed the meaning to some, but not to all (the divine doctrine of selection is unmistakable here).

Parables are a judgment, a way of withholding truth as well as disclosing it. Matthew sees this as a fulfillment of prophecy (Isa. 6:9-10). See also 13:34-35. Isaiah 6:9-10 is in the context of the prophet's great call into the ministry. After he cries out, 'Here am I! Send me' (v. 8), he is told that he will go to a people who can hear and see, but God will not allow understanding and insight because He plans judgment.

'The secrets of the kingdom' concerns the emergence of the kingdom into history, gradually now and finally in the eschaton. God is selective as to whom He reveals these mysteries; however, they are not hidden truths in the sense that it is to be openly declared and people are invited to hear and believe. The Old Testament background of the use of 'secret' is likely Daniel 2:18-19, 27-30.

The structure of Jesus' reply to the disciples' inquiry is a wonderful example of the artistry of Matthew's work; it is a chiasm (vv. 13-17). Each line parallels its counterpart in reverse sequence (1-7, 7'-1'); 7 is the number of completion (in this case a complete thought); and 7 and 7' are the focus or emphasis.

In verse 18 Jesus says that the prophets of old desired to understand more clearly when they described the coming of the kingdom but were not enabled to do so (Dan. 12:8-9; 1 Pet. 1:10-12). His coming into the world is the fulfillment and culmination of the prophecies of old.

Here is the truth of the electing, selecting grace of God; it is a mystery beyond the grasp of our minds. God asks us to marvel at it, marvel that He included us in it, find security in it, and worship Him for it. Jesus did not throw the pearls of the kingdom before swine (7:6).

The meaning of the parable is given in verses 18-23. It is about various reactions to the preaching of the gospel that we are to expect in the inaugurated kingdom. The emphasis in this section is upon 'hearing the message'. It explains the mixed responses Jesus received throughout His Galilean ministry and that of His followers until time is no more! The 'anyone' of verse 19 is highlighted by its position in the verse; the use of the plural indicates that Jesus is speaking to the disciples.

The seed on the hard paths (vv. 18-19) concerns seed that takes no root; the hardness of the soil permits no penetration and birds (the devil [6:13; 12:45; 13:38-39]) snatch it away. It depicts people whose only response is hostility and rejection through a lack of understanding (v. 19). They are careless hearers.

The seed on the rocky soil (vv. 20-21) reflects those who initially respond, even joyfully, but not from the heart. The pain involved in discipleship is too much and the seed comes to nothing. Time reveals their lostness.

The seed among the weeds (v. 22) represents those who superficially embrace the gospel, and then become choked as the cares of life turn them away. These are people who may think well of the truth, but the complexity and affairs of life take precedence, aborting any serious attention to the Word of God. Time reveals false converts. These seem to embrace Jesus, but with time find something more attractive; they simply have never truly encountered Him.

The seed in the good soil (v. 23) describes those in whom it is planted with understanding, resulting in a lifestyle of commitment. Seed in good soil produces genuine saints; they endure and produce the fruit of righteousness (v. 23). While there is a variance of fruit-bearing, there is no variance of destiny since it is eternal life.

It seems that the public instruction ended in verse 10, but it resumed in verse 24 as the crowds are once more mentioned. The three following parables are grouped together; two continue the theme of seeds and the third leaven, a cause of expansion in bread-making. The mustard seed and leaven parables emphasize growth, the sower and the weeds variance. The mustard seed and leaven parables are not interpreted.

The parable of the wheat and the tares, which distinguishes between possessors and professors in the kingdom, is found in verses 24-30. It is stated to the crowds, but interpreted privately to the disciples. What we have here is a case of sabotage in a field. It is not about the farmer or the slaves, but a situation that arises in the field. The weeds are darnel, a ryegrass that resembles wheat in its early stages of growth, but its narrower black flowers, called spikelets (5 to 7 in number on each stalk), suggest otherwise. It is poisonous and when mixed with wheat renders the crop worthless. The only solution is to carefully separate the wheat from the darnel by hand, a slow painstaking process that only can be done at harvest. To preserve the wheat the owner allows the weeds to grow with a view to a separation at the time of harvest, the darnel to be destroyed and the wheat preserved.

Applications

1. In the parable of the sower, Jesus says that there will always be different responses to the gospel. Opposition to the Word comes from the devil, insincerity, and the distracting cares of the world. We are to expect varying results from the scattering of the seed of the gospel. Sharing the gospel does not always lead to good results. This should be expected. In each case within the parable, it is not a problem of poor seed dispersal, but external factors such as the devil's work of blinding, the hardness of the human heart, or the crushing effects of the exigencies and troubles of life.

2. You and I can neither cause nor prevent how people receive the gospel. It is not within our purview to know. Our task is to sow the seed; the condition of the soil is

another issue that we do not have the ability to alter. We can have assurance that some of the seed we sow will fall on soil prepared by God and will be receptive. Is that not great? So, it can be said that our job is to sow, not bring about the results. From our sharing, there will be wonderful consequences as well as sad ones.

3. There is evidence of receiving the Word rightly; it is not joy or enthusiasm, but endurance and fruit. This tells me that a time element is important before a Christian can be identified since profession is outward and may not be rooted in the heart. Have you found cases of people who at one time professed faith in Christ, and showed every evidence of being genuine, but after time simply lost interest! In the judgment of Jesus' teaching, it is hard to be sure whether they are true believers or not. It is not past works or childhood experiences that are the ground of assurance; it is enduring faith and moral conformity.

4. The community of the faithful will always prove to be a mixed assembly of people, according to Jesus. False crops, such as darnel, and good edible crops, like wheat or barley, look the same by external appearances at times. There are differences, but they are difficult to identify. We should not be surprised when we find darnel in the basket of wheat. Darnel, which looks so much like good stuff, is fatal to those who identify with that metaphor and potentially hazardous, though not fatal, to those who truly believe. False professors of the faith are to be expected. By their fruit you shall know them, not by their smiles, sincerity, or enthusiasm.

5. It is amazing that Jesus spoke so as not to be understood. With His increased rejection by the nation's leadership, He turned to the multitudes to draw some from among them to faith. Some hear only with their ears, not their hearts. Only God can do the latter, open the heart. He did not intend for all to come to Him. That is rather amazing. Have you expressed appreciation lately that He allowed you to understand the message of the gospel?

6. There is a wonderful promise in the parable. Some people will receive the seed and the soil of their lives will produce fruit. In every scenario the seed is the same and the efforts compatible, but the consequences beyond our effort. We have the promise of God that the seed we sow, in some people's lives, will produce multipliers! Have you not seen this illustrated in your own life? Have you seen it in people that you know?

7. The sobering side of the wheat and tares parable is not only that the external community of the Lord is a mixed assembly of look-alikes, fakes, and the genuine, but that God will sort them out in the last day. His judgments will be correct and those who are not His, but living in His community, will be cast out. There is coming a day when the crop will be expunged of its weeds and the community will exist as the unadulterated, cleansed, pure bride of the divine redeemer. Are you looking forward to that day?

The emphasis in *the parable of the mustard seed* is on the growth of the kingdom, the rapid development of the church from very small beginnings (vv. 31-32). From a small seed, a huge tree will emerge. While Jesus says that the mustard is the smallest of all seeds, we know that it is not. However, in Jesus' day it was a common saying, a proverb. Further, this is a parable, and the nature of the genre is that things are often overstated for effect. 'Birds' may suggest an evil element; they seem to represent 'the evil one'. I think here it indicates or emphasizes the largeness of the tree from small beginnings. The kingdom of heaven will have a small beginning that is deceptive relative to its ultimate size and destiny. In this sense, the 'birds' would suggest the believing community.

The background for this parable may be Daniel 4:12, 21. It contains the account of birds in the branches of a tree symbolizing Nebuchadnezzar's vision, the birds being the nations that took shelter under the might of the great Babylonian Empire. It was a huge, though short-lived, empire. Obviously, the 'tree' in this case that shelters the nations, the people of God, will endure forever.

The parable of the leaven and the loaf is told in verse 33. Leaven is contained in unused dough; it is not strictly yeast. It functions to intensify transformation; it does not grow, it permeates. Like the previous parable the point is growth from small beginnings. However, the emphasis here is not so much rapid growth as the expansiveness of it, from a little comes much. The normal method of leavening bread dough in the ancient world was to place a small amount of leavened dough into a batch of unleavened dough. Here leaven is not a symbol for an evil element (it is often used that way in the Old Testament); if so, the parable would be saying that the kingdom is evil. Further, yeast was used in sacrificial offerings (Lev. 7:13). The point seems to be that the kingdom will grow and extend throughout the entire world in its final form, not that evil will permeate it.

Parables to the disciples (vv. 34-52)

In the privacy of a house, the disciples ask for the interpretation of the wheat and tares parable. Previously, and privately in the boat, Jesus had explained the meaning of the parable of the soils.

Matthew restates the function of parables to emphasize the selective purpose in Christ's teaching (vv. 34-35). This time the use of parables is stated as almost an editorial comment, not in the words of Jesus. He quotes from Psalm 78:2, where Asaph, a musician responsible for worship in the tabernacle in David's day, speaks in parables of the righteous acts of God in redemption. Matthew's point is that in the use of parables to teach about Himself, Jesus is standing in the tradition of the Hebrew prophets.

In what sense was Asaph a prophet and in what sense is the psalm a prophecy? Matthew makes the point in 11:13 that all the Hebrew Scriptures are in some sense prophetic; they look forward to Christ.

Jesus here spoke privately to His disciples in 'the house,' just as he left from one in Capernaum at the beginning of the chapter (v. 1). He begins by interpreting the parable of the wheat and tares (vv. 36-43). Perhaps the reason Matthew adds the editorial comment on parables in verses 34-35 is that the disciples asked not about the function of parables, but the specific interpretation of one.

The parable is about constituents in the world, believers and unbelievers (two kinds of seed that have been sown). The emphasis is upon the end of the parable, the separation of them that comes at the end of the age.

Jesus' reference to Himself as the Son of Man is again rooted in Daniel's vision (7:13-14). He uses it here because the emphasis is upon the end-time judgment. In the end of times, the Son of Man will gain supremacy and reign forever.

It would be a misapplication of the parable to suggest that we should not be concerned with weeds in this the initial phase of the kingdom. There is too much Scripture instructing us to deal with the errant. The 'field' is the world (v. 38), not the church. The 'field,' being the world, suggests a mission greater than Israel (10:16-18, 28:18-20). The good seed is not the gospel as in the soils-parable, but here it is people, the sons of the kingdom, those who respond to the gospel.

The implications are described in verses 40-43. The 'so' suggests a shift from the meaning of the symbols to the implications of them.

The Son of Man, through the auspices of His angels, will gather the 'weeds' for destruction, unbelievers described as 'all causes of sin' and 'all lawbreakers' (an allusion to Zephaniah 1:3). At that time, the wheat, the righteous, will shine suggesting blessing and delight (Dan. 12:3). The kingdom of the Son becomes the 'Kingdom of the Father' (v. 43) as well.

The parables of the hidden treasure and the pearl, which follow, are a couplet in that they teach the same lesson. In both parables there is something hidden that must be found, something of enormous value. These parables have to do with priorities. The point of the repetition is emphasis.

It was common in those days to protect valuable possessions from looting by burying them (cf. Matt. 25:25). With the passage of time and life (particularly in times of war), when no one survives to remember the buried valuable, others may stumble upon it. In this case, a person finds a treasure, but he may not own the field (v. 44). If the treasure is important enough, he may purchase the field to become its legal owner. The treasure is the realm of God's rule, redemption through the Messiah; the field is the world; the man is anyone who finds it; the giving up all to purchase the treasure is because of its perceived, supreme worth; and the joy of obtaining the treasure is true life.

The merchant who finds this pearl (vv. 45-46) recognizes instantly its greater value compared to all other pearls (Judaism) and gladly gives up all else for it (the Christ). Unlike the previous parable where the treasure was stumbled upon, here it is sought. In both cases decisive and sacrificial action was required to obtain it. Notice that the treasure had first to be revealed, and when it was, it was recognized as wonderful, and it called for diligence to get it.

The parable of the dragnet is concerned with the judgment at the end of the kingdom (vv. 47-50). This parable is much like the wheat and tares, placing the emphasis upon the intermingling of types of fish and a final judgment. Separation of the fish (like wheat from tares) comes at the end of the age (the consummated kingdom, not the inaugurated kingdom). Judgment awaits bad fish, incorporation into the kingdom the good fish. The angels will do the separating; it will be sure and accurate. That the net is not pulled from the lake until it is full suggests that there will be no premature division of the fish. Verse 50 is identical to verse 42.

The householder deals with both old and new things in the kingdom (vv. 51-52). Here the emphasis is upon the people in the kingdom. To speak of the householder as a scribe indicates one learned in the Scriptures. The 'storehouse' refers to a person's innermost being, the heart (12:35). The true disciple brings things that he/she has learned, the Hebrew Scriptures, to the light of the newer revelation of God. He/she recognizes that the Old Testament is a pointer to a fulfillment that takes precedence over it. The old is renewed by the new. A disciple has this understanding; this knowledge, however, does not make a disciple. It is the essence of being a disciple. Jesus may also be saying that the old should not be neglected in the acquisition of the new.

Applications

1. We can be assured that the Lord's church, though small in beginnings, is destined to be large. We should

not judge things by the beginning of things, the end may not be indicative of the beginning. Though there are times when we wonder if God is in control of our fractured and destructive world, times in which we wonder if God is doing anything, this world and God's purposes in and for it are exactly on schedule. When you and I stand in heaven, we will see far more clearly than we do today. Today is the day of faith, hope, and love; tomorrow will be the day of love because all that we trusted in will have come to fruition as well as all the things comprising our hope!

2. The gospel is the most precious treasure that can ever come into our possession. When discovered, it should be pursued at any cost. Those convinced of its truth should give up anything for it. Here is the meaning of discipleship; it is discovering the wealth of the gospel. Not that the gospel is a source of wealth, the path to material accumulation but, since it is so intrinsically overpowering and delightful, everything else is secondary. A disciple is that person who values the things of God over everything else. Can that be said of you?

3. There is a day coming, actually the last day, when God will stand in judgment over the earth and its inhabitants from over all the centuries. At that time, He will separate His people from all the other peoples, the wheat from the tares. It will be a day, the greatest of all days, for us; it will be the day of the ultimate triumph of God over His enemies; it will be the beginning of unsullied, unbroken delight and worship. It will be a day of awakening for all of us, some to life and some to the realization that they missed the greatest of all treasures.

4. Jesus repeatedly emphasizes the reality of hell. It is a terrible realm of suffering. Nevertheless, our culture remains skeptical of its reality though frequently referencing it. It is increasingly popular in the Christian community to denigrate divine justice and wrath by creating the illusion that justice and love are

opposing concepts. Without justice love cannot exist and without love there can be no justice. Universalism destroys the possibility of grace. If the treasure is not found, tragedy will be certain. Do you tell people where to find the treasure?

5. Jesus asked the disciples a very serious question. 'Do you understand these things?' (v. 51). The Lord expects us to be serious students of His teaching. The disciples indicated that they grasped what He was saying, but subsequent events should cause us to think that there must be levels of understanding. It seems that there must be degrees of grasping things for all of us. This indicates that learning requires diligence as well as time and experience. Learning is another component of being a disciple.

6. The treasure of the gospel is both new and old. It is new in the sense that the clarity of the substance and surety of the promises are much clearer now because the promises have been fulfilled in the coming of our treasure, procured through His death, and verified by the resurrection as having accomplished His task. It is old in that the promises were expressed in the multiple repetitions of the Abrahamic promises of a land (heaven ultimately, Palestine temporally), an heir (Jesus), and blessing (redemption) then unfolded in the Mosaic, Davidic, and New Covenants; the treasure has been in the field for a long, long time. Whenever it is found, it is new! Does that not thrill you?

7. It is possible to recognize profound wisdom in Christ, yet not possess heart affection for Him. The townspeople of Nazareth were offended by His claims just as the Gadarenes were by their loss of revenue (8:28-34). Though admired, Jesus was an embarrassment to them. Is that not sad? Have you ever been embarrassed because of Jesus? I guess we all have to some degree, but hopefully it was but a brief, sad moment.

7

The Final Ministry of the King in the Galilee

(13:53–16:12)

Jesus' movement from Capernaum marks the beginning of the end of His ministry in the Galilee (13:53). It is also a fulfillment of 13:14-15. As the nation's leadership increasingly opposed Jesus, He turned increasingly to the instruction of His disciples. It is interesting that the first of the incidences of our Lord's rejection by the general populous was in His hometown (the second deals with the rejection of John the Baptist). Also, it is the last time that Jesus is said to be in a synagogue. From this point Jesus operates outside the traditional structures of Judaism until He reaches Jerusalem at the triumphal entry. This verse comprises a standard formula that marks the close of a section and the transition to a new one (see 4:23-25; 7:28-29; 11:1).

The Rejection in Nazareth (13:54-58)

Jesus' rejection in His hometown is indicative of the general reaction to Him, though in this case it is by those who knew Him from His childhood. The last episode before the parables of chapter 13 was an incident suggesting alienation from Jesus' earthly family (12:46-50). The narrative now enumerates His rejection in His hometown just as had happened in Bethsaida, Capernaum, and Chorazin (11:20-24).

At this point, the family had grown to four sons and several sisters (vv. 55-56); the absence of Joseph suggests that he may have died by this time (Joseph does not appear in the narrative after the return from Egypt and the settlement in Nazareth [2:19-23]). The villagers viewed Jesus as the carpenter's son (v. 55), a mere earthling though with unusual power that they were unable to understand.

Like the people of Gadara (8:28-34), after the healing of the demoniac, the people of Nazareth were 'offended'. So very tragic! So much light, yet so much blindness! Jesus seems in His rejection to be similar to the Old Testament prophets in that regard (v. 57).

The sentence, 'And he did not do many mighty works there because of their unbelief' (v. 58), is related to our Lord's mission. As He would not turn stones to bread because it would violate His mission (4:1-4), so He could not do miracles indiscriminately without turning His mission into a sideshow.

Rejection of the Forerunner Remembered (14:1-36)

The murder of John by Herod Antipas must have been recent to the event recorded here (11:2-6); it is suggestive of the prominence and popularity of John for Herod since he made a connection between him and Jesus. Jesus seems to have followed the trajectory set in John's ministry. John's imprisonment signaled the beginning of Jesus' public ministry (4:12-17) and word of John's death signaled Jesus' rejection. Jesus' miraculous powers caused Herod to think that He was John resurrected. It is interesting that there is no record that John performed miracles. Somewhat misleading is the phrase 'about John' (v. 1) in the NASB. It is in italics indicating that it is not in the original text but inserted by the translators. However, what Jesus heard about was not John's death, but Herod's association of him with Jesus.

Herod Antipas and Jesus (vv. 1-12)

Herod Antipas, the son of Herod the Great, ruled as tetrarch (4 B.C.–A.D. 39), the term king, as well as tetrarch, being used loosely; he ruled as one of three over Herod the Great's divided domain, over the Galilee and Perea (the Transjordan).

He lived mainly in Tiberius on the western shore of the Sea of Galilee. Reports of the miracle-working career of Jesus called for an explanation; all that Herod could think of was that John the Baptizer had been resurrected from the dead.

Herod Antipas had been maneuvered into John's murder by drunkenness, ego, and the subterfuge of his wife Herodias. She was a daughter of Herod the Great's son Aristobulus (a son that Herod the Great murdered for threatening his throne rights). His brother Philip is not to be confused with Herod Philip, the tetrarch, who ruled a region north and east of the Sea of Galilee. Herodias was previously married to Herod's half-brother, Philip, the son of Mariamne, whom Herod Antipas murdered for threatening his rulership. Herod Antipas and Philip were half-brothers who both married sequentially a niece, Herodias. In visiting his brother Philip in Rome, Herod Antipas seduced his wife and subsequently convinced her to leave him. Philip and Herodias had a daughter, Salome[1] (the dancer); she became Herod Antipas' stepdaughter.

Herod's first wife was the daughter of Aretas, an Arabian king of the Nabateans, a kingdom immediately to the south of Perea. John's rebuke of Herod Antipas was not for the divorce from the daughter of Aretas, but for incestuously marrying his half-brother's wife. The couple were an 'Ahab and Jezebel'. This society lacked the right of free speech; to criticize a ruler's character was suicidal.

Herod's divorce had led to war with Aretas and the Nabateans; it was a political defeat for Herod Antipas, and he was rescued only by the intervention of the Romans under whom he ruled as a client king. Many felt Herod's defeat was a divine judgment for the execution of John, so there were social and political ramifications.

Herod was a political creature; he did what he did to secure his own self-interest. It was political expediency over

---

1. Josephus Flavius, *The History of the Jews*, 18:5.4. He wrote: 'Herodias, their sister, was married to Herod [Philip], the son of Herod the Great, who was born of Mariamne, the daughter of Simon the high priest, who had a daughter, Salome; after whose birth Herodias took upon her to confound the laws of our country, and divorced herself from her husband while he was alive, and was married to Herod [Antipas] ....'

fleeting pangs of conscience. Antipas wanted to murder John, but John's enormous popularity among his subjects prevented it (v. 5).

Salome was now fourteen. She consulted her mother either before or after Herod's magnanimous gesture (suggesting, perhaps, that she was too young to make decisions of this nature or was simply as wicked as her mother and stepfather). Thus, Herodias was presented with a way of getting rid of an old nemesis. Birthday parties were a Hellenistic custom, not a Jewish one.

Herod is a case-study in greed, a weak conscience, and fear. He was a troubled man without convictions except for self-promotion. He seems to have embraced the Pharisaic concept of life after death contrary to the Sadducees.

John was given no trial and beheading was contrary to Jewish law (not Greek or Roman law however). Josephus tells us that it took place in the fortress at Machaerus (one of Herod the Great's refuge fortresses) in Perea, near where John preached. Others have suggested that the execution took place in Tiberius; the banquet scene seemingly more likely to have taken place in his capital (this speculation is largely based on Mark 6:21 because the guest list included lords, the upper echelon of the military, and 'leading men of Galilee'). It seems a large and diverse contingent to track southward. Further, Josephus leaves out such pertinent details as the banquet, the dance by Salome, and Herod's oath from his account,[2] perhaps suggestive he was amiss of important details.

Christ's Withdrawal and Further Teaching (vv. 13-36)

Jesus was last noted in Nazareth (13:53-58), but He at some point returned to the northern Sea of Galilee area. Apparently, the flashback of Herod Antipas posed a threat, so Jesus withdrew from the immediate area where He continued to instruct His disciples and demonstrate His claims.

---

2. ibid., 118.5.2. Josephus wrote that 'accordingly he was sent a prisoner, out of Herod's suspicious temper, to Macherus, the castle I before mentioned, and was there put to death. Now the Jews had an opinion that the destruction of this army was sent as a punishment upon Herod, and a mark of God's displeasure to him.'

The lesson of sufficiency: the feeding of the five thousand (vv. 13-21)

Matthew's account of the miracle, a miracle recorded in each of the accounts of our Lord's ministry, is particularly crafted to emphasize the instructional component of the incident. Absent is the circumstance of having a meager supply of food to feed the crowd, or the response of the crowd perceiving that the feeding had Messianic portents. The crowd is de-emphasized while the lesson of faith and trust is emphasized for the disciples (the leftover food being greater than the original supply, as is the great faith of Peter later when walking on the sea). However, what Matthew records is the great affirmation of the disciples, 'Truly you are the Son of God' (v. 33).

The location of the miracle has puzzled the scholars. The most likely place is on the eastern side of the Sea of the Galilee in the area of Bethsaida, or today's Bethsaida Julias. This would make sense in that the progress following the miracle was east to west on the sea, the disciples with Jesus arriving at Gennesaret (a region on the northwest corner of the sea). Luke tells us that Jesus took His disciples to Bethsaida (9:10); Mark tells us it was 'a lonely place by themselves' (Mark 6:32) and, after the miracle, the disciples departed for Bethsaida (Mark 6:45). John tells us that the disciples' destination was Capernaum, which is a short distance further west on the lake (John 6:17). (To reconcile the two destinations, it seems that Jesus was to meet them at Bethsaida, and they would proceed together to Capernaum.) If Bethsaida is the area, it would be in the territory of Herod Philip. Archaeologists have recently discovered at Hippos, a city on the east side of the lake, the ruins of an early church with a mosaic of the feeding that may have been constructed to commemorate the general site.

General statements of multiple healings have been recorded by Matthew (4:23-24, 8:16, and 9:35). It is little wonder that John could write at the end of his gospel: 'Now there are also many other things that Jesus did. Were every one of them to be written, I suppose that the world itself could not contain the books that would be written' (John 21:25).

The context concerns Jesus' increasing instruction of the disciples in light of mounting rejection. Here, He is teaching them a wonderful lesson: God's provisions have no limitation. He is the 'New Moses' who gives 'bread' from heaven ('true manna'). He is also 'the prophet', doing a far greater array of miracles than Elijah (1 Kings 17:9-16; 2 Kings 4:42-44).

That Jesus had the crowd organized into groups (Mark 6:39-40; Luke 9:14) emphasizes the enormity of the miracle with perhaps as many as ten thousand gathered over a vast landscape in groups of fifty. The typical loaf of bread would feed three people in that day. Not only was a huge crowd fed from a small amount of food, twelve baskets of food were taken up afterward. When the disciples took up the leftovers (v. 20; John 6:12-13), each held in his hands an individualized lesson of God's provision.

The lesson of His presence: the calming of the sea (vv. 22-33)
The verb describing the dismissal of the disciples is demonstrative, 'made' or 'constrained' (v. 22). The reasons may have been several: to quell the Messianic uproar following the miracle of the five thousand, to gain some solitude for prayer, and, more likely from Matthew's perspective, to further His instruction of the disciples. However, Matthew gives us no clue as to the cause for the abrupt dismissal of the crowds or the disciples, but John tells us that the crowds became frantic in the assertion that Jesus was the Messiah (6:14-15). To quell the enthusiasm, a premature recognition before Jerusalem, Jesus sought to diffuse the circumstance.

That night they would have traveled from the northeast side of the lake to the northwest, the area called Gennesaret (Mark 6:53, today Ginosar). The subsequent storm may provide evidence that the feeding was east of the sea. Violent storms emerged when barometric pressure plummeted, forcing a downdrift of winds upon the lake. Energized by western winds on the northwest corner of the lake through the Valley of the Doves, the sea suddenly could become dangerous.

The Roman night was divided into four three-hour units beginning at 6:00 p.m. The fourth watch would be from 3:00–6:00 a.m. The disciples had rowed several hours into the dark, increasingly noisy, tempestuous night.

That Jesus came to them is beyond compare, expressing His sovereign power over nature, but also His incomprehensible compassion and care for His fear-ridden friends ('Take heart; it is I. Do not be afraid' [v. 27]). Mark adds the interesting comment that Jesus was passing by the disciples when they noticed Him (6:48). The reaction of the disciples was not that Jesus was coming to them, but death ('It is a ghost,' v. 26).

The account of the great faith of Peter (vv. 29-30) is the first of three episodes that focus on Peter (see also 16:13-23; 17:24-27). Peter's faith only crumbled when he focused on the waves. Amazing!

The storm's stilling and the disciples' worship is described in verses 31-33. This is the first time the disciples addressed Jesus with His full, divine title. 'Son of God' language appeared in the comments of the Father at Jesus' baptism (3:17) and in the confrontation with demons (4:3, 6; 8:29), but this is the first time from the disciples. They are putting the composite picture of Jesus together through His names, words, works, and titles. Later (16:16), Peter will make the same confession, but add to the title that Jesus is the Messiah, the Christ.

A transitional summary and Jesus' popularity (vv. 34-36)
Jesus and the disciples crossed the lake to a more populated Jewish area, Gennesaret (along the northwest corner of the lake from Magdala to Capernaum). Once again, Matthew discloses another instance of numerous miracles in a summary fashion. Touching the tassels of Jesus' outer garment reminds one of a similar healing in 9:20 (the healing of the woman with an issue of blood).

Applications

1. The past has a way of coming back on us. Often present, similar experiences are interpreted through the lens of past ones. Herod Antipas did wrong and knew it, only to be haunted later. The conscience is not strong enough to prevent action, but it can remind us of past inappropriate action. How many of us are haunted by past, poor choices that we cannot get out of our minds at times? Sadly, the past colours the present. The only

answer for bad memories is the cross of Christ and far better memories of what Christ has done for us. There is no past that cannot be forgiven; only an awareness of forgiveness can heal memories. Do you have some memories that you need to carry to Jesus? What kind of baggage did you bring into your marriage that needs the touch of God?

2. Rash promises often are a source of regret, particularly when combined with fear and insecurity. Antipas is a case study of some people you meet. He was powerful on the outside, but weak of moral character, a prisoner of his own brokenness. He feared personal embarrassment more than what was right. Have you met people that were so gullible that they could prove dangerous if the circumstances proved conducive? Perhaps you know some of this type. Perhaps some are in your family and among your friends. In a crowd they change and become so vastly different than when one-on-one. Are you like that to some degree?

3. The paucity of resources is not a problem for God. He wants us to know that He is the great provider. You and I have a God who has promised never to leave us or forsake us. When storms come upon the 'sea' of our lives and in the darkness and loneliness of fears, we frequently feel abandoned by the Lord. That is simply not true. The Lord may wait till the 'fourth watch' of your night, until your fears and pain have rendered you helpless, but He will come to console you, to comfort you. God sends us into storms, never as punishment, but to reveal Himself to us. Hear the words of God, 'I will never leave you nor forsake you.' Is that not great? Is that not true?

4. Is it not a great source of comfort to know that God truly knows when we are afraid, and He cares so much that He brings us relief? When Jesus came that night He said literally, 'Do not go on being afraid.' What a wonderful statement. Jesus knows when you and I are filled with anxious thoughts. Then He said, 'It is I.' Here is the reason. When Jesus is with us it matters not that storms

rage, because our focus suddenly changes to Him. Jesus drew the conclusion from His presence that we should 'take courage'. Wow! Here is something that you and I can tuck in our pockets for all of our tomorrows. Are you in the middle of a raging storm? Are you being battered in the night? Jesus will never leave you. What a grand comfort and joy!

5. Often it is not in the best of times that we learn the most cherished lessons, but in the worst of times. When Jesus fed the five thousand, and the disciples held twelve baskets of leftover food, they made no response of worship. In fact, they were swept along in the emotion and passion of those who saw in Jesus a source of meeting only temporal needs. However, when He cast them into a storm and they were overtaken in fear, they responded with recognition of His worth by saying, 'You are the Son of God.' They bowed in worship though by the wee hours of the morn the miracle of the loaves was but a distant vague memory. Our most lingering lessons come in the midst of pain and sorrow. Have you noticed that? Is that not true of you? What are some of the lessons you have learned from difficult experiences?

6. Peter is a great example of the benefit of focusing on Jesus rather than on our circumstances. As long as he looked to Jesus, he did not sink. Jesus allowed Peter to come in order to show him the faltering nature of his faith. Our problem is often not faith, but its constancy in our lives. One moment we can be filled with trust, confidence, and hope and within a brief period sink in faithlessness. Are you glad that it is not the potency of faith that saves and keeps us, but the object of our faith, Jesus?

7. Many people experience the mercies and generosity of God; grace is extended to all peoples every day. Some people understand that tangible things, such as health and family, are pictures of the greater fact of divine care for us. Good things remind us that God cares infinitely for us. Most people take good times for granted, welcome them, and never turn to the Giver

in thankfulness and praise. They like the benefits, but not the Benefactor as much. Can that be said of us? Are there times when we desire His benefits more than Himself? It seems that there are a lot of these types in our world.

Tensions with the Pharisees and Scribes (15:1-39)

As Matthew developed the narrative, the conflict with the religious leadership became more strident and focused. They were on a collision course. Whereas conflict between the Pharisees, scribes, and Jesus seemed to have been of local origin, in this chapter Matthew tells us that they came 'from Jerusalem' (v. 1).

The dispute over tradition (vv. 1-20)

In this section, Jesus clashes with Orthodox Judaism, particularly over the origin of corrupting influences. The Pharisees adopted the view that pollution had an environmental or external cause; Jesus says that it springs from mankind's innermost being. The flashpoint of conflict was over ceremonial cleansing before eating. Was washing necessary in the avoidance of pollution or not? Is corruption of external or internal origins? What is the nature of true righteousness? How is true righteousness distinguished from hypocrisy? If pollution finds its origin in external circumstances, the Pharisees had a point in the erection of cleansing and separating legislation. If they were wrong as Jesus asserts, they were making a grave religious mistake.

The connection between the confrontation over the authority of oral tradition, so much a part of the Pharisaic view of Judaism, should be read in light of Jesus' comments (11:28-30) that His yoke is easy and his burden light. In Pharisaic Judaism, Sabbath restrictions, dietary laws, and circumcision were essential; Jesus opposes all three! See also Colossians 2:16.

What is interesting is that hand washing, the issue in the conflict, was not a legal requirement for ordinary Jews, but only for priests in cultic performances. The scribes extended the requirement to all Jews under all circumstances before eating. Jesus did not challenge the hand washing of priests in their cultic duties (Exod. 30:17-21), but the unbiblical extension of it.

The religious leadership raise a question (v. 2). 'Tradition of the elders' refers to the body of additional teachings that 'explained' the 'true' meaning of the Law and applied its meaning in minute detail, often reflecting the diverse opinions among the rabbis. Jesus' point is that He is not in violation of the Mosaic Code because the accretions of the scribes go beyond it and are not part of it.

In part, the motivation behind the creation of elaborate commentaries on the Mosaic Code by the scribes was to avoid another tragedy like the Babylonian exile. Being careful to avoid dereliction, Jews in the intertestamental period constructed elaborate 'fence laws' to prevent violations. In so doing, they went well beyond the intent of the Law; in fact, the consequence was the creation of a false means of righteousness (obedience) and shackled the people with burdens they could not carry.

Jesus' rejoinder is that the development of such traditions was a perversion of the Law (vv. 3-6). He cited two Scripture-texts to illustrate the point (Exod. 20:12 and 21:17). Both texts are said to be the very Word of God. The first demands the care of parents and the second is more specific dealing with their proper treatment, in this instance the avoidance of denigrating them. However, according to scribal tradition, the use of wealth to care for family was not required if one claimed that their material wealth was dedicated to the Lord (this is called 'Korban', meaning 'dedicated to the Lord' [Lev. 27:9, 16]). It was a subversive way of not fulfilling one's duty to care for parents while supposedly avoiding violation at the same time.

Jesus' reply shows that the inquirers were advocates of the very action that they condemned in the action of the disciples. The principle that Jesus rejects is that tradition, the elaborations of the nation's religious leaders, is of the same authority as the Mosaic Code. He validates His teaching by the witness of Scripture. It was not the disciples who errored in religious practice; it was the Pharisees and scribes because they embraced things not taught by Moses.

Indication of the mounting crisis was the heightened strident discourse. This is the first instance in the book that Jesus uses the word 'hypocrite' (v. 7), a theatrical term meaning 'one who plays behind a mask', specifically of the religious leadership (though clearly implied in Matthew 6:2, 5, 16). The evidence of the falseness of their religious claims is that of consistency with their forefathers. Just as the great prophets found the leadership of their day (Isa. 29:13), so did Jesus.

This is also the first time in the gospel that Jesus speaks specifically of the religious leadership in denouncing their understanding of the origin of corruption (vv. 10-11). Defilement is not so much external in origin, the outward being only solicitation, but inward, human thoughts motivated by inordinate desires.

The consternation of the disciples is mentioned in verse 12. They were stunned by Jesus' evaluation of the religious leadership either out of fear of the consequences or by ignorantly having embraced the Pharisaic understanding of the source of human sinfulness.

The response of Jesus must have been as shocking as the disciples' perceptions (vv. 13-14). Jesus perceived that the leadership was in gross error; they did not reflect the true religious understanding of the origin of human corruption and, thus, taught falsely its remediation; their teachings were not of divine origin (the use of a metaphor, blindness). They were ignorant of the truth; and they faced divine retribution. The 'if' clause (v. 14b) indicates a probability, not a factual certainty, meaning that if they remained ignorant, a certainty awaited them. This suggests the possibility of divine grace for them such as in the cases of Joseph of Arimathea and Nicodemus (Luke 24:50-51; John 3:10; 20:39-40).

Peter's follow-up inquiry is detailed in verses 15-20. He designates the metaphor of planting as a 'parable'. This indicates that the term has a broad range of meaning beyond a detailed story (see a further explanation of the term in the comments on Matthew 13).

Matthew tells us that Jesus was shocked by the self-revelation of Peter's ignorance (v. 16). What is also clear in Jesus' reply is that He assigned to Himself the role of the true interpreter of the Law (vv. 17-18). A greater than Moses is here!

Four of the sins that Jesus lists (v. 19) are taken from the Decalogue in the order presented in Exodus 20:13-16 –

commandments five to nine. The two others, false witness and slander, are extensions of false testimony. All these sins originate in the heart; all are violations of the intent of the Law (22:38-40).

Wickedness is rooted in the heart of mankind, not in the external environment (v. 20). External factors may present options and ideas to the mind, but the motive for selection is interior, the 'heart' being the mechanism of human choice-making. It is the 'heart' also that is the fundamental sphere of the Holy Spirit's act of regeneration!

The withdrawal of Christ (vv. 21-39)

As tensions mounted with the religious leadership, and perhaps also the consternation of the disciples, Jesus left the northern Sea of Galilee area to journey northeast to Gentile areas, and then returned (a journey that would likely have taken an extended period of time). Jesus must have realized that it was not the moment to challenge the Jerusalem religious leadership further, preventing a crisis before the appointed time. Tyre (11:21) offers a remarkable contrast to the reception of the Jewish religious leadership to Jesus. Gentiles received Him as did the Roman centurion in Capernaum (8:5-13), but the Jews offered resistance! These two miracles have some remarkable similarities. In both cases:

- The request came for someone close to the person healed.
- The request came for someone under his or her charge.
- The subjects were Gentiles.
- The people making the request had greater faith than those in Israel and were commended by Jesus.
- The cure came by a word spoken from a distance.

The two miracles that follow are important in the greater narrative of Matthew's book. A clue is in Matthew's insertion of the visit of Gentile astrologers from Babylon (2:1-2) and then the account of God's grace to the centurion's servant (8:5). Here, after the increased hostility of His own people ('He came to his own and his own did not receive him' [John 1:11]), He

withdraws in this section to the Gentiles, finding great faith
in a woman (as he had done in the centurion at Capernaum)
and feeds an enormous crowd (14:13-21). Clearly, Jesus is
making the point that grace is being extended to the nations.
Jerusalem and death loom in the near future, but beyond that
is the resurrection and the command for His disciples to go
to the nations (28:18-20).

To Tyre and Sidon: healing of the 'Canaanite' (vv. 21-28)

This is one of the few healing stories outside of Israel. Tyre and
Sidon are located on the Mediterranean coast about thirty-five
miles northwest of the Sea of Galilee. Matthew is careful to
say that Jesus came into the region, not any specific city. In
addition, there are no instances in which Jesus inaugurated a
conversation. Here, a lady came to Jesus in the context of His
reluctance to converse, reminding us, perhaps, of a similar
situation with an encounter at the well of Sychar (John 4:1-26,
there Jesus initiated the conversation).

Matthew refers to the woman as a Canaanite, Israel's ancient
enemy (the Hebrew Scriptures, on occasion, speaks of 'Tyre
and Sidon' as a synonym for Gentile territory [Isa. 23:1-4]).
In a parallel account by Mark, you have the designation
'Syrophoenician' (7:26). An outsider comes to a Jew for grace!
This is not the first recorded healing of a Gentile (4:24-25;
8:5-13); it is the first healing of a Gentile outside Israel.

The unnamed woman revealed deep insight though she
likely had not previously met Jesus. She repeatedly calls
Him 'Lord' and the 'Son of David' (v. 22). Further, she seems
to have a deeper knowledge of Jewish religion than many
Jews; Jesus is the sovereign One and the greater Son of David
(divine and human, God and royalty).

The disciples' request can be taken two ways: to send
her away because she is annoying or to send her away with
her request (vv. 23-24). The former seems to be the better
option contextually. The disciples seemed to be consistently
ignorant of the real meaning of events swirling around them.
They also seemed to find children a nuisance. These are
interesting men for they have been with Jesus for some time
(remember, they also feared, or at least too highly respected,
the Pharisees).

Jesus initially appears to be acting towards this Gentile as would be expected of the contemporary Jewish perspective. He says that He was only called to 'the lost sheep of Israel', a statement consistent with His instructions to the disciples when He initially sent them out (10:6). 'To the Jew first' was the basic principle since they were the ethnic heirs of the promise. As the Jewish leadership increased their descent, there are hints that, in light of His rejection by them, the door was increasingly opening to Gentiles. However, the ploy actually appears to be a method by a master teacher.

This woman has amazing insight (v. 25). She called Him 'Lord', a divine title, and she worshiped Him. Three times she calls Him 'Lord'. Here is the earnest cry of a mother ('Lord, help me!').

Clearly in verses 26-27 Jesus wanted her to understand the distinction between Jews (children) and Gentiles (dogs). His point is one of preference; 'children' are to be fed first! 'Crumbs' do not refer to the quality of blessing bestowed since it fell from the dining table. Further, even dogs have a right to be fed! This dear lady accepted the fact that salvation was of the Jews, but they had failed in sharing the blessings of Abraham with the nations!

This discourse with the woman on Jesus' part seems harsh. Yet Jesus was probing the lady's depth of knowledge and He concludes that it was great. Further, the reference to 'dogs' may simply be a statement about how animals are treated in a household (Jews had dogs in their homes; it was not an unclean animal). Jesus may have been engaging in a comparative metaphor with ethnic or religious connotations of inferiority. Further, it may have been a statement of Jewish precedence in the program of God.

This is only the second time that Jesus calls a person's faith great (v. 28). Her faith, as also that of the centurion (8:10), suggests a time when Gentiles will join Jews on an equal basis before the Lord (the criteria being faith in the promises and provisions of God through Christ). The de-emphasis on the healing itself, the few words describing it, suggest that the main point is not the miracle. The issue is the foreshadowing of the extension of the gospel of Jesus to the nations after His rejection by the nation to which He had been sent.

A summary of miracles follows in verses 29-31. On returning from the region of Tyre and Sidon, according to Matthew, Jesus taught and performed miracles along the Sea of Galilee. Mark tells us that Jesus was on the eastern side of the Jordan River in Gentile territory, the Decapolis, doing these things (7:31) and that the Gentiles 'glorified the God of Israel' for what they saw. The blind, the lame, and the speechless were healed (Isa. 61:1) among many others.

The feeding of the four thousand (vv. 32-39)
What is clear is that Jesus engaged in teaching as well as miracle-working; words and works. If I were guessing the scenario would look like this: after Jesus' rejection by Pharisees in Galilee, who argued that His miracles were of demonic origin and plotted to kill Him (12:14), Jesus turned to instruction through parables (13:1-52) and miracles (14:13-33). With the heightened animosity caused from confrontation with the leadership from Jerusalem over the role of tradition (15:10-20), He withdrew from the Galilee both to diffuse mounting tensions and to teach the disciples the importance of reaching out to Gentiles. After returning to the Galilee and further ministry in Herod Philip's territory, He would make his way to Jerusalem, where He experienced death and resurrection, and then sealing the point of His journey into Gentile territory (15:21-28) with the Great Commission (28:18-20) to go to the nations!

The location of this miracle is a point of considerable discussion. It seems that it was on the eastern side of the sea, in largely Gentile territory (outside Herod Antipas' jurisdiction in the Decapolis [Mark 7:31], the realm of his brother Herod Philip). Only Gentiles could utter the phrase, 'they praised the God of Israel.' The location is remote (v. 33, wilderness [KJV], desert [ASV]), and, when Jesus left, He went by sea to Magadan (v. 39, most likely Magdala located on the northwest corner of the lake). If so, here is a case where Gentiles received more than crumbs. The blessing of the Gentiles is beginning to dawn!

As was frequently the case, Jesus' conversations with the disciples have a pedagogical purpose more so than the solicitation of information (vv. 32-34). Again, as in the previous feeding of the 5,000, the issue seems to be the heightening of awareness of human inadequacy in light of a huge need. The parallel with the feeding of the 5,000 suggests that Jesus wanted the disciples to know that the claims of Jesus were for the Gentile as well as for the Jew. God is extending 'bread' to the Gentiles.

There are differences between the two feeding miracles:

- The audience in ethnicity and size
- The number of loaves and fish
- The size of the leftovers
- The disciples stressed the fact of inadequacy to a greater degree in this feeding.
- Less detail of the feeding arrangements
- The season (the ground was parched suggesting that it was late summer. If the 'Feeding of the 5,000' was in the spring around Passover, it would suggest that Jesus' journey to the Gentile region took several months).
- Jesus clearly spoke of the feedings as separate events (16:9-10).
- The word 'satisfied' (14:20; 15:37) literally means stuffed. Both groups were equally and abundantly fed.

Again, it seems that 'Magadan' was a town on the shoreline, since Jesus and the disciples came there by boat, and in a Jewish area since the religious leadership of the nation confronts Jesus once more (16:1), this time by Pharisees and Sadducees (perhaps in today's Migdal Nunya, ancient Magdala, the town of Mary Magdalene). It seems that they were awaiting His return to continue the confrontation. It might also explain why Jesus almost immediately left to return to Gentile territory to diffuse the tensions until He would re-enter in order to go to Jerusalem.

Applications

1. Jesus would be as misunderstood in our day as He was in His own. He was politically incorrect, straightforward, and critical. It takes tremendous courage, rooted in

a deep sense of what is right and wrong, of what is beneficial and detrimental, to speak your mind. We live in a decaying, immoral culture and yet the virtues of it seem to be tolerance and 'open mindedness', at the very time when there is no moral compass to give direction. Can a disciple of Jesus not speak up when we see our children making terrible mistakes, families torn apart, and destruction abounding? The place to begin is in our homes and families!

2. According to Jesus, environmental or external factors do not cause us to sin. Sin emanates from our corrupt hearts or affections. It is not what enters us that causes sin; it is what is within us. Jesus' understanding of basic anthropology is fundamental for our lives and society as a whole. The improvement of external circumstances is helpful, but it is not the solution to reversing bad choices and behavioral patterns. This is a point where the Christian faith differs radically from secular or other religious or social explanations of deviancy. We claim that the problem is within, though the stimulus is often without, and that the individual is responsible for his/her choices. We simply believe that the responsibility for bad choices resides within the individual.

3. Jesus' understanding of sin makes salvation by self-effort impossible. If the problem of evil choices is within the human immaterial faculties, the heart or affections, then the improvement of social choices or a sedate personality is not the solution since its absence is not the real problem (only the symptom). Salvation is something outside of us and must come to us as a gift; we have no capacity to improve our religious condition before a holy God. Only God can cleanse the heart. Have you turned to God for religious peace or are you seeking refuge by controlling your thoughts and environment? Human methods to relieve pain and discomfort have a temporal value but lack a durative quality. Have you noticed that?

4. It is a dangerous thing to add to the Word of God. Jesus would have us define religion by the Scriptures alone; men tend to add to the Scriptures their own insights

only to enslave themselves and others. Knowing your true moral freedom as a Christian is to become acquainted with the Bible. There is a tendency in all of us to add to the Bible things that are simply not there. The problem is that when we add to the stipulations of the Bible, we tend to think that God is more pleased with us by emphasizing the 'do nots' of cultural religion. God saw what the scribes did as destructive of the freedoms of true religion. Do you find yourself making up rules that are beyond what the text actually proscribes or prohibits?

5. Sometimes affliction, sickness of our children, leads to great blessing as in the case of the woman of Tyre. It is in the darkness that light shines the brightest, often not when the 'sun' is at its height. There are important insights that come to us through pain and disappointment. A stream of water without rocks simply does not sing; rose bushes without thorns do not flower. None of us desires pain or should ever seek it out, but it is a reality in a fallen world. God turns tragedy into opportunities for wonderful insights. Has that been true in your religious experience? Can you see ways that hurt has brought peace?

6. A lesson not to miss in the feeding of the four thousand or the healing of the centurion's servant is God's love to reach out to the nations; ethnicity is not a delimiting barrier to divine mercy and grace. In the dawning of the new age, the creation of the new community of God, the barriers of nationality have been broken to pieces. Our text says, 'I (Jesus) have compassion' (v. 32). What a wonderful statement! Jesus truly cares for us spiritually and materially, Jews and Gentiles. God's great desire is to gather His new people from the nations. Do you share the same concern? What are you doing consciously to expand the borders of Christian faith and confession?

7. Jesus delights in engaging His people in conversation with Him. It is not merely to enjoy our attention and fellowship, but to extend understanding to us. One

of His methods is to employ the tool of questioning. Probing another person through the art of inquiry is a powerfully illuminating and engaging tool. Do you employ this method in your social conversations with your children, with your mate, with your friends, with people you meet? Is your conversational pattern more of a monologue then a dialogue? Perhaps you would learn more about people by engaging them in discourse (talking *with* them rather than by talking *to* them). Some people talk too much and listen too little!

Tension with the Pharisees and Sadducees (16:1-12)

In this section, after Jesus returned to the Galilee, He is confronted by the Pharisees and Sadducees. A sense of stridency emerges from Jesus' comments. The leadership is focused on dealing with Him; the curtain is falling. Jesus returned to the Galilee but spent little time there before taking the disciples into Gentile territory once more (v. 5).

Common purposes make diverse people companions. Sadducees and Pharisees often clashed over theology and practice (Acts 23:6-10). The former were aristocratic, powerful, strict law constructionists, and liberal; the latter were the populists, embraced traditionalists with the law, and conservative. Both were in the Sanhedrin along with scribes and elders (powerful laymen).

The request about a sign was for evidence of His claims to be 'from heaven' (v. 1). Earlier, in 12:38-39, scribes and Pharisees came to Jesus with the same motive, that is to confront Jesus and show Him to be a fake. This is the last confrontation with the religious leadership in the Galilee. In point of observation, the most severe conflicts seemed to emerge from the Sadducees who resided in Jerusalem, but they had no discernible presence in the Galilee (this being the only time they are mentioned outside Judea).

In His reply, Jesus observes that the leaders are better at weather prediction than they are spiritually insightful (vv. 2-4). He refused to give any other evidence of His claims except one that is yet to come, the resurrection, and rebuked them for asking (v. 4). The religious leadership were better with the natural sciences than they were with religious understanding. If they had been, they would not have asked for a confirming sign; they would have embraced Jesus.

Jesus can be blunt when He encounters unbelief and rejection (v. 4). 'Adulterous,' being an adjective, suggests unfaithfulness to one's vows (see 12:39 where Jesus upbraids the Pharisees for rejecting His claims by rejecting the source of His authority). Their demand for evidence is foolish unbelief because they had seen so many of His miracles. Unlike the reference to the sign of Jonah previously (12:40-41), He does not explain its meaning here. Obviously in retrospect, it was the resurrection.

This is a major turning event in Jesus' ministry; the Sadducees have crossed the point of no return. His ministry in Jewish Galilee has ended; He is about to confront the religious leadership in Jerusalem!

Private instruction of the disciple in light of the inquiry (vv. 5-12)

This is Jesus' final withdrawal before the journey to Jerusalem. He seems to have gone into Gentile territory ('other side' of the sea [v. 5]) where further conflict with the leadership could be avoided for the time being. Jesus had important further insights to communicate to His disciples.

Once again the disciples find that they had not made adequate provision for their journey. You would think they would have remembered to prepare properly, but perhaps Jesus' previous feedings of the crowds had made them lax or that the instructions of 10:9-10 had them thinking of securing hospitality to meet any needs.

The lack of bread gives the Lord an opportunity to speak to the disciples about the 'bread' of the national leadership (v. 6). Leaven can be a symbol of a wide variety of wickednesses, always with the idea that a little of it results in far reaching devastation or penetration. The emphasis here seems to be on its pervasiveness.

The disciples erroneously thought that Jesus' warning was about their failure to bring bread for the journey (v. 7). In contrast to the Canaanite's 'great' faith (15:28), His disciples have little insight. They have completely missed the point (vv. 8-9). Jesus is not talking about literal bread, because the lack of it is no great issue. On two occasions there was great insufficiency and He fed thousands with baskets of leftovers. He may also be asking the disciples to remember that He bountifully provides for Jews and Gentiles in banquet-style and will do so in His kingdom (v. 10).

The memory of the two miraculous feedings should have put the disciples' minds at ease when they discovered their forgetfulness (v. 11). Jesus used the opportunity to teach a lesson. While Jesus disagreed with both religious parties on some things, His condemnation was not a blanket one – He recognized the Pharisees' acceptance of the resurrection and the Sadducees' rejection of oral tradition; it was about their 'yeast' as a composite whole. The 'teaching' that Jesus was concerned about was the attitude of unbelief towards divine revelation, specifically that He was the Messiah.

Finally, the disciples get the point of Jesus' warning; it was not about bread, but about the teachings of the two major religious parties (v. 12). Both groups refused to recognize the claims of Jesus. It seems that Jesus wanted the disciples to understand the failure of first-century Judaism!

8

The Final Instructions of the King in the Galilee

(16:13–18:35)

In this long section Jesus continues the instruction of His disciples in light of His rejection in Galilee. Jesus is intensively preparing them for His departure.

Disclosures in Light of Opposition (16:13–17:27)

Jesus again withdrew to Gentile territory, to a region twenty-five miles north, at the foot of Mount Hermon. A pagan temple to the god Pan was there. The city was called Caesarea Philippi in honor of Augustus Caesar and Herod Philip, the local governor (tetrarch) and son of Herod the Great.

The King's person (16:13-17)
In this setting, Jesus asked the disciples their general opinion of who the 'Son of Man' may be. Though Jesus' favored designation of Himself, rooted in Daniel 7:13-14, the title does not engender a unified definition. It is a broad term subject to various nuances. Perhaps this is why Jesus used it; it avoids the specificity that would lead to premature confrontation with the religious leadership.

Herod Antipas' opinion was that the Messiah was John risen from the dead (14:2). Some thought of Jesus as the fulfillment of the prophecy that Elijah would come

(Mal. 4:5). Others thought He might be Jeremiah. Still others perceived that Jesus was simply one in a succession of a long line of prophets. By implication, few were thinking of Jesus as the Messiah.

Jesus asked the disciples who they thought He was. The words 'but you' is the point of emphasis and 'you' is plural. Jesus asks the disciples as a group. Simon Peter answered for them. He replied that Jesus is the Messiah (God's anointed One), God in the flesh! The several titles of Jesus that Peter groups together create a portrait. The common conception of Messiahship at the time was that of a political deliverer sent by God to deliver the people. Generally, the meaning of the title connected 'Son of David' – a royal, kingly redeemer, the fulfillment of the promise to King David (2 Sam. 7) – with a merely human deliverer.

Further, Peter says that Jesus is 'the Son of God', an allusion to Psalm 2:7 ('… You are my son, today I have begotten you'). In the aftermath of the storm incident in Matthew 14 the disciples collectively acclaimed Jesus as 'the Son of God' (v. 33); here Peter declared Him to be 'the Christ, the Son of the Living God.' He is the promised One, the fulfillment of the ancient promises. The kingly redeemer/deliverer is deity in flesh! 'Son of the living God' tells us that He is not a mere idea of hope and deliverance; He is real. It is interesting that Peter says this in a region where false gods were worshiped. Jesus combines teaching with settings that support the things He desires to convey; He knows the value of visualization.

'Blessed' (5:3-11) literally means 'the one upon whom divine approval rests'. Peter is 'blessed' because he knows something that could only come by revelation (v. 17), and he believed it (unlike the Pharisees and Sadducees who repudiated revelation when they saw it [16:11]).

Matthew refers to Peter by his full name, Simon Peter; also Jesus calls him the 'son of Jonah', likely a figurative designation (He will subsequently speak of him as 'Satan' [v. 23]), as a likeness between the prophet and Peter and not that his father was named Jonah (Peter will preach to Gentiles like Jonah to the Ninevites – both witnessed large ingathering of repentant peoples, and both found the results uncomfortable). However, this is conjecture on my part; yet it is intriguing, given Jesus' often employment of words with double meaning. Peter, like Jonah, initially proved derelict in his testimony, but later demonstrated obedience. Peter was called to a Gentile, Cornelius, introducing Jewish-Gentile mission outreach (Acts 10), Jonah to a city of Gentiles!

That stated, it must be recognized that many commentators take 'son of' as a statement identifying Peter's father (it is common to identify a person by his father's name). In two parallel passages of this account found in John, Peter is referred to as 'son of John' (1:42; 21:15, 16, 17); perhaps Matthew selected 'Jonah' because he wrote for a Jewish audience that spoke Aramaic (in that language 'son of Jonah' meant 'son of John').

Peter's insight was not the result of his cleverness. How could it be? Jesus is from a place that human wisdom is unable to penetrate, 'flesh and blood' being a figure of speech for humanity in general.

The King's program (16:18-28)

There has been much discussion concerning the meaning of 'this rock'. The name 'Peter' does mean 'rock'. It would seem that Jesus is making a pun (the distinction between the masculine *petros* and the feminine *petra* is poetic). It would also seem that Jesus is calling Peter a foundation stone of the church. Peter is the rock or foundation stone in his confessional capacity as the leader in the early church (clearly the other disciples did not understand Jesus' statement as suggestive of Peter's superiority in light of the discussion that shortly follows in 18:1 and Jesus' extension of authority to all the disciples in 18:18). The following points can be made about Peter and his position in the church:

(1) If Jesus wanted to make a distinction in the size of rocks, He could have used 'lithos', meaning a large rock. Jesus did not say, 'You are Peter, *but* on this rock ....' He said, 'You are Peter, *and* on this rock ....'

(2) The foundation of the church is 'the apostles and prophets' (Eph. 2:19-20, Rev. 21:14); Christ is the cornerstone.

(3) In this passage, Jesus is the builder of the church (v. 18), the disciples the foundation. John was the last living apostle to have direct apostolic authority from Jesus. Peter died before

John; it is illogical to think that, if Peter had a successor in Rome, he would have had authority over a living apostle.

(4) If the disciples understood that Peter was the head of the apostles, the question in 18:1 would not make sense. Peter would be considered the greatest in the kingdom.

(5) Peter was prominent in the early church (Acts 1–12), but the other apostles sent Peter and John as equals (8:14). He was accountable for his actions to the Jerusalem church (11:1-18) and was openly rebuked by Paul (Gal. 2:11-14). Peter is one among equals and on the foundation of these men Jesus would build His church.

(6) This approach to the issues is consistent with later statements in the New Testament that Jesus is the foundation of the church (Rom. 9:33; Eph. 2:20; 1 Pet. 2:5-8).

'Gates of hell' is difficult to understand since gates in the ancient world were part of the defensive walls of a city. The gate of a city was its most fortified place, so it may be used here metaphorically for strength. Further, 'gates of hell' seems to refer to death and the 'city' refers to the place of defeat where the dead reside. Satan, his minions, and even the destruction of the saints cannot prevent the Lord's church from being built.

The matter of the 'keys' is also quite a subject of debate. The 'keys' are relative to the 'kingdom of heaven'. The kingdom and the church are two distinct concepts, though not separable. 'Church' refers to a gathering of people, 'kingdom' to rule or reign. The kingdom has dawned, light has broken forth; the strong man is being bound and God is calling out of the world (the sphere of His rule) a people. 'The keys' are to the storehouse and the image is that Peter's role will be to secure provision from heaven for the early church in the gospel (though it is used in reference to all the disciples in 18:18). 'Keys,' then, refer to admission or exclusion, the right to declare those to be God's children who embrace the message as well as to declare as lost those who do not receive the apostles' message. The instructions here appear to be an elaboration of the directive given when the disciples were initially sent out (10:11-15).

The meaning of 'whatever' is important in understanding 'loosing/binding'. It can be things or people. 'Whatever' is clearly used of people here (the neuter gender refers to groups or categories of people, not individuals [18:18]). The 'loosing/binding,' then, refers to the regulation of conduct in the early churches; 'to loosen' means to permit a particular action and 'to bind' to prohibit. The reception of the gospel, or its rejection, is something Peter is to declare because it is something already settled in heaven (the verb is future perfect passive, a future reality considered already done by God) and the churches possess authority in regulating their internal affairs ('binding/loosing' refers to decision-making, judgments). The apostles had the authority to announce what heaven had declared already!

Instructions concerning the immediate future (vv. 20-21)
As with Jesus' withdrawal from religious controversy, as well as the inappropriateness of the adulation of the crowds, the instruction to tell no one is a matter of the immediate context. The real confrontation must await Jerusalem! The disciples' understanding of Jesus as the Messiah is still in the developmental stage; they will put all the pieces together after the resurrection (see the following verses). Then it will be time to make Him known!

The instruction concerning His death and resurrection is a key marker in the book, the transition to Jerusalem. Following the recognition that Jesus is the Messiah, He announced, for the first time, what that meant (not glory, but suffering and then glory).

This is the first of three times that Jesus informs the disciples of what lies ahead in Jerusalem (17:22-23; 20:17-19), each time adding greater detail. The 'Son of Man' is both to die and reign! Three Old Testament passages are alluded to in Jesus' statements here (Pss. 22; 69; Isa. 52:13–53:12). 'Must' (v. 21) indicates His willingness to fulfill His divine mission. 'The elders and chief priests and scribes' refer to those in authoritative positions in the nation, the Sanhedrin. Pharisees would have been classified with elders and scribes; the chief priests were Sadducees.

Verse 21 is intriguing because of the phrase 'from that time'. It appears in 4:17 at the commencement of Jesus' ministry and may appear here to indicate the impending conclusion of His ministry. Some divide the book based on this phrase: (1) the introduction of Jesus (1:1–4:16); (2) the ministry of Jesus (4:17–16:20); and (3) the climax of the ministry of Jesus (16:21–28:20).

Peter's rebuke of Jesus (v. 22) reveals that though he confessed that Jesus is the Christ, he had little grasp of the nature of biblical Messiahship. In fact, he failed to grasp how Jesus could be successful, yet die (the dilemma of the prophets). In Peter's view, Jesus was mistaken and needed correction. For Peter, Jesus would reign, but suffer He would not. Clearly, Peter's mind was not set on the things of God, but only conceived of an earthly geopolitical figure.

Peter so quickly turned from a rock on which the new community is to be built into a stumbling block, literally a trap. Jesus' reply is deeply severe (v. 23); Peter is called Satan because, like the devil, he thought of a kingdom without suffering, a crown without a cross (4:7-10). Jesus came to do the Father's will; the only way to do that was the Father's way. This means Jerusalem and death, and then resurrection and reign.

Jesus' further instruction on discipleship (vv. 24-28)

The Jewish leadership renounced Jesus' claim to Messiahship; now Jesus asks His disciples to deny themselves (v. 24). To take up a 'cross' meant carrying a burden. The image is that of self-denial even to the point of death, loyalty to Jesus above self-preservation. The notion of self-denial is supported in that the 'if' clause is a first-class condition, meaning it is a fact! The two imperatives ('deny' and 'take up') suggest definitive action; the imperative 'follow' is present tense, suggesting continuous action.

The rationale for obedience is given in verses 25-26. As for the Lord, so for us: the way to glory is a road called self-denial. The soul is more precious than the totality of the world's wealth. In death, the values of this world have no value.

Jesus drives home His point with two questions: the first appeals to the profit motive. Is gain at the expense of one's life worthy of the loss afterward? The second question comes from the world of commerce. Nothing in that world has a value comparable to that of one's life.

There is comfort in obedience (vv. 27-28). The reward at the coming of Christ is entrance into the fullest manifestation of the kingdom; it is the gift of eternal life. While the Son of Man is enthroned on the clouds of heaven today, one day He will come to judge the inhabitants of the world. The basis of the judgment, not the cause of life in the Messiah, is works. Works cannot save us, but they do indicate our true values and priorities. Judgment will be based on our attitude towards God's Son, and the evidence will be in our self-denial for Him. The 'Son of Man' will return to the earth in glorious splendor unlike the circumstance of His initial coming. When He comes, judgment will follow.

Verse 28 is a difficult one to understand. It seems best to take 'coming in his kingdom' to refer to the extension of the inaugurated kingdom (the resurrection, Pentecost, and gospel proclamation afterwards). Remember: the concept of 'kingdom' in the gospels is flexible. Here it means the multiplication of disciples, including Gentiles. The cross will inaugurate the kingdom. Again, the way to glory is through suffering. The structure of the passage may help; it is a chiasm.

v. 24 The challenge: take up the cross and follow Jesus

v. 25 The incentive: reward and punishment at Christ's coming

v. 26 The important: the soul, not all the wealth of the world

v. 27 The incentive: reward and punishment at Christ's coming

v. 28 The promise: the power of God in the immediate future

Another way to interpret the phrase, 'there are some standing here who will not taste death until they see the Son of Man coming in his kingdom,' is to connect the verse to what immediately follows ('six days later,' 17:1). The 'some' would refer to Peter, James, and John, and the event would be the Transfiguration, a preview of Christ in all His glory. Peter seems to confirm this as he states that he, and others, on 'the mountain' saw the majesty of Christ and heard the testimony of God from heaven, 'This is my beloved Son ...' (1 Pet. 1:16-18).

Applications

1. It is a sad commentary that some people are better at discerning physical things than spiritual things. Have you met people who can endlessly talk about politics, the global crisis, the weather, and television programing, but have little discernment when it comes to spiritual things? It seems to be a waste of wisdom, not that such topics are not enlightening and helpful, but they have no eternal value. Since life is more than the accumulation of stuff, even knowledge being limited, and the material side of life being the least important, it is a shame. Do you know people like that?

2. When you think about people, you come to the realization that they are capable of great heights and great depths, of wisdom and stupidity, of strength and weakness, of helpfulness and destructiveness. What is also amazing is that we can pass through these various stages quickly. We can stand in criticism of Peter, but we can see Peter in all of us. A profound expression of wisdom and insight does not guarantee that the next insight will be helpful. We have all had these types of experiences. Can you name some out of your experience?

3. There is a question that every one of us must answer: who is Jesus Christ? This is the greatest and most important question in this world because it should determine how we live, what priorities control our lives, and it certainly determines our destiny. Peter had been given remarkable divine insight. Jesus is the Messiah, the deliverer; the Son of David, the ultimate expression of royalty; and the Son of God, deity. Here expressed is Jesus' origin, humanity, and deity; here is His person and His work declared. Is Jesus to you all these titles? Since He is the Son of the 'living God', He lives today! Has His life been expressed in your life? Do you possess the life of God in your innermost being?

4. You and I as representatives of Jesus have a special privilege that He initially disclosed to Peter and the other disciples. That is, since the Bible discloses the

mind of God and we can know and study it, we can declare to people God's mind on things. The authority to speak the truth of God is predicated on the fact that what we teach has already been declared to be true in heaven. Our privilege of speaking on behalf of God is real and powerful. The authority to speak does not reside in the speaker, but in the God who has spoken! We need not fear to speak the truth to people because God has already spoken it. What a privilege you and I have to speak for God and what wonderful authority has been granted to us to do so. We never need to feel inadequate, fearful, or intimidated!

5. The church is built upon Peter as the head of the apostles. In the early church Peter took the lead in the extension of the message among the Jews and the Gentiles. That is valid and we as Protestants should give credit where it is due. However, the uniqueness of Peter was his place at the beginning of the church because the same privilege of authority was granted to the other disciples (and to us as well). Together those disciples are the foundation, and Jesus is the cornerstone. It is not wise to misuse the gift of privilege. Peter was flesh and blood, a sinner and a saint. Let us admire God's grace to him, but not twist it beyond biblical warrant. We have only one great hero to honor and that is the one who Peter adored! Do you adore Him daily?

6. True biblical discipleship in its essence is self-denial expressed in emulation and obedience to the person and directives of Jesus Christ. Whether it is about conduct in our families, places of business, or the assembly of believers, a disciple constantly deals with a personally rebellious heart, seeking to subdue it because of his desire to be a worthy follower of Jesus. We must daily come to the place where we die to our own selfish desire and take up the restrictive burden of service to others. It is a new hill to climb every day and in the many confrontations that come to us in it. 'Following' comes after dying. Have you made progress in dying daily? In what areas have you seen

progress lately; in what areas would you like to see better progress?

7. The glory that comes with following Jesus comes at the end of our sacrifices for Him. To gain all that the world has to offer and fail to gain heaven is to lose too much. In this life we are self-denying followers of our Lord; in the next life we shall share in His rule as His sons and daughters. We must always remember that Jesus taught that the glory comes after the grind, the cross before resurrection and enthronement. Do you live in the expectancy that your greatest joys lie in the future and that the best of them today or tomorrow are broken shadows of good things to come? Have you learned the lesson that to gain life you must lose it and to lose it in Jesus is to gain what time and circumstances cannot remove?

The King's Kingdom (17:1-27)

The event of the Transfiguration at this point in the narrative, with Peter's grand confession of Jesus behind them and Jerusalem facing them, functions to enhance the fact of Jesus' Messiahship in the minds of the disciples. The Transfiguration demonstrates to three of the disciples that Jesus is far more than a human teacher, that His relationship to Moses and Elijah shows that He is the Messiah-figure, and that He is the Son of God as He is confirmed once more from heaven (cf. Matt. 3:17). Jesus clearly wanted the disciples to later tell what they saw (v. 9; 2 Pet. 1:16-18). For a time, heaven came to earth, the harbinger of an ultimate future fulfillment; Jesus for a moment appeared enthroned, in anticipation of future events.

The kingdom foreseen: the Transfiguration (vv. 1-8)

The baptism of Jesus and the Transfiguration, one at the inauguration of His earthly ministry and the other at its impending completion, are linked. In each case, the Father commends the Son with the same words ('This is my beloved Son with whom I am well pleased' [3:17; 17:5]), though Matthew adds here, 'listen to him.' The reason for the event might have been to recognize the worth of the Son as He was about to end His mission. It may also have been to encourage the disciples, sustaining them through the dark days ahead.

The phrase 'and after six days' seems to connect with 16:28. The similarities between this account and the receiving of the Law on Mount Sinai (Exod. 24:15-18) are significant. A greater than Moses has come, the argument also made in Hebrews 3. In both accounts the location is a mountain, six days are mentioned, Moses appears, and God speaks (in the one the Law is stated; in the other the New Law is identified). Jesus came to fill the Law with its true meaning (5:17). The Law revealed the divine standard of a relationship with God, Himself; the Law was impossible to keep so that all humanity has failed to meet the standard; the standard was met for us in Jesus, the divine/human substitute; and in Him the Law has been and is being kept!

The location of the mountain here is uncertain. Jesus was last in the region of Caesarea Philippi. The traditional sight at the top of Mount Tabor in the Jezreel Valley, not far from Nazareth to the southeast, seems questionable though possible, because six days is sufficient time to walk from the region of Caesarea Philippi. Following the sequence of Jesus' movements, He returned to Capernaum (v. 24). It does not seem logical that He would travel to the Jezreel Valley and then back to the Sea of Galilee. The episode narrated in verse 22, the second explanation of His pending demise in Jerusalem, is simply stated as being in the Galilee. There are two other suggested sites: Mount Hermon with Caesarea Philippi nearby, and Mount Meron, southwest of Caesarea Philippi.

'Before them' implies that the event was largely for the disciples, as does the 'them' of verse 5. The radiance of Jesus would suggest that He is the 'New Moses' in that when Moses descended from the presence of God his face glowed also (Exod. 34:29-35). However, Moses' glory was reflective; Jesus' was intrinsic.

Moses and Elijah have eschatological import. Moses was a prophet-figure (Deut. 18:18), Elijah a forerunner-figure and a prophet. Both had strange experiences at the end of their lives. Both were men of God in transitional times (the first, to introduce the Mosaic Covenant; the second, to renew obedience to it). Both had a vision of God's glory on the same mountain (Sinai or Horeb). Both experienced suffering through rejection from the people to whom they were sent.

Both ran for their lives to the wilderness of Horeb and met God there. Together, they illustrate the Law and the Prophets, and their presence, conversing with Jesus, suggests that He is the 'New Moses' and the 'New Elijah', though far greater. Prophets were sent to the ancient people to warn them of the potential of judgment; Jesus, the greatest of the prophets, warns of far more severe judgment in the last day.

Also, in the parallel account by Luke we are told that this event occurred at night since they went down the mountain the next day (Luke 9:37). Peter's suggestion about building three shelters is suggestive of the celebration of the Feast of Tabernacles (v. 4). He may have thought that the Messianic kingdom was about to appear. A cloud, not a dark one but a bright one, covered them with light and God spoke (v. 5). A 'cloud' is an eschatological image, suggesting the presence of God, as at Sinai (Exod. 13:21-22). The message is the same as that at our Lord's baptism (3:17), a mingling of Psalm 2:7 and Isaiah 42:1. 'Listen to him' is an allusion to Deuteronomy 18:15 and connects Jesus to Moses as the fulfillment of an eschatological type. Moses and Elijah are subservient to Jesus!

The visible glory of God brings terror (vv. 6-8), but Jesus comforts His disciples with the words He used in the Galilee storm incident (14:26-27 [in that incident Peter took his eyes off Jesus, but here he did not. There Peter cried out for help [14:30]; here he worshiped]).

The explanation of 'Elijah' (vv. 9-13)

This explanation brings greater understanding to the disciples concerning the event of the Transfiguration. This is the fifth and last time that Jesus commands silence. He says this to prevent a premature confrontation with the nation's leadership and to indicate that the greatest evidence of His Messiahship is the resurrection, the sign of Jonah.

Since Elijah, not Moses, was anticipated to have an eschatological role, this seems to be the grounds of the disciples' inquiry. Jesus affirms that the scribes are correct about the role of Elijah. However, Elijah has already come in the person of another who announced the coming of the kingdom: John the Baptist.

If Elijah's role was to restore true worship, why would Jesus need to die (16:21)? How could Elijah have come first if violence follows? The disciples cannot grasp why Jesus would need to die.

The word 'all' (v. 11) should not be taken as in Elijah's day or in John's day, but rather in the complete manifestation at the end of time. The 'all' of John's day is greater than Elijah's day because the kingdom is dawning in Jesus. Elijah must come first, but the 'true Elijah' is John. There is a connection of the restoration motifs between the 'true Elijah' and Jesus. If the restoration did not prevent the death of John, it need not prevent the death of Jesus. Why should He be better received?

Jesus also connects the suffering and death of John with His own that is to come. The 'they' seems to implicate the nation's leadership in John's demise; certainly, they would have been glad to see him pass off the scene. Just as our Lord's forerunner suffered death, so it is of the One he announced!

The disciples had gained a little more insight (v. 13), but the resurrection will be the ultimate teacher (26:50-56). The 'lights' will finally come on!

The deliverance of the demoniac (vv. 14-21)

Here is a case of an attempted exorcism gone wrong! The nine disciples could not perform what Jesus indicated they could in chapter 10. It is not a case of the lack of faith in the person needing healing or in the father, but in the nine disciples. Again, and common to Matthew's narrative, the focus is not on the miracle, which is treated with brevity, but a teaching moment for the disciples.

Though the son evidenced symptoms associated with epilepsy, the text is clear that demonic possession was the cause. The wording of verse 15 suggests that this was the man's only son ('my son'). 'Your disciples' most likely refers to the nine that Jesus left behind before the Transfiguration event.

Jesus' response is even more blunt than that of the father (vv. 17-18). He addresses a greater audience than the disciples, extracting a principle from their failure. Jesus seemed let down and shocked by being confronted with a helpless boy by a helpless father in the context of helpless disciples.

'Generation' probably refers to the people of Jesus' day, perhaps an allusion to Deuteronomy 32:5, 29 (a text quoted by Jesus in His temptations). The failure of the disciples, their lack of faith, was characteristic of the response of the people as a whole. However, Jesus says that the people of the day had twisted minds and were faithless. Thus, the incident of the failed healing was a picture of the failure of the nation, as well as of the disciples.

The disciples were hurt by their failure (v. 19), certainly in light of Jesus' commands in 10:1, 8. They expected to be able to cast out a demon. Jesus' answer (v. 20) to the disciples' ('your' is plural) failure is that of their 'little faith' (ESV, ASV, NIV) or 'unbelief' (KJV). 'Little' does not look at quantity, but quality; it was impoverished. It seems that what was missing in their faith-life at this point was dependence, a degree of trust. The words, 'little faith,' were on Jesus' lips in the episode with Peter on the sea (14:28-31). There it was spoken of one disciple, here of the twelve. The 'if' clause indicates that the disciples would have faith; it is now in the developmental stage.

That the mustard seed was the smallest of seeds was a proverbial saying in Jesus' day. The size of faith is not as important as the object of faith (not quantity but quality, not the size of our faith but the greatness of our God). 'Faith to remove mountains' was also a proverbial saying meaning a problem beyond human solution; Jesus was using the idea metaphorically. While mountains have not been moved by faith, mountainous difficulties have. It means the ability to do tremendous things, but not all things (see also, Phil. 4:13). In context, it means an ability to do those things that extend the authority of the kingdom.

The disciples were given authority over demons (10:1, 8), but they seem to be using it as magic, something done by the waving of the hand, so to speak. What the disciples needed was not giant faith, but true faith – a faith that consists in deep, personal trust expecting God to work. It is a faith expressed in dependence, not presumption.

(Verse 21 is not found in some major, ancient manuscripts and this is reflected in the ESV. It is assumed to be a later scribal addition.)

The second prediction of His death (vv. 22-23)
The first prediction of Jesus' death was prior to the
Transfiguration (16:21-23), immediately after Peter's
confession of Jesus' identity (6:16). This is the second. Jesus
prepares His disciples for what is ahead (it could be said
that this is the third since Jesus commented on His death
in the Transfiguration [17:12], but it was cryptic and offered
to only the three disciples present). This time He adds two
details not in the first declaration. He will be 'betrayed' or
'handed over'. Also, the person doing it could be God or a
man since the verb is passive ('will be'); it will be done to
Jesus. Also, the statement of the disciple's emotional reaction
to the announcement this time is new.

The issue of the temple tax (vv. 24-27) is a lesson in humility
on our Lord's part, assurance for the disciples (strangers, not
sons, pay taxes), as well as God's provision of our needs. The
tax in question was a tax levied on all adult Jews from twenty
to fifty years old to support the temple and its services; it was
not an issue of Roman law. Originally, it was to be paid at
the time of census-taking (Exod. 30:11-16). In Jesus' day the
tax was two drachmas or a half shekel (also called a 'stater')
per person. After the exile, the tax was reduced to one-third
shekel annually. The half-shekel coin was rarely minted, so
two adults would pay the tax together with a four-drachma
coin. Since a shekel was equivalent to a denarius, and a
denarius was a day's wage, the tax was equal to a half-day's
work per male adult.

The tax was paid annually at the celebration of Passover
while the pilgrim was in Jerusalem. If he was not able to go
to the city, it was collected in each town. The Jewish people
considered it a patriotic tax.

If the tradition is valid that Jesus resided in Peter's home
in Capernaum, it would be natural for the collectors to
approach the head of the house about the tax. This is the
last reference to Capernaum in Matthew.

Jesus was of the opinion that He was not obligated to pay
this tax since He is Lord or a son of the temple, actually the
true one, but He submitted (vv. 25b-26). To Him, it was a
case of personal privilege, not obligation. Verse 27 implies
that neither He nor Peter was obligated to pay the tax,

since both have the status of sons. If Jesus did not pay the tax, He would be seen as those who were not ethnic, free, adult, male Jews; He was not opposed to what the temple stood for. If He paid the tax, it would indicate that He was a mere son of Israel, one among equals (which He was not). Jesus paid it because of the claim of love (not duty since He was the Son). Further, the money for the tax was not His personally. Freedom from a requirement is restricted by circumstances sometimes!

Here is the only reference to fishing with a hook in the gospels; the net was the common method. What a great way to finance taxes! Scholars have suggested that the fish was likely a catfish that scavenges near landings, having a large mouth and attracted by bright objects. Having no scales, the fish was unclean. Is Jesus indicating something about the future consistency of the kingdom?

Applications

1. When Jesus was upon the earth, He hid the manifestation of His deity; it was condescension on His part to be with us. This is grace because who could behold the divine presence in mortal flesh and live! 'Veiled in flesh the Godhead see, Hail the Incarnate Deity,' wrote Charles Wesley. At the baptism of Jesus, a voice spoke from heaven declaring that He was the Son of God with no transformation of His appearance. In the Transfiguration three disciples saw a tiny glimpse of His radiance and again heard a voice from the throne of God declaring Jesus to be the Son of God. That Jesus is God is unmistakable. Does that not bring you delight and pleasure?

2. There is life after death; death is not the end of existence, and that existence is not the mere memories of those still living. It is real. The Transfiguration is proof of the resurrection of the body, that there is life after death (Moses and Elijah). Death brings us a new body somehow shaped in a recognizable form as our old ones. This means that we will see our loved ones and friends who have gone on before us. Death is more than

the loss of physical existence, as we know it now; it is the beginning of a new existence. It is unimaginable because there are no earthly analogies of comparison. It will be beyond comparison. Can you not rejoice?

3. The disciples could not grasp the relationship between suffering and glory in our Lord's message. They thought the two were antithetical and were confused. Jesus gave us the biblical pattern for life; in this life there will be adversity, but a crown will follow, the crown of life, though we die now. This is the true concept of being a follower of Jesus. We have not been promised ease and comfort as we walk this life. Problems, pain, and anxiety are part of the path of discipleship and the way to glory. Jesus said, 'Foxes have holes and birds have nests, but the Son of Man has nowhere to lay his head' (8:20). The path that Jesus taught us is one of legitimate denial at times because our hope and delight is elsewhere. Is this true of you? Your delights are your priorities. Where are your delights?

4. It is interesting that Jesus took three disciples with Him to see His Transfiguration. The three were of the four Jesus initially called in the book, the exception being Andrew. This tells me that discipleship has degrees and even in the discipling process the mentor is more intimate with some than with others. Peter recorded the incident in his second letter, John wrote several canonical writings, and his brother James endured martyrdom. Later Peter was killed, and John exiled in old age. Jesus uniquely prepared these men with special privilege to sustain them in special duties and pains. For Jesus, discipleship was tailored to the person and task. One size does not fit all; one method is not the only method.

5. It seems that the disciples used their privilege as a sign of their own significance at least in the case of the demoniac boy and troubled father; giftedness to heal was a source of pride. Giftedness and privilege can lead to a lack of dependence on God. This seems to have been the problem with the disciples. Ability

without humility and dependence will not accomplish great things. Abilities, occasions, and good outcomes are gifts from God. You and I have nothing that we have not been given. All is a gift, and any usefulness should lead to praise and thankfulness. None of us have it natively; all things come as gifts from God. Has privilege proved ever to be a stumbling block to you? Has opportunity caused you to think more highly of yourself than you should?

6. Jesus, being God, had and has a perfect knowledge of the future. If Jesus knows an event will happen, it will not happen otherwise. We can rest in this and not fear any tomorrow, because God has envisioned all tomorrows from eternity. We speak of accidents and luck because we cannot fathom causes, but in the mind of God 'all things work together' in ways we shall never understand. God is absolutely in control of the events and circumstances of life; He knows the future. Does that not cause you peace and rest in the turmoil and pains of life? Tears are real for all of us yet through them we can have the peace of knowing that God is working out in fine detail a master plan for 'his good pleasure'. In God is our comfort and delight, not in seeking to figure out the whys of sad events.

7. It is better to make concessions than give offense sometimes. When the issue is not unwarranted or prohibited by Holy Scripture, we are free to engage in it. At times, it is prudent and wise to do so. Jesus may have been a Son, but the privilege did not obscure the fact that He was a human being and a Jewish son as well. So as a citizen of a nation, He was willing to pay the tax. Jesus is saying that at times it is right to relinquish our rights and be seen as loyal in our social circumstance. You and I have dual citizenship, and both should be taken seriously. Resistance to laws that do not violate Scripture is quite unwarranted. Are you careful to obey the laws of your land even if it seems to be frequently wasted by unscrupulous people just as the temple tax was put in greedy pockets in Jerusalem? There are

some things we must stand for and many that are not worth fighting over! Sometimes, it is prudent and wise to make a discernment in the matter.

The King's Instructions (18:1-34)

This chapter contains the fourth discourse of Jesus recorded by Matthew. The discourse was prompted by an inquiry of the disciples; the instructions are private. Jesus stresses the importance of humility in the kingdom. The values of the kingdom are not of this world. Uprightness and readiness to forgive others are important. Perhaps this discourse should be called 'life in the Messianic community or kingdom'. It is about the importance of humility and forgiveness, two of the great Christian virtues.

Two questions seem to carry the discourse (vv. 1, 21), while the general theme is the corporate or relational life of individual disciples in the community of the faithful. It is about conduct in light of the stresses and strains of social life, of people living together at a basic level.

The connection of this subject with the previous issue of the temple tax is that of the privilege of sons being exempt from it. Jesus' argument was that of the status of sons in relationship to others. It was about place and privilege. If life in the kingdom is like life in normal life, there is stratification and privilege. So, the question seems to be twofold: Is there special status in the inaugurated kingdom? Can that be obtained by the asking? It would seem from the previous events that Peter would have the most prominent place in the kingdom since Jesus paid the tax for him and called him a 'son'.

A re-occurring theme in Matthew's narrative is the misperception and ignorance of the disciples. They gained some grasp that Jesus was the promised One but remained woefully slow in putting all the implications together; they only understood pieces such as the nearness of His kingdom, not His suffering to obtain it. The emphasis in this section is upon the correction of the disciples' perspectives and values, so preparing them for the near events in Jerusalem and ministry after the resurrection (such as the crucial importance of understanding our role in humility and service to others as opposed to place-seeking, prominence, and accolades [vv. 1-14], as well as the importance of forgiveness in the community of the faithful [vv. 15-35]). In subsequent chapters Jesus discussed the indissolubility of marriage, the value of the insignificant, and the problems of wealth accumulation (19:16–20:16).

Instruction concerning humility (vv. 1-14)
It seems strange that Christ predicts the tragedy of His death while the disciples focus on their place in His kingdom. This can be seen even more sadly in 20:20-28. The disciples became increasingly sure that Jesus is the Messiah, the Christ, but they are still confused about the time of the fullest manifestation of His kingdom (see Luke 19:11). The best you can say is that they figured things out slowly.

Since a child is used as an object lesson, Jesus is saying that there are some things we can learn from them: non-preoccupation with status, simple trust, and dependence (vv. 2-4). Concern for significance or self-importance is pride. It is destructive. It is the opposite of the best features of a child. They are not the ideal of innocence or mental maturity, but they do exhibit simple trust. Being in the kingdom does not mean competition for prominence, but humble service. It is interesting that the word for 'child' here can also mean servant. Those who possess the kingdom possess the characteristics of a child.

Pride, seeking self-significance, and the quest for prominence are destructive, not only to oneself but those to whom we express it of ourselves. It seems from Jesus' comment in 10:42 that 'little children' is being used here as a metaphor for His true followers (vv. 5-9). All of God's people have child-like qualities!

Those who humble themselves, acting in a godly manner, giving prominence to God's children, honor the Lord (v. 5). The negative parallel is stated in verse 6. Catastrophic judgment awaits anyone who purposefully harms God's children. Hanging was a Jewish form of punishment; drowning was common among Gentiles. A millstone was a heavy, chiseled stone pulled about by donkeys and used for grinding. It seems that Jesus is overstating the consequence of such behavior to make the point of its importance (a not too uncommon literary technique). Such behavior is simply awful! Remember the text is not about the loss of our salvation; it is about the inappropriateness of self-centeredness.

The origin of opposition to God's 'children' is the world (v. 7). The disciples are told that it will come, but they are given the assurance that justice will be served in the end. 'Woe' was used by the prophets and in funeral dirges, suggesting the judgment of God.

The disciples were warned that they must beware of failing to deal with similar sins in their own lives. Pride must be dealt with as severely as lust (cf. 5:29-30). The physical severity of the correction is figurative, suggesting the seriousness of the endeavor (vv. 8-9). The eye or foot does not cause sin; it is found in our blighted affections, the heart. Jesus says that a serious problem must be handled in a serious manner. Jesus' mention of 'eternal fire' (v. 8) and 'hell of fire' (v. 9) are instances of hyperbole; this is evident by the fact of pridefullness in His disciples (20:20-28), for example. The severity of the error is established by the severity of judgment for it. He is certainly not saying that all perpetrators face eternal judgment, but that an unrepentant heart could!

Are verses 10-14 a good 'guardian angel' passage? The context is not about 'little children'; it is about conduct towards other believers. Further, it is about a positive action in heaven, not on the earth. I take it that 'angels' in heaven beholding the face of God are departed saints, their spirits. The evidence is not overwhelming, but we 'will be like angels in heaven' (Matt. 22:30). When Peter was released from prison, the assembled saints thought it was his angel (spirit) at the door (Acts 12:15). The parable of the lost sheep (vv. 12-13) illustrates God's great love for His 'children'. He sees His 'children' as so valuable that He will not allow a single one of them to be lost (v. 14).

Instruction concerning forgiveness (vv. 15-35)
Here Jesus deals with the treatment of a brother/sister who has offended a 'little one'. The 'against you' suggests sins against the community from the perspective of the one sinned against. It seems that there may be a connection with the previous

paragraph; the quest for privilege through prominence often is at the expense of hurting others, fracturing the bond of unity among believers.

The instructions concerning a sinful brother are fourfold (vv. 15-20). First, go privately to the offender (v. 15). The allusion here is to Leviticus 19:17. This is not with a view to casting judgment, but to making the grievance known so that it can be resolved. Second, if the issue is not resolved, take two or three and go again (Deut. 19:15). It seems that the function of the 'two or three' is not merely to lend support for the offended, but to provide further evidence of error (v. 16). Third, tell it to the assembly of 'children' (the church) (v. 17a). Fourth, separate from such a person. Perhaps an example of this would be found in 1 Corinthians 5, though the separation here seems to call only for personal action (v. 17b), not corporate.

If it becomes a church matter (vv. 18-20), the binding/ loosing is the same idea as in 16:19. There it was in reference to Peter; here it is in reference to all the disciples and the church. Decisions made on earth in conformity with Scripture are those already made in heaven. The mind of God and the Scriptures are the same on issues. Therefore, it has been settled (the verbal form is future perfect passive); heaven will confirm the righteousness of the action taken on earth.

Verses 19 and 20 are not a promise of answered prayer; the context is not about that. It is about decisions rendered towards an offending brother/sister. In rabbinic literature, forgiveness should be extended three times for the same offense (perhaps an allusion to Amos 1:3, 6). Peter is being generous extending forgiveness to seven offenses (v. 21).

Jesus in His answer (v. 22) alludes to Genesis 4:24. Lamech's revenge is transformed into a principle of forgiveness, the act of an unbeliever in contrast to the believer. Forgiving a person 'seventy-seven times' (some translation renders the words 'seventy-times seven' or 490 times). In either case, the number seems to be metaphoric for the need to always forgive.

The need to forgive because of having been forgiven is illustrated by the parable of two debtors (vv. 23-34). The unwillingness of the forgiven slave to forgive proves that his heart had never been changed (v. 35). This is illustrated by the prayer our Lord taught us, 'Forgive us our debts as we also have forgiven our debtors' (Matt. 6:12). True forgiveness should generate a forgiving spirit (v. 33).

The debt of the servant was beyond repayment; it was huge (between 60-100 million denarii, 30-100 million days of labor, or 275,000 years of wages). The most expensive slave was sold for a single talent. David gave 3000 talents of gold and 7000 talents of silver towards the construction of the temple (1 Chron. 29:4, 7). Selling all his assets, including the freedom of his family, would not have helped. The compassionate king is willing to consider the debt a bad loan.

However, the forgiven servant refuses to forgive; the debt accumulation is small in comparison. The smallest price for a slave was 500 denarii. This man owed only 100. Further, a person could not be sold legally for an amount greater than the debt. This indicates that the man was hard-hearted, revengeful, and greedy.

The consequences of the servant's unforgiving spirit are described in verses 31-34. Remember that a parable conveys a single point wrapped around a story. The details of the story function to support the point. Doctrine should not be derived from the story itself, only a principle. This text, within its context, cannot be about the insecurity of the believer. Salvation is not earned; it is a gift. It cannot be lost by not continuing to earn it since it cannot be purchased or obtained by any human endeavor or ingenuity.

The point of the parable is given in verse 35. Jesus sees no incongruity with the Father acting as a compassionate father and as a just judge. One who refuses to forgive shows that he/she is incapable of receiving forgiveness. The point of the story is that we who are God's children should not count offenses against us by others; we who are forgiven should understand human failure to do right, since it is so much a part of us, and be willing to forgive.

Applications

1. It seems utterly amazing that the disciples were with the Lord observing His manner of living and His profound care for others, and yet seemed unable to apply what

they must have observed to their own demeanor and social interaction. The incident Matthew recorded in this chapter, taking an entire discourse to do so, must have impressed him. Before we become too harsh with the disciples, could it be that they are a mirror of our actions at times? Have you ever been in a situation when a person wanted to express something deeply important to him, but you had other interests and needs and were insensitive to his/her needs? Think of wife/ husband relationships.

2. The surest mark of true conversion is humility, a change of affections. It is the opposite of pride and self-orientation. It is the essence of discipleship, a true follower of Jesus. Greatness in the kingdom is not determined by stupendous acts of service, but in the quiet, lowly service to others. Jesus is not impressed by the size of our deeds, the amount of our giving, or our status in the Christian community; He is impressed with the size of our hearts!

3. Jesus sees abusive conflict among His people as a grave thing. He came to save them, so they are precious to Him (vv. 11, 14), bringing to them peace and forgiveness. If we have been wronged, our first care should not be for the adjudication of the grievance or justice, but care for the offender and the damage that mistreatment can do. In the case of offense, the first step is not the airing of the problem before others, but to go personally to the offender. Harmony among believers is a mark of true forgiveness. Has someone, someway offended you and you are holding it resentfully within? You need to go to them, tell them that you will forgive them, and start the healing process.

4. The second surest mark of a child of God is a willingness to forgive others. The necessity of humility and a forgiving spirit are the two major emphases made in this chapter. Is it not amazing that Jesus has Jerusalem before Him and yet the discussion of importance with the disciples is forgiveness and humility? Are there people in your background that you are unwilling to

forgive? Think about how much God has forgiven you. Do you carry an unforgiving spirit toward something your mate has done or failed to do? Think of the love of God!

5. Interpersonal conflict is the primary cause of divisions in our homes, workplace, and church. It must be a source of sorrow to our Lord when He sees His children fussing and fuming with each other. Jesus values social cohesiveness and that is why forgiveness is so very important. We all do things that hurt others, but we must never cherish revenge. It seems that a forgiving spirit is far more of a rarity among Christians than bitterness, unkindness, and spite. Why do you think that is so? How do you think this can be addressed in our homes, among siblings and parents alike?

6. Jesus gives us a fourfold procedure in dealing with a fellow Christian who acts inappropriately: a private talk, a second talk with others present, an explanation to the church, and separation if there is no repentance. The purpose of such a procedure is the restoration of the offender; it must be motivated by a willingness to help a person see his weakness and help him rise above it. Have you found help when a person came to you with a valid behavioral miscue? Confronting a person with the proper motive is a mark of true discipleship.

7. If we are not willing to forgive others, there is little chance we have been forgiven ourselves. You can only extend what you have received. 'Forgive us our debts as we have forgiven our debtors' (6:12). A willingness to forgive is not the cause of forgiveness; it is the consequence of having been forgiven. The change that God causes in our affections by redeeming grace is so great that it changes heart attitudes. The presence of new attitudes that reflect the character of God demonstrates that God has placed His life in you. Could it be that you harbor an unforgiving spirit towards those who hurt you because you have never experienced the love of God in His forgiveness of you?

9

The Journey of the King to Jerusalem
(19:1–20:34)

Beginning in 19:1 Jesus departed from the Galilee to make His way to Jerusalem. He interacted with the religious leaders, performed miracles, and taught His disciples as He made His way. He traveled on the eastern side of the Jordan below the Sea of Galilee and crossed over the Jordan somewhere north of the Dead Sea – John performed his baptisms on the east side of the Jordan, perhaps near the crossing site – and came through Jericho. Is it not interesting what Jesus determines to talk about in the last weeks of His life: issues of humility and forgiveness, even family? Quality interpersonal relationships are to be maintained in the family of God.

Verses 1-2 are a summary of Jesus' ministry. There are similar pointers in 4:23; 9:35; 14:14; and 15:30. Some scholars divide the book by these markers. They each seem to introduce a section containing one of the five discourses of Jesus.

The Journey Commenced (vv. 1-2)

In Matthew's account of the life and claims of Jesus, this is the only journey to Jerusalem. The Galilean ministry is at an end; however, the Lord will return in triumph to the Galilee and launch the international missionary enterprise at the end of the gospel.

The indication that Jesus entered the region of Judea beyond the Jordan can be taken in two ways ('beyond the

Jordan River' is Perea, not Judea; it was ruled by Herod Antipas, not the procurator Pilate). The term 'Judea' may be used loosely to indicate a region of ethnic population that was true of Perea or that Jesus traveled in the Transjordan and entered Judea from there. The second option seems preferable since He passed through Jericho (20:29). This was the normal pilgrimage route to avoid Samaria.

Instruction concerning divorce (vv. 3-12)

The context of the discussion on marriage and divorce is a question posed by the Pharisees (this is not the first time, see 16:1); it is clear that their motive was to discredit Jesus by showing that He differed in His teachings from Moses. For the Pharisees, Moses and their understanding of Moses was the same thing.

It is also of interest that the Pharisees chose to confront Jesus with the same issue that brought about the demise of John the Baptist (John had been incarcerated over his stance on Herod Antipas' marriage to Herodias after she divorced his half-brother [14:3-5]). While the motivation was to discredit Jesus, the angle of approach may have been to cast Jesus in a similar political controversy as John.

Divorce was accepted in Judaism for men, not women (women could divorce in Roman culture, hence the difference in Mark's account of this incident). A man could be ordered in Jewish courts to divorce his wife if he proved to be derelict in his duties or life-threatening; so there was some protection for a wife from the caprices of a husband. However, there was a division over the proper grounds within the two major religious parties. One party argued that it could be granted only for a serious offense (Shammai); the other for any offense (Hillel). Jesus was closer in His opinion to the school of Shammai, though He approached the matter with a different perspective. While Jesus recognized the brokenness of mankind, he prioritized the enduring unity of the marriage commitment.

The genius of this question is that no matter how Jesus would answer it, He would offend some in the leadership. He takes a position that the Pharisees would not have anticipated. He simply sees divorce as a violation of the creation mandate.

For Jesus, Genesis 1:27 (one-man/one-woman relationship) takes precedence over Deuteronomy 24:1-2, a concession by Moses to the brokenness of human relationships.

This discussion by Jesus has three parts: the principle that marriage is a permanent creation ordinance (vv. 4-6), the fact that it is not always permanent (v. 7), and the resolution to the apparent discrepancy (vv. 8-9). Jesus' view was stricter than either of the parties within Judaism. He is opposed to divorce (v. 6) so, in effect, he aligns with Malachi (Mal. 2:16), not Shammai.

Jesus quotes several Genesis passages: 1:27 concerning the original creation (v. 4); 2:24 concerning the sexes (v. 4); and 2:24 concerning the uniqueness of marriage (v. 5). He later sets Deuteronomy 24:1 within the context of Genesis 1, suggesting two levels of ethical instruction, the ideal and the broken, but real, at times. Genesis 1 takes priority over Deuteronomy 24, but does not eliminate it. Deuteronomy 24 deals with a situation that had already gone wrong and deals with it in a different context than God's ideal. Deuteronomy 24 is a 'trouble-shooting' text.

Jesus argues that the creation ordinance is God's ideal. Though men and women are different by creation (v. 4), the two independents (v. 5) enter into an indissoluble bond (v. 6). The fall, however, has exacerbated the differences between males and females in the marriage bond, creating trouble.

The test question posed by the Pharisees is not about the permissibility of divorce (that was established by Moses), but on what grounds it is permissible. This was a sensitive issue in Perea, near the Dead Sea, where John the Baptist had spoken against Herod Antipas' divorce and was murdered by a resentful Herodias, perhaps at Machaerus nearby (14:1-12).

The Pharisees asked a follow-up question about Deuteronomy 24:1. In His reply (vv. 8-9), Jesus said that Moses permitted divorce to protect the wife from the evil of her husband. Since divorce was practiced within Jewish society, a begrudging husband could put a wife away from his home and prevent her from remarrying. Without legal protection, she would be reduced to an uncertain future. A man could have more than one wife, but a wife only one husband. Moses' concession prevented extreme spousal abuse from happening

(v. 8). Remarriage was permitted if the first marriage was dissolved for appropriate reasons. It was viewed as the lesser of evils, better than prostitution, perpetual heartache, and broken promises. Jesus agreed with Moses. Divorce is not the rule; it is a concession to protect the innocent from the dehumanization of the guilty party.

The grounds for divorce in a fallen world of broken promises is sexual perversion. The term translated 'immorality' is a broad word covering lesbianism, incest, bestiality, prostitution, and adultery. In Jesus' day, divorce for sexual perversion was demanded. A man who divorced his wife and marries another, without just cause, entered into an adulterous relationship (v. 9a). When one married an illegitimately divorced woman, since she was not separated legitimately from her first husband, he entered into an adulterous relationship (v. 9b). Otherwise, to remarry is not sin, but it is the lesser of two evils.

In verse 10, the disciples make a comment. Since marriage is a unique institution requiring faith-keeping, and is indissoluble, they wonder if it is worth marrying in the first place (we already had a hint of their attitude towards children, which will become more evident in the next paragraph). Jesus answered their concern (vv. 11-12) by saying that it is not possible for many to remain single; most simply do not have that ability, though marriage can have its problems (a cantankerous, sickly, sexually frigid, or undomesticated partner is not grounds for divorce). Some should not marry because of their make-up from birth (physiological issues, the inability to procreate). Some have been made eunuchs, a reference to castration (such were excluded from the 'assembly of the Lord' in Deuteronomy 23:1), and others are called to special work for God that requires singleness.

Instruction concerning children (vv. 13-15)

Just as the disciples did not initially share Jesus' attitude towards the marriage bond, or at least were shocked when they understood it, they did not seem to embrace His view of children. The disciples seemed to view parents who troubled Jesus about their children as nuisances (v. 13b). In the busyness of the Lord, the disciples must have felt that children were an intrusion to Jesus and sought to protect Him from parental requests. They could be utterly self-centered when it came to their places in the kingdom (18:1), but had no time for caring parents and chattering children!

Jesus enjoyed children. He observed their games (11:16-17), spoke of them in His teaching, and used them as illustrations (18:2). It is clear that these are literal children as in 18:5, but with the use of 'such as' (v. 14) the thought extends beyond them (those of simple trust, the 'least in the kingdom').

The topic is not child dedication or baptism in this section though such practices may be seen as applications or extensions of Jesus' care for children. Taking children to a rabbi in first-century Jewish culture was not so much to obtain a blessing as to secure help. What is evident in the instruction here is that in the emergent kingdom children have a welcome place!

Instruction concerning wealth (19:16–20:16)

In this section, another attitude of the disciples is observed and corrected. They are shocked that Jesus seemingly turned away a potential recruit who by his status could be 'great' in the kingdom. Desiring to be a disciple without discipleship is impossible. Further, earning the right to be one is equally false. Discipleship is a gift from God; the privilege is not universally granted. Since wealth was a sign of God's blessing under the Mosaic covenant (Deut. 28:1-14), the reward of obedience, affluence, is in the disciples' minds the evidence of divine favor. This well-to-do man wanted both God and the pleasures of materialism (6:24); the error was that of supposing he could have his affections attached to both with each the evidence of the other.

This rather long section is a unit of discussion that begins with a question about eternal life and how to obtain it. There are four subsections in it: the question posed by a scribe, a teacher of the Law, who had wealth but not life (19:16-22); the discussion of Jesus with the disciples about wealth and salvation (19:23-26); Peter's inquiry about rewards (19:27-29); and an answer in the form of an illustration (19:30–20:16).

A scribe, Jesus, and eternal life (vv. 16-22)
This teacher of the law, called a rich, young ('young' being between twenty and forty years of age, v. 22) ruler, reveals his understanding of salvation; it is practical, not theoretical, and Pharisaic. He seeks to earn a place in the kingdom by doing something. He wants a reward, understanding nothing of grace. In the context of the chapter, that of challenging questions from the nation's leadership, it is likely that he is seeking to demonstrate that Jesus is at variance on the issue from the Pharisees. The Pharisees' teaching is that of Moses, at least as they understood the teachings of Moses. Jesus opposes Pharisaic teaching because, He argues, it is contrary to Moses.

Jesus' focus on the commandments (v. 17) was intended to reveal to the man that he lacked the internal goodness requisite for life (the law revealing human incompetency), but this scribe was so conditioned by the Pharisees' reinterpretation of Moses that he was convinced he had kept the Law. He likely kept it in the twisted way Jesus described in 5:21-48.

It is important to hear what Jesus did not tell this scribe. He does not say that if you keep the commandments you will enter into spiritual life. He simply says that life requires obedience, but obedience does not guarantee the gift of life in and of itself ('if'). Obedience is a necessary element in acquiring salvation, a heartfelt response; it is not the cause of salvation. Jesus is seeking to help the man understand his own words.

The logic of the question goes something like this. At issue are two points: the role of the 'good', and entrance into eternal life. Jesus indicates that the man is correct in his focus on the 'good', but 'good' is defined by the will of God as revealed in the Scriptures that he possessed. Eternal life comes by doing the will of God, by keeping the commandments. 'Keeping the commandments' means heartfelt devotion with a consistency as perfect as the divine character. Jesus offered the correct answer, but the man did not realize the impossibility of it. He did not recognize the need for a substitute and did not want to turn from the delights of self-sufficiency.

In his second question, the scribe made two errors (v. 18). First, he was under the impression that he had kept the Law and he likely did so in the manner that the Pharisees interpreted it, by turning it from inward attitudes to outward acts (5:17-48, the one commandment in the Decalogue that could not be externalized was the tenth, 'do not covet' [20:17], being a spiritual attitude).[1] This is the one commandment that Saul-turned-Paul could not reinvent (Rom. 7:7-11). Second, the ruler failed to determine right and wrong by the criteria of divine perfection, God's character as revealed in His commands. He did not realize that God's demands are absolute because God is absolute perfection. The criteria of right and wrong, acceptable and unacceptable, is determined by the very nature of God, an absolute and unchanging standard, the perfection of holiness.

In response, in clarifying what was meant by the Law, Jesus cites the sixth, seventh, eighth, and ninth commandments respectively, following the same order as in chapter 5, and then adds the fifth. In addition, Jesus ends with one not in the ten – love of neighbor (Lev. 19:18). What these commandments have in common is that they are observable by others (vv. 18b-19).

The scribe never gave a thought to the fact that he had not kept the Law, but he did know there was emptiness, a void, in his life though he was rich (v. 20). To get this difficult fellow to see His point (v. 21), Jesus asked about material wealth (the tenth commandment). Possessions do not earn eternal life (this stipulation is not in the Old Testament, it is not something for purchase), but our attitude towards it reveals our heart. This dear fellow loved physical possessions more than God; he believed that the two were interconnected. Salvation cannot be earned! The word 'perfect' or complete does not suggest moral flawlessness as it does moral maturity.

The scribe's disappointment is stated in verse 22. He illustrates the truth of Matthew 6:24, 'You cannot serve God and money.' He had no higher priority than what he could put in his pockets, though he recognized a hole in his life. He had the cultural appearance of divine blessing, but not the reality of it.

---

1. According to general Jewish scholarship, the Hebrew Scriptures are said to consist of about 613 commandments, the 'ten commandments' being only a part, though in Christian tradition they have received considerable emphasis (Exod. 20:2-17; Deut. 5:6-21).

Applications

1. Marriage is a holy institution and is only dissolvable under extreme circumstances. The creation mandate is the basic instruction of the mind of God in the matter. It is to be entered into with enormous dedication and is dissolved by death of one or another partner. Our culture is quickly being eroded by neglect of God's design for marriage; children are being neglected and promises trivialized. The emphasis in our teaching should be on the permanence of the institution; it should be modeled with integrity and purity and should be our chief comfort and joy in this life. Do you view marriage as God does? Are you teaching and training your children by precept and example its importance?

2. While our first and governing thought should be that marriage is permanent and indissoluble, we live in a broken world. Promises are often not kept, moral exclusivity not preserved, and spousal abuse takes vicious forms. In such cases, the escape clause of Deuteronomy 24:1 is as valid as it was in Moses' sin-scarred era. A broken marriage is not the end of the possibility of a wholesome relationship; it is simply not the divine ideal. But when you think about it, sin is not what God ordained but it is a very real intrusion, and its effects are a reality. God is merciful and knows the horror of failure to keep our promises. Sometimes it is better to end a marriage than continue in it. It tells us that we live in a fractured existence, far from the divine ideal. Are you laying a foundation of instruction to help your children make good choices in a mate?

3. Marriage is not for everyone though we live in a culture that places pressure on adults to marry, particularly in Christian circles. Marriage is for those who understand that their calling in life and the structure of their personal needs are such that singularity is not a wholesome choice. Some simply do not see the need or urgency to marry; others see the importance but not the priority above other values such as service

for the Lord in places and circumstances that make it prohibitive (at least in their estimation). Singularity can have the benefit of undivided service to God, but that requires a special giftedness and is rare. Do you tend to think that single people are odd for some reason, not normal? What are you doing to embrace those who chose singularity in your family, in your church?

4. When a person takes time to love children, it says a lot about their character. Children are restless and reckless, often possessing abounding energy with a lack of skill and awareness of others. They tend to be noisy and disruptive with little to contribute but interruption to adults. They offer little but demand a lot. It takes time to appreciate the contribution that they make; often that comes to us in the graying years. Jesus took time for them and so should His followers. They are precious and important. As a parent, do you take time to talk to your children, enter into their worlds, and see life through their eyes? Do you take time for kids in your neighborhood, showing kindness and acceptance?

5. It is also interesting that Jesus recognized that parents want the best for the children and did not feel imposed upon when they desired Him to show kindness to them. Do you realize that a potentially productive way to reach a parent is through a child? A person of some recognized authority, such as a teacher, can have an enormous influence on parents by enjoying their children. Do you purposefully talk to children in the presence of their parents? Do you sit next to children at meals, talk to them, and help them if necessary? You can have an influence on them that neither they nor their parents will soon forget. One of our greatest needs is acceptance. Do you extend that to parents by being aware of their children, or are children a hindrance to you, and your view is like that of the disciples?

6. The most important question to ask is not, 'What good deed must I do to have eternal life?' However, it is on the right track and the assumption behind the inquiry is fairly natural for all of us. We all connect the attainment

of a desire as a consequence of doing something; it is very much a part of our social conditioning and personalities to think that way. Since eternal life is beyond temporal existence, it cannot be obtained by pursuing what we know in this life to acquire it (the infinite cannot be obtained by even a magnitude of the finite; it cannot be earned by human endeavor). However, it can be obtained. Jesus earned it through His substitutionary death on the cross. He could earn the infinite because He came from heaven; He possessed infinitude in the flesh (John 1:14). The good news is that it is free; it has been obtained; it only requires a response to the claims and affirmations of Jesus, not merit or an endeavor. Have you asked?

7. The commandments of God are the litmus test of our moral rectitude. What is clear is that we cannot keep them if defined as heart attitudes. Who has not been angry? Who has not coveted? Who has not used deceptive speech? The scribe thought that he had kept them because he defined the demands of God through the lens of distortion. If we could keep the commandments, we could earn eternal life. However, no one has done that, except Jesus, and He did that for us because we could not do it for ourselves. Is He your righteousness? Are you still seeking to manufacture your own? Do you fall in the trap of comparative righteousness, feeling right before God because you know people less right than you are? As Christians, we need to constantly realize that our righteousness is through our divine substitute, Jesus. It is not our own; we have been bought with a price! How has this insight helped you to understand your faith, and how has it informed your walk before God?

8. For some people, material things or temporal things are more important than eternal values. The things that can be seen are of more value and importance than the things that we cannot see. The consequence of such an approach to life is that it is shortsighted. The scribe in our story went away from all that could have filled

his life with meaning because he highly valued money and what it could procure in status and creaturely comforts (that is what possessions can afford). Do you have a mindset more on today than on eternity? Disappointment will be your lot because what you can clutch you cannot keep.

Jesus' comment on wealth and salvation (vv. 23-26)

The episode of the scribe's materialistic orientation, that he cherished things more than trusted in the Lord to care for him, as he does the birds of the field (6:26), raised the issue of wealth as a hindrance to faith. The disciples show themselves once more to have been deeply impacted by their culture; wealth to them was evidence of divine pleasure. Jesus' view astounded them. Jesus generalized from this opportune encounter to comment on the negative issue of affluence.

Wealth can be a hindrance because it has the lure of self-sufficiency and the false value culture places upon it is deep (vv. 23-24). Most Jews expected the rich to inherit eternal life, thinking that physical prosperity was evidence of spiritual prosperity. Jesus finds wealth an obstacle, though not an impossible one, as illustrated by his reference to a camel. The camel was the largest land animal in Jewish culture. Since Jesus' point is the impossibility of the self-reliant to enter His kingdom, the 'needle' should be taken literally. It cannot be a small door in a city gate for latecomers because the metaphor would conflict with the point Jesus makes in verse 26 (if so, you can get in with extreme effort!). It is a ludicrous illustration used to make a point as in the parable of the debtors (18:21-35) or the metaphor of a log in the eye (7:3-5).

This is one of a few instances in Matthew that He uses the term 'kingdom of God' instead of 'kingdom of heaven' though the terms appear to be general equivalents. He may have chosen 'kingdom of God' here to express the fact that you cannot serve two kingdoms, God's and man's.

The disciples then ask about who can be saved (v. 25). 'Saved' conveys the same idea as 'entering the kingdom' (v. 23). If the rich are not saved (meaning as a class of people), the disciples wonder who can be saved. There is still a lot of 'Pharisee' in the disciples!

Jesus' answer in verse 26 is that self-sufficiency is a stumbling block to heaven and only God can lift us above ourselves. Salvation is a work that only God can do; it requires a change of heart (the inside), not hands (actions, the outside). It is 'hard' for the rich (v. 24); it is difficult because the lure of mere cultural values, coupled with the blight of human pride, is weighty. However, with God it is possible! Ultimately, salvation rests in the hands of God. For us, it is a matter of willing submission and following Him in a life of discipleship, not to earn or maintain redemption, but the pursuit of a heart-rooted change of values, perspectives, and priorities that it brings!

Peter's question shifts the focus of the discussion to the matter of rewards for the faithful servant (vv.27-29). If salvation is unearned and unmerited, then what is the benefit of obedience since it does not bring one into the kingdom? The reward for Christian faithfulness is eternal life; it is given to all of God's children regardless of talents, circumstances, or successes. Heaven is a classless society. Productivity in this life is a gift from him; some do more in outward appearances, and some are called equally to less. It is about God's individual callings, not a better life later based on the 'bigness' of our task now or in the final expression of the kingdom.

Since salvation is not earned, not being the fruit of our labor, how can one know that he/she is saved? What do we get for all the work we do as a result of this free gift? If salvation is not earnings-dependent, what is the point of works?

There is a reward for following Jesus, partly now and much later (vv. 28-29). The part now is that the authority of Jesus as the enthroned king is being shared with us. We have the privilege of representing the Lord on the earth; we are His ambassadors and, as such, have been given the right to do God's work on the earth now (16:18-19; 18:18). Later, we will receive the crown of eternal life from the king when our earthly sojourn ends.

Jesus first applies the answer to the disciples and then He universalizes to all Christians. The first applies to the inaugural era of Jesus' reign and the second to the fullest manifestation of the kingdom in eternity.

Jesus' answer is that the reward will be great. For the disciples and us after Christ would be enthroned by virtue of the ascension. Now, He shares His authority with us in the growth of His kingdom. 'Age to come' and 'in the regeneration' refers to Daniel 7:13-14, the vision of the enthronement of the Son of Man. Jesus is sharing His rule with His disciples now, yet more is to come! Judgment has been given to us (18:18); we are to do and declare what heaven has ordered to be done!

The reference to 'twelve thrones' is a metaphor for authority (though Judas is excluded). It is to be taken in a non-literal manner suggestive of shared authority on earth with heaven (16:18-19). The disciples, not only Peter, after the ascension, will share in the implications of Christ's enthronement. They, and all who follow them, will reign with Christ to be what Israel failed to be, a light to the nations.

The answer is that we, the disciples of Jesus, receive much: glory, honor, and eternal life. The reward of our work is the gift of eternal life after the temporal work is finished. We do not earn it by working; we receive it when the work is over because Christ has merited it for us!

An illustration of the point (19:30–20:16)
The story of the workers in the field illustrates the grace of God in granting to us far more than we deserve and demonstrably merit. It answers Peter's question (19:27) in illustrative, parabolic form within the context of the scribe's quest for salvation through merit.

The phrase in 19:30, which is repeated in 20:16 in a slightly different order, is the point: the last will be first someday. The repetition encloses or frames a unit of thought. The story is about a wealthy, eccentric landowner, who hired day-workers under various arrangements as a day progressed. Some were employed with a binding bilateral contract; some had a promise; and some had a command with a promise attached. The landowner is the 'Lord', and the workers represent mankind as a whole. God can do as He pleases with His workers (the 6 a.m. hires) and also in grace (the 5 p.m. hires). In grace, He grants the unexpected!

The context of the story (v. 1). 'Kingdom of heaven' means salvation (19:25); it simply is not entered through the merit system. The vineyard owner illustratively is the Lord, the vineyard is his kingdom.

The arrangements with the day-workers (vv. 2-8a). Day laborers were hired to work from 6 a.m. to 6 p.m., the normal Jewish workday. However, workers were employed during the day at three-hour intervals (the 5 p.m. workers excepted). The standard wage was a denarius. The six o'clock hires (v. 2) agreed for an increment of pay for twelve hours of labor. They went into the vineyard with a binding bilateral contract. The nine, twelve, and three o'clock hires (vv. 3-5) are not important in the story; they are 'filler' to emphasize the point of what happens to the last hires. They are given a promise of equity, not justice or grace. We are not told how they fared at the end of the day. The five o'clock hires (vv. 6-7) had waited all day; no one requested their services. They are the leftovers (a point the landowner seemed to recognize). They are told to go and trust the landowner to be kind. Likely, the vineyard owner was being pressed to complete the harvest accounting for his urgency. There were no wage clarifications; they trusted the owner to do what was right by them; he will do far more, exceeding their expectations (as God will do with us).

The payment of the day-workers (vv. 8-10). As day-workers the various hires were paid at the end of the day. The last, those who worked one hour, got a full day's wage (clearly the landowner was a compassionate man recognizing the need of the workers and their families; these were the destitute). They who worked a full day got what they contracted. The point is not the perceived injustice rendered to the first hires, but the grace extended to the last ones. Against the backdrop of justice, God displays unmerited grace.

The complaint of the earliest hired day-workers (vv. 11-12). The early workers filed a double grievance with the landowner, the inequity of the renumeration when compared with the five o'clock hires and the harsher working conditions in the heat of the day as opposed to the cooler late afternoon. The tense of the verb 'grumbled' indicates continuous action; they put up quite a fuss.

The answer of the landowner (vv. 13-15). The vineyard owner was not persuaded by the arguments of the workers. He addressed one in the grumbling group arguing that he had a right to do with his possessions as he pleased. He treats his 'hires' as he will, but always righteously, and sometimes graciously.

Discrimination is the prerogative of the owner. Life experiences in the kingdom may not be equal, but it is not based on merit either. All will not judge the nations with Jesus; true disciples will (19:28). In the final expression of God's kingdom, no one will be greater than another and no one will receive a greater reward than another. Salvation is not a commercial transaction! Life is grace as well as the privilege of service. Now we enjoy the privilege of serving the King and later we will have the privilege of being in the presence of the King.

The complaint of the 6:00 a.m. workers concerned the generosity of the landowner to the later workers; it seemed to them to be a matter of injustice on the part of the owner! 'Do you begrudge my generosity' reminds the reader of our Lord's comment on wealth and masters in the Sermon on the Mount (6:23, the same word translated there is rendered 'bad').

I cannot resist quoting Blomberg once more: 'we are fools if we appeal to God for justice rather than grace, for in that case we'd all be damned.'[2]

Instruction concerning His death and resurrection (20:17-19)
This is the third time Jesus predicts what will happen to Him in Jerusalem (16:21-23; 17:9, 22-23 [if the comment at 17:12 is counted, this would be the fourth announcement of His death. However, it seems cryptic in comparison to the other three]). The first prediction was while they were in the region of Caesarea Philippi (16:21) and the second likely in Capernaum on the Sea of Galilee (17:22-23). Here is the most detailed explanation and was given to His disciples privately, away from the Galilean crowd, while going up to Jerusalem for the Passover. The disciples made no comment. This is the first reference to crucifixion, which was a means of execution that only the Romans practiced (they learned of it from the Carthaginians). This is also the first hint of the involvement of Gentiles.

---

2. Carl Blomberg, *Matthew*, p. 305.

While the disciples were thinking that entrance into Jerusalem would mean the inauguration of the Messianic kingdom, as evidenced by the episode that follows, Jesus wanted them to know that glory follows suffering. Again, the disciples' thinking was twisted by their cultural/religious heritage.

Instruction concerning positions in the kingdom (20:20-28)

The question raised in 18:1-4 by the disciples ('who is the greatest in the kingdom of heaven?') is raised once more. This time it is not generic; two disciples asked for prominence over the others. The assumption of the disciples, as they approach Jerusalem, is correct, but not as they suppose; the King will approach Jerusalem and His reign will commence. Two errors persist in their thinking, however. First, while Jesus will be enthroned, it will be after His death; the glory and crown come after suffering. They failed to recognize the reality of the meaning of His resurrection. Second, they did not understand that Jesus would inaugurate the kingdom, evidenced by the resurrection, but will remain absent until the kingdom's inhabitants have all been called and then the Lord will return and establish His reign completely and forever. They had not grasped the now/not yet aspects of Jesus' rule. What is found here is our Lord's instruction not only on a proper perspective relative to what would unfold in Jerusalem, but on the error of self-promotion, desire of positions, and the struggle for position rather than dutiful, contentment for the privilege of service.

An important insight in this paragraph, and stated in a passing manner, is the purpose of His death. He came to serve, not to be served, and the manner of His serving was to be a ransom, a death-substitute and purchased-price for many. Here is stated for the first time in Matthew, and rarely in the gospels, the reason for the death of Jesus (v. 28).

The request of Salome (vv. 20-21)

While Jesus is focused on the upcoming events of death and glory, the disciples are concerned about the implications of glory for themselves ('... one on your right hand and one on your left, in your kingdom'). They believed that the fullest manifestation of the kingdom would come immediately; James and John wanted the most prominent places in it. The clue for this discussion may have been Jesus' comment in 19:28. Salome was probably the sister of Mary, Jesus' mother, making her Jesus' aunt and the brothers His cousins.

Their mother makes the request. It is uncertain whether she was prompted by her sons or did it on her own. She quickly drops from the scene and the brothers become the focus of the discussion, suggesting that they were behind the request. Again, the disciples are shown to be ignorant of what was happening, selective of memory, and poor listeners.

The answer of Jesus (vv. 22-24)

To ask to reign with Jesus is to ask to suffer with Him; the disciples had not learned that lesson. The 'cup' is frequently an Old Testament imagery for suffering (Ps. 75:8; Isa. 51:17-18; Jer. 25:15-28). Their later flight from Jesus in the Garden of Gethsemane (26:56) evidenced the fact that the brothers might have been sincere, but also quite naïve. James was later martyred (Acts 12:1-2) and John exiled in old age to Patmos (Rev. 1:9).

The place of honor is assigned by the Father; it is given 'for those for whom' (v. 23), indicating more than one. I take it to be the collectivity of all the redeemed from all the ages who will reign with Christ and, thereby, all will be honored with the metaphoric significance of authority (thrones).

What they were asking for was to usurp Peter's place as head of the disciples (16:17-19). They desired only two thrones in the kingdom, not twelve (19:28). 'Throne' is a figurative expression for authority in the kingdom. The reaction of the ten was jealous indignation (v. 24). It would be understandable in Judas, who has no heart affection for Jesus, but not with the others. However, it does reveal their humanness.

The instruction of Jesus (vv. 25-28)

Jesus' point is that the values of the kingdom are radically distinguishable from worldly values. It seems that from the beginning of the Lord's move towards Jerusalem, following Peter's pronouncement at Caesarea Philippi of

Jesus' identity, that His focus was on teaching the values of the kingdom that He would inaugurate with the resurrection, and they should emulate.

Greed of place and prominence is the way of the world (v. 25). In the world, you can expect 'push and shove'. Remember chapter 18! The first characteristic of a kingdom member is humility; the second is a forgiving spirit (the two being interrelated).

The way of the disciple is that of a servant (vv. 26-27), service being the essential duty of a Christ-follower. In 18:1-4, Jesus made the point with the status and demeanor of a child, but here He uses the social convention of master and slave. The way of eminence in the kingdom is the way of lowly service, not significance-seeking.

The grand example of a proper view of our life and work is that of Jesus who came to serve, pointedly in the ransom He became (v. 28). 'Ransom' means 'to purchase or buy'; it was commonly used of buying slaves. What is interesting about our purchase is that it was to make us sons, not slaves, to provide elevated status for us. A ransom was paid to recover those captured in warfare; Jesus paid the ransom fee for us who were held captive also. This verse helps us understand Jesus' view of His death. His death is the supreme example of service. He died to redeem; He died to purchase us by paying the debt (1:21). Matthew is alluding to Isaiah 53:5-6, 11-12. 'For' can be translated as 'in the place of' indicating the meaning of His death as the substitution for ours.

The healing in Jericho (20:29-34)

At this point, Jesus was within eight hours' walk (16 miles, 25.75 km) from Jerusalem; He was about to make the ascent through the Wadi Kelt or Judean wilderness to the city via Bethphage, Bethany, the Mount of Olives, and the Kidron Valley. It concludes the record of Jesus' journey from the Galilee. Further, the miracle, done before a large entourage of people journeying for the Passover feast, affirms His credentials as the Messiah. Most likely, many in the group will shout 'Hosanna' in the triumphal entry shortly to come. The emphasis in the narrative is upon the miracle, thus raising expectations.

Though blind, these men, one we know as Bartimaeus (Mark 10:46), had deep insight! Their use of a Messianic title is important. Jesus is David's greater son. The title has been introduced in Matthew's narrative previously, so its presence is not to reveal new insights into Jesus (9:27; 12:23; 15:22). They must have heard of Him through reports of His activities in the Galilee.

The plea of the two men is for pity. It is interesting that on three other occasions (two blind men [9:27], the Canaanite woman for a daughter [15:22], and the man for a deranged son [17:14-21]), they all cried out in the same manner. In all four cases, the pleading person refers to Jesus with a Messianic title, 'Son of David'. In the two episodes of the blind men, they ask for themselves, but in the other two they ask for one of their children.

Jesus' question was not to elicit the desire of the men, but to draw attention to it. Again, the concern of Jesus for two men without status, being beggars, teaches the lesson of the value of people in the kingdom. The attitude of the blind men is in stark contrast to Jesus' disciples in the previous paragraph; the disciples sought prominence while these men sought mercy.

A second title for Jesus is used in answer to Jesus' question (v. 33). He is 'Lord,' a sovereign, all-powerful master.

The term 'pity' (v. 34) suggests deep emotional feeling. It is found in the story of the healing of the leper in Mark 1:41, the miracle of the deliverance from death of a son at Nain (Luke 7:13), and in Jesus' comment about the tragedy of the nation having no shepherd to lead them (9:36). As in the miracle of the leper (8:3), Peter's mother-in-law (8:15), and the blind men (9:29), Jesus touched them.

These men join the entourage to Jerusalem with Jesus. They must have shared in the triumphal entry, so witnessing to His kingship-claim.

Applications

1. Status in the Christian community, spiritual giftedness, even prolific results, do not determine one's reward in heaven. The reward in heaven is uniform and universal;

it is eternal life. Heaven is a classless society of praise. Accomplishments as Christians are gifts from God; this is not a reflection of degrees of the love of God (meaning God loves those who obtain the greater results), nor of greater or lesser rewards in heaven. All saints will have an abundant entrance into glory regardless of calling, gifts, or circumstances. Productivity in the Christian's life is a privilege. We seek to be productive because of our love for the Lord, not with a view to any gains, unless it is for His pleasure alone. How does this insight affect the way you think about serving Christ? Do you serve to receive a reward or because you have been given a gift to do so?

2. The reward for following Christ is an incomparable gift; it is eternal life. It is like working for a single hour and receiving a full day's wage. Can anything compare with the fact that we are so wonderfully blessed with everything that will count when time shall be no more? That tells us that our lives should not be lived in dread of God, but in gratitude for His unspeakable gift of His life, eternal life. Do you find yourself depressed by circumstances of life and family? Perhaps your focus is misplaced. We do not need to look within to find solutions; we do not need to look to others (they can only be temporal solutions); we all need to look up! Do you?

3. For a while, the disciples were slow to grasp spiritual truths. This should be a comfort to us in our failures since they lived with Him and missed clues. The disciples are a testimony to the blindness of our eyes and the hardness of our hearts. Jesus was not pleased with the slowness of their learning process, but His displeasure did not imply a lack or diminishment of care for them. That should be an encouragement for all of us who are slow learners. Jesus' love for us is not dependent on the depth of our insight, our moral conformity to the ideals of kingdom life. God determined to love us when we had nothing to offer Him, and He continues to love us for the same reason.

This is security for you and me. God's love is not based on our insight or performance!

4. The essence of true discipleship is expressed in the service of others. The desire for status or acclaim is not what the Christian should value. The essence of discipleship can be captured in the idea of denial, self-denial. We are people who have been called of God to die daily, die to our desires and wants in the service of others. Every mother knows much of this in the birth, nurturing, and rearing of children. Can it be said of you that you are a disciple, a follower of Jesus in the way He defined it to be? What steps are you taking to be a better disciple?

5. When we seek positions of prominence, it causes dissension with our friends. Jesus said that the desire to be number one is the way of worldlings. In the world, pushing and shoving to reach the 'top' is to be expected, but not among kingdom people. God calls us to be servants, not privilege-seekers over others. Jesus came to serve, not to be served. If called upon to list words that described your Christian life would 'servant' be among the descriptions?

6. Some who cannot see have better vision than those who can see. It is better to see with the heart than with the eyes sometimes. The two blind men have three important lessons for us. First, when our need is great, there is no greater person to come to than Jesus. Second, when you come to Jesus, you come to someone full of care and compassion. Third, when you come to Jesus, you come to one who has the ability to address your deepest needs. Do you see better with your heart than with your eyes?

10

The Official Presentation and Rejection of the King

(21:1–27:66)

This section of the narrative is interesting in that it encompasses a single week, yet it is eight chapters in length, culminating in the Lord's death. The shadow of His death became apparent in chapter 16 while He was still in Galilee; it ends here in Jerusalem.

The Official Presentation of the King (21:1-22)

Three symbolic actions comprise this section: the triumphal entry (vv. 1-11), the entrance into the temple (vv. 12-17), and the cursing of the fig tree (vv. 18-22). The first symbolically asserted Jesus' claim to be the promised One, the second affirmed the spiritual emptiness of Israel's worship, and the third graphically symbolized the failure of the nation. In the first of these, Jesus likely was supported with the accolades of the Galilean crowds, many in His entourage being from the north; in the second and in the third He was with His disciples. The first and second actions were met with consternation and hostility ('the whole city' [v. 10], and in the temple the 'chief priests and scribes' [v. 15] respectively).

Parenthesis: It is important to pause to consider some historical background before proceeding.

The Temple: This magnificent structure was one of Herod the Great's huge building projects (others being Caesarea Maritima, the Herodian, and Masada); it was an architectural wonder both in size, engineering, and beauty. The complex, the temple mount, comprised a very large courtyard (thirty-three acres), the Court of the Gentiles, and the building itself with the temple (Court of the Women, the Holy Place, and the Holy of Holies). Rimming the temple area were porticos, called the Porticos of Solomon, that provided shaded meeting places. It was in the Court of the Gentiles that the moneychangers set up business.

The Passover: This was one of three major pilgrim festivals in Israel's religious life requiring all males to appear before the Lord. Passover was an early spring celebration commemorating the deliverance from Egyptian bondage; Pentecost, Feast of Weeks, or First Fruits came fifty days after the Passover celebrating the early harvest; and Tabernacles, or Feast of Booths, that commenced with the Day of Atonement occurred in the autumn. While the normal population of the city of Jerusalem in the first century has been estimated at 30,000, the city swelled for Passover to some 180,000. With limited accommodations many camped in the environs of the city.

Galileans: Judeans viewed Galileans as a lower caste nationally and religiously. Galilee was a racially mixed area with major Gentile centers in Tiberius and Sepphoris. Geographically, Samaria and the Samaritans separated the two. After A.D. 6 with the deposition of Archelaus by the Romans, Judea was ruled by Roman procurators; Galilee was ruled by Herod's son Herod Antipas; and the Decapolis by another son, Herod Philip. Culturally, Galilee was considered a Judean backwater! Judea rejected 'Jesus the Galilean' (26:69), but it is from Galilee that he would launch a global movement (28:16-20) after defeating the nation's religious leadership in Jerusalem.

The entrance of the King into Jerusalem (vv. 1-11)

While it is customary to speak of Jesus' procession as the 'triumphal entry' (perhaps we should call it the 'Triumphal Presentation'), He only entered the city later. The crowd that hailed Jesus was perhaps largely Galilean (20:29). Further it is not proper to say that the people who welcomed Him as their Messiah changed the view later in the week and said, 'Crucify Him!' Their view of Him was likely mixed, some embracing the hope that He would deliver the nation from Roman oppression, another 'Judas Maccabeus'.

The instruction for the entry (vv. 1-3)

Bethphage was a town on the western side of the Mount of Olives (the term designates an area of large fig groves [the term means 'House of Ripe Figs']). There were also olive groves on the slope of the mount facing the Kidron Valley ('Gethsemane' means the place of an olive press). The town, along with Bethany, was considered the outer limits of Jerusalem (within the limitation of a Sabbath walk). Matthew's mention of the town and the mount may be rooted in an allusion to King David, thus recalling his exile and return in triumph after the death of Absalom (2 Sam. 19–20). David rode on a mule when returning to the city, as did Solomon at his coronation as David's successor (1 Kings 1:38-40). This is the first time we hear of Jesus riding on a donkey.

The account of the securing of a donkey and her colt is one of those instances that suggest that Jesus pre-arranged it (only Matthew recorded it). 'The Lord needs them.'

The fulfillment of prophecy in the entry (vv. 4-5)

Jesus' riding on the colt, the foal of a donkey, is seen as the fulfillment of prophecy; actually, Matthew combines two passages, a portion from Isaiah (62:11) and another from Zechariah (9:9). He takes as his introduction a phrase from Isaiah, 'Say to the daughter of Zion,' and joins it to lines from the Zechariah passage. Matthew recognized that, while presented to the inhabitants of Jerusalem, they would not receive Jesus as the Christ, contrary to the full verse in Isaiah, so he ends his validation of the event by quoting portions from another prophet whose words were clearly Messianic as well.

A donkey was a lowly beast, a beast of burden, and also a symbol of humility and peace. Jesus is no political threat, but palm branches cast before Him by the crowd is an allusion to Maccabean triumphs. The crowd saw Him through their political aspirations. Notice: He did not ride on a warhorse yet a conqueror of nations He will be!

The preparation for the entry (vv. 6-7a)
Matthew mentions two animals, a female donkey and its offspring. He rode on the foal, an animal that had not been ridden (this would explain the presence of two animals since a female donkey would accompany its young offspring). The disciples placed their coats on the animal; the people placed their coats and palm branches in the street, both suggestive of a high status being accorded to Jesus. These actions are very expressive: to cast garments, making a path, was an indicator of homage, a recognition of an exalted position; the waving of palm branches implied welcome or acceptance.

The entry into Jerusalem (vv. 7b-9)
The crowds that received Him with adulation were likely composed mainly of the multitudes that came with Him up to Jerusalem; many had heard His teaching and seen His miracles (e.g. the two blind men [20:29-34]) or had been attracted by an event that had arrested their attention. That Jesus rode on a colt, an unbroken animal, is itself a miracle; the animal remained calm.

The praises of the people come from Psalm 118:25-26. It is praise, a blessing by priests, and a prayer, a cry for deliverance. The psalm was used at the feasts of Dedication, Tabernacles, and Passover. By such reaction, the people understood that Jesus was presenting Himself as the Messiah, the Son of David, though varied in their understanding of the office.

The discussion of His person (vv. 10-11)
All that 'Jerusalem' was willing to say is that he was a prophet from Nazareth. However, His claim is unmistakable. He is David's son, royalty, Messiah! What can be said is that the Jerusalemites were shaken by the manner and accompanying circumstances of Jesus' coming into the city (the only other occurrence of the city being stirred as a whole was following the inquiry of the wise men as to the location of the birthplace of the king [2:3]), the first at the beginning of His life and the other near its conclusion.

Since Judea was under direct Roman rule, acclamations that Jesus was the promised king would pose a political threat to the religious leadership, the Sanhedrin, which tended to be sensitive to the plight of their subjected nation (if not unwarrantedly concessive for power and prestige). Further, the Galileans were firebrands, so to say that Jesus was from the Galilee made the fear of Roman retaliation and imposition a plausible response. To speak of Jesus as a prophet, likely said by the Galileans, was understood by most to say that He was the prophet like Moses (Deut. 18:18).

The entrance of the King into the temple (vv. 12-17)
If the triumphal entry is interpreted as the presentation and claim of Jesus to be the nation's Messiah, the Son of David, Israel's royal deliverer, His appearance at the temple is His claim to be Israel's great High Priest, the one who is in authority over religious life.

The cleansing of the temple (vv. 12-13) occurred on the day following the triumphal entry, making the claim that Jesus is both king and priest. Matthew places the two events in succession and states that the withering of the fig tree happened 'in the morning, as he was returning to the city …' (21:18). Mark tells us that the fig-tree event occurred 'on the following day' (11:12).

Stalls were erected in the Porticos of Solomon that surrounded the Court of the Gentiles (this was the largest area on the mount, the place where Gentiles could gain access). There, animals were sold for Passover sacrifice, the annual temple tax was paid (the half shekel), and currency was exchanged since purchases were in a special coinage at an additional fee (Tyrian coinage being the most stable and exacting in weight and value of the day [coins had intrinsic value determined by metal and weight, not a numeric printed on them]). Moneychangers were needed to convert Greek and Roman currency into temple currency, at least to pay the half-shekel tax. To allow such commerce in the temple made it a place of merchandizing rather than of worship.

Jesus' disgust was not that trade was taking place, but the motive and location. The leadership was making money, so Jesus referred to the area as a 'den of robbers'. Here the allusion is to Jeremiah's sermon (Jer. 7:11) in which he decried the fact that the people had desecrated the temple on the eve of the judgment of the nation and the destruction of the temple. Simply put, a second judgment is about to descend upon the nation!

This is the second time that Jesus acts as though He possessed the temple. Matthew, Mark and Luke record this incident; John only records the previous one (John 2:13-17). Were there two temple cleansings? There are references to oxen and sheep in John, here to money only. Also, the terms for money and the moneychangers are different in the two accounts. It seems that the moneychangers simply had returned to their business in the temple courtyard after Jesus initially put them out.

This event probably took place in the Court of the Gentiles since this was the only place Gentiles could go in the temple complex. If so, Jesus cleansed the Court of the Gentiles from Jewish defilement! The quotation from Isaiah 56:7 is from a context in which the prophet looks forward to a time when the temple would be called a 'House of Prayer'.

The temple cleansing occurred in the context of numerous healing miracles by our Lord (v. 14, 'the blind and the lame', and, thus, they could immediately participate in temple worship), so verifying His Messianic claims (11:2-6). The cleansing of the temple seems to be a fulfillment of Zechariah 14:21 that at a future time no 'merchandizer' would ply his trade in the house of the Lord.

The consternation of the leadership is described in verses 14-16. After Peter's confession of Jesus as 'the Christ, the son of the living God,' Jesus spoke of His opposition in Jerusalem for the first time (16:21), specifying that rejection would come from the elders, chief priests, and scribes. Here the last two of these groups are specifically mentioned as opposing Jesus. Prior to the cleansing of the temple, Jesus spoke of the high priest three times. From this point on there will be thirty-two additional references.

In His reply Jesus rejects the leadership's plea to quiet the praise offered by the children to Himself as the Son of David by quoting from Psalm 8:2. In the psalm, the praise is for

God; Jesus claims the verse speaks of Him! 'The children' is masculine in gender indicating that those praising Him were boys.

Jesus probably stayed in the home of Lazarus, Mary, and Martha in Bethany (which was located on the eastern slope of the Mount of Olives), though He could have stayed with Simon the Leper (v. 17). It is possible that Simon was their father; we cannot be sure. Another option is that He stayed in a garden, the garden where He was later arrested.

Applications

1. The titles of Jesus in our passage tell us much about who He claimed to be. He is the Son of Man, the fulfillment of Daniel 7:13-14, the One who will stand in judgment over the nations in the end of times. He is the Son of David, the truest and greatest of rulers. He is the Messiah, the One who will bring deliverance to His people. He is Jehovah, the LORD. He is God and claims to be so. Do you know that these titles are true of Him? Have you experienced the meaning of each of these terms and titles in your life?

2. While Jesus had numerous titles, He had one purpose in His coming – it was to give His life in death for us. The purpose in His death was to be our ransom price. He came not to be served, but to serve and He did that by offering His life as our sin offering. It was for you that He came. He came to pay a ransom price for you. Have you paused to thank Him lately?

3. Jesus had zeal for the things of God and God's house. It pained Him greatly when religion became a form of exploitation rooted in greed and expressed in pious superficialities. Are we jealous to preserve the holiness of our houses of worship? Does the majority of televised religion, being materialist quackery and base entertainment, bother you? Do you have a passion for authentic worship? Is it a priority for you and your family? What does true worship look like?

The King's symbolic rejection of the nation (vv. 18-22)

The triumphal entry into Jerusalem occurred on a Sunday, the cleansing of the temple on the following day, Monday. This makes the fig tree incident a Monday event. Mark has the cursing of the tree on Monday (11:12-14), but the recognition of its withering on Tuesday (11:20-26). What Matthew combines, Mark separates into two incidents. (Remember, the gospel writers often take a topical approach to a subject rather than a chronological one.)

It is important to view the withering of the fig tree from the perspective of the prior cleansing of the temple courtyard. The parallels between a fruitless, but a professing-to-be-fruitful tree, and the leadership's pious professions, but emptiness of reality, are keys to the passage. First, the tree had leaves, but did not have fruit. Leaves suggest fruit, but there was none, even though it was not fig season. Second, Matthew emphasizes fruit as a metaphor for moral behavior consistent with kingdom life. Third, the fruit of the fig tree in the Old Testament is an image of the life God expects of His people.

Thus, Jesus was saying with the tree withering that contemporary Judaism was a failure. Jesus has authority over the city (vv. 1-11), the temple (vv. 12-17), and the coming judgment (vv. 18-22) reflective in these three symbolic events.

The fig tree (a figure for Israel), in having leaves, should have had fruit on it, but it did not. Though not the season for figs (see Mark's account), the tree with its leaves, suggesting fruit, would have stood out. Jesus reacted because the tree, like the nation, made a false profession.

Fig trees in Israel bear two crops. In the spring, as is the case here, it bears a bitter, small fruit that is edible. Since the fig tree had leaves, it should have had figs. The time for sweet, larger figs is June, but the poor ate the March/April fruit. Jesus came in a humble fashion identifying with the downtrodden even in His diet. In this, the tree was like the nation of Israel. It should have borne the fruit of righteousness, but it did otherwise (Isa. 5:1-7).

The response of the disciples was amazement (v. 20), captured by the suddenness of the tree's withering. The same term appears in 8:27 ('marveled') describing their reaction to the stilling of the storm on the Sea of Galilee.

Jesus takes the opportunity in the cursing of the tree to speak of the efficacy of faith (vv. 21-22); however, He does so in symbolic and hyperbolic language (see 17:20). There is no record that any disciple moved a mountain, nor that Jesus did. The 'whatever' is an incentive to prayer, but it must be qualified by the permissive will of God.

Obviously, God does not answer all our prayers because some of them are amiss of His will and pleasure. The kind of faith that receives answers to prayer is stated in the negative ('does not doubt'); it is a practical trust in the power of God. Prayer and fruitfulness, not temple rituals, are the ways to God. In speaking of faith, Jesus puts the emphasis on the source of Israel's failure; they refused to believe.

The Rejection of the King by the Nation (21:23–22:46)

From the time of the triumphal entry, Jesus was in the last week of His earthly life and hostility towards Him was mounting. If Mark's chronology is followed, the incident recorded here took place on the Tuesday of Passion Week. The first attempt of the leadership was to discredit Him through intellectual arguments without the need for violence; the second was to falsely accuse Him and demand His death. They had rejected His claims, viewing Him as detrimental to the well-being of the nation.

This lengthy section is composed of the challenges by the religious leadership to Jesus. Three questions are posed by the leadership, three parables are spoken by the Lord after the first question, and one question by Christ ends the section. With it, the leadership became silent, though scornful and murderous.

The conflict with the chief priests and elders (21:23–22:14)

In this section, the chief priests and elders, the powerful elite, confront Jesus. Both groups are members of the Sanhedrin. The 'elders' were wealthy, lay aristocracy. They pose a question and Jesus answers them with three parables to illustrate His point.

The question of authority (vv. 23-27)

'These things' (v. 23) likely refer to the Messianic implications of His entry, the disruption of commercialism in the temple complex, and the numerous miracles He performed there. His actions imply a personal authority greater than a mere 'Galilean prophet' and, thus, a right to speak. If the leadership, reflected corporately in the Sanhedrin, was the religious authority in the nation, the implication is that Jesus was acting without sanction. They claimed to be the highest authority. Since Jesus appeared to them to be unsanctioned for what He was doing, meaning He lacked official national approval, He was viewed as a false, deluded messiah-figure and an ultimate threat to national security. While this is not specifically stated in the text, it is a clear inference in the three parables that follow.

Jesus answers the inquiry by linking His authority to that of John's, implying that, like His forerunner, His authority came from heaven (vv. 24-25). He evades a direct answer, but it would have been incriminating to admit that He lacked the sanction of the religious authorities. If the leadership answered His one question, He would answer their two.

Jesus turns the tables on His inquirers (vv. 25-27). He will answer them only if they will tell Him the source of the authority of John. They are on the horns of a dilemma because either answer would involve grave consequences. They refused to reply. If his authority was from heaven, John should have been listened to, but the leadership did not, although many in the populous did (11:25). They had a high regard for John, so the leadership feared an uprising if they denied the heavenly origin of his message. By their refusal to answer Jesus' counter-question, they gave witness to their lack of spiritual insightfullness and their sullied, hostile motives.

They refused to answer and so did Jesus (v. 27); there was a stalemate. They raised a question of Jesus' authority. By raising an alternative question He diffused the focus away from the initial hostile question. His alternative question concerned their ability to judge an important religious issue (He made the same point earlier [16:1-3] when contrasting their wisdom in discerning the weather with their ignorance of deep religious issues).

Jesus, then, seized the initiative with three parables (21:28–22:14) aimed at the leadership for the hardness of their hearts; all three have to do with the failure of the nation's leadership to respond properly. In each of the three parables there are two contrastive groups: those who assumed they had a right to a privileged position (but did not) and those who were lowly but were unexpectedly promoted. The point seems to be that in Jesus' judgment the current leadership would be replaced, an era is ending, and a new one is about to begin.

In each of the three parables, the focus is upon the failure of a person or persons to fulfill their promises to another (a father, a vineyard owner, a king). In each case, there is an indication of compliance, but a failure to do so with no repentant attitude for dereliction. The point is that these types of people (a son, tenants, and a king's subjects) followed the path of those who listened but rejected John's plea for repentance. They were acting like those who despised John's message, but a greater than John was now speaking with the implication that the leadership was making a similar, though far graver, mistake.

An additional way of viewing the three parables as a single unit is to envision a progression of emphasis. In the story of the two sons, it was the disobedient one who repented and obeyed his father's instructions. The 'obedient' son, the nation's leadership, perceived no necessity for repentance, being self-righteous moralists. In the second, the 'obedient' sons paralleled the tenants with the emphasis on their rejection of the owner's rights and forfeiture of privilege; they will not enter the kingdom. The final parable speaks of the judgment of the unrepentant (the son, the tenants, the invited guest).

Parable 1: the story of the two sons (vv. 28-32)
The issue of authority in the previous paragraph connects thematically with this first parable. The obedient son was the one who went into the field; words alone do not reveal the heart. Jesus is saying that the leaders were disobedient sons upon whom the Father's wrath will fall. The life-changing trust of tax-gatherers (e.g. Matthew) and harlots brings to them the kingdom.

Two questions from Jesus frame the story: 'What do you think?' (v. 28) and 'Which of the two did the will of his Father?' (v. 31). In a Jewish mind, the vineyard metaphor would speak of the nation (Isa. 5). The obedient-son image is that of only some in leadership capacity, the godly remnant (e.g. Nicodemus). The mere outwardly conforming son was the current majority of the leadership of the nation. They speak well but act conversely. Jesus' questions demand a singular answer, and with it He mounts His criticism of Israel's spiritual leaders. In answering the question posed by Jesus, the leadership stood self-incriminated. They claimed to be sons, but their actions revealed that they were not.

In His conclusion, Jesus for the first time makes a personal application from a parable. Public sinners, tax-gatherers and prostitutes will make it into the kingdom before the religious leadership. He made a similar statement in 8:11-12 when saying that Gentiles will enter the kingdom to sit with Abraham while the 'sons of the kingdom' will be left out. True profession is a heart-felt change resulting in actions, not mere words.

The issue is not religion, but heartfelt attachment by faith that leads to repentance and obedience. The disobedient son repented and obeyed; the outwardly conforming son did not. As the leadership refused John's message, they refused Jesus' message. Jesus places His authority and that of John's on the same basis; it is from heaven (here is the answer to the questions posed by the chief priests and elders, v. 23).

Jesus is not mincing words. The leadership ('you') are disobedient fakers and will not enter the kingdom. Simply put, the leadership of the nation, in Jesus' view, are religious hypocrites!

Parable 2: the story of the vineyard owner and the tenants (vv. 33-46)

This parable highlights the iniquity of the leadership and their peril because of it. Land was rented out to tenants with a view to the owner's receiving a portion of the fruit it produced; however, when the owner sent for his share, the tenants abused and killed his servants, and they even killed his son (first, the prophets of the Old Testament and now Jesus). Judgment will befall them; that is, the nation. Israel is pictured in the Old Testament as a vineyard that God planted with a view to fruit; it failed to produce any (Isa. 5).

In the story, the current tenants are the religious leadership of the nation. They are acting in continuity with those who rejected the prophets before them. Here is clear evidence that Jesus knew that the intent of the leadership was to murder Him. The consequence of Israel's failure to heed the prophets is about to be repeated by their killing the greatest of those sent by the Father!

This parable answers the issue of the origin of Jesus' authority in that He is the 'son' sent from the vineyard owner (the Father). Again, the Old Testament referent is to Isaiah 5. God planted a vineyard, a nation, and looked for a good harvest (righteousness and justice), but what He found were wild grapes (iniquity, unbelief) so He destroyed the vineyard.

Seeking a fair return for his investment, the owner expected a portion of the fruit of the land. When he sent for it, the tenants failed to listen, abused, and killed his messengers. This is a synopsis of God's dealings with Israel, His enormous display of mercy and grace, and their hardheartedness and rebellion.

The sending of the owner's son was something of a last resort in the story line (short of his personal return). The son, of course, is Jesus. In an ultimate act of defiance, the tenants killed him. The leadership murdered Jesus. If they killed the son in the vineyard, spilling out his blood, the land and produce would have become unclean. This is why, it seems, the text states that they 'threw him out of the vineyard'. They, like the truly disobedient son in the previous parable, made promises but refused to keep them! That the son was killed outside the vineyard, having been first cast out of it, can be taken as an allusion to Jesus' death outside the city (Heb. 13:12)!

The leadership's response to Jesus' question (v. 40) reveals that they had the correct answer, but were blind in applying it to themselves (v. 41). The tenants should not be merely evicted but punished for their crimes. Did they not know they were rendering their own sentence?

In His response (vv. 42-44), Jesus quotes from Psalm 118:22-23. The quotation, at first glance, seems out of place, because it was a psalm that Matthew previously cited in his account of the triumphal entry (21:9), though not these specific verses from the psalm. The builders rejected the cornerstone, the key to the structural integrity of a building, just as the tenants rejected God's choice Son. The point is that Matthew used an Old Testament passage to draw an analogy. Just as the tenants and the builders rejected the best, so the nation's leadership denied Jesus' claim to be the best. The consequence would be awful judgment for them and the nation (the destruction of the temple in A.D. 70 and the great judgment later). This text is quoted in Acts 4:11 and 1 Peter 2:7.

The initial phrase in verse 44, which concerns the judgment of A.D. 70, reflects an allusion to Isaiah 8:14-15. God is described there as a rock of refuge for those who trust in Him and a crushing stone for those who do not. The stone in Psalm 118 is applied to Jesus in verse 42. Here is another claim of Jesus to His deity! The second phrase, the crushing action of the stone, is an illusion to Daniel 2:34-35, 44, the vision of a series of empires broken by a stone from heaven that becomes a new kingdom.

The leadership's reaction is described in verses 45-46. The Pharisees replaced the 'elders' (v. 23) in Matthew's description of the audience. They and the chief priests knew that these stories were about them (v. 45). They reacted with violence, which only proved that Jesus' claim was correct.

Parable three: the story of the wedding feast (22:1-14)
The third parable in the trilogy hammers home the danger of the leadership's course of action. If, in the previous parable, Jesus faulted the religious leaders for neglecting their covenantal duties, He now chastised them here for neglecting God's grace. The flaunting of the banquet invitation led to the invitation of others. The nation could have entered the kingdom of God; though given ample opportunity, they refused. The seized and murdered slaves are the prophets. Again, as in the other two parables, the point is that the loss of privilege is the fruit of disobedience, a failure to repent.

The parable not only speaks of the loss of Israel's privilege, but the nature of the 'nation' that would replace it. Being 'in' the new nation is parallel to being 'in' Israel. Not all in either outwardly professing groups would enter the kingdom. It belongs to those who bring forth the fruit of righteous living rooted in the wonder of a heart-change called regeneration.

The son's wedding banquet (vv. 1-2) hints at the Messianic 'Supper of the Lamb' (Rev. 19); the king's son is clearly the Messiah. A wedding feast would commence with a banquet, which is envisioned here, and could last over a week. The invitation in the story is a call to faith and fellowship in Jesus, the Messiah.

The invited group in the story were the nation's leaders – the elders, Pharisees, and chief priests (vv. 3-4). Twice the king invited the guests, but they would not come. The assumption is that they agreed to come when called to do so, but they refused ultimately. They simply had other, temporal interests.

The calloused guests not only had selfish excuses; they mistreated, even killed, the king's servants (that is, the prophets) who came announcing a gracious invitation, not realizing that they were answerable to the king for their actions (vv. 5-6). In essence, they simply did not care about the will of God!

The consequent reaction of the offended king points to the destruction of their city, Jerusalem, a reference to the holocaust of A.D. 70 (vv. 7-9). It is interesting that Jesus says that the city would be burned, and it was by the Romans (making no mention of the burning of the temple complex). However, the temple was set on fire by the Jewish defenders, not the Romans, according to Josephus.[1] Jesus calls Jerusalem 'their city'. It is no longer God's.

The king invited others (vv. 8-9). In fact, his servants were to call as many as they could find. The call was an indiscriminate action to any and all they could find wherever they were located. The clear inference is that the invitation was non-discriminatory (Jews and Gentiles, the righteous and unrighteous). The servants called all kinds, the good and the bad, to the banquet (v. 10). The difference with the new list of guests was their willingness to come, an attitude the religious leadership lacked.

A wedding feast presupposed proper attire; clearly Jesus is making a point based on an analogy (v. 11). It would seem that the acceptance of an invitation entails the consequent recognition of appropriate respect relative to the

---

1. Josephus Flavius, *Wars of the Jews*, 6. 2-3.

importance and dignity of the occasion. The meaning of the 'man not dressed in wedding clothes' is unclear (vv. 12-14). However, even secondarily invited guests must be clothed properly. Ethnicity and status are no criteria for entrance, yet righteousness is crucial. Proper clothing was available, but this man entered wearing his own attire! The man knew immediately that he was guilty; he 'was speechless'. He knew that he was in the wrong, but he simply refused to come in a respectful manner.

The symbolism suggests that even those invited to the banquet must fulfill certain obligations, such as proper attire (respect for the privilege of being invited). Entrance into the kingdom is free, but there are many that slip in with only outward profession that will be separated out, because of them having no change of heart affection (remember the parable of the tares and wheat, 13:24-30, 37-43).

None who were invited to the banquet could remain there without the proper clothing. Improper clothing is the grounds of dismissal from the banquet. The host provided the clothing, but one refused to put it on. Though he came, he did not come clothed in the proper manner. The judgment of the improperly clothed man is graphic (v.13), Matthew using the same terminology in several instances throughout his gospel (8:12; 13:42, 50; 24:51; 25:30).

The 'many called' were both sets of guests, but the invitation is only an external thing. One must have a willingness that comes from God's willingness to make us willing (v. 14). Willingness does not save; God saves us in calling us by His divine power and prerogative. Not all the called will turn out to be the chosen, as evidenced by the unwillingness and lack of respect of some. However, these are not our thoughts, but God's thoughts, which are final and alone true. What is clear is that God chooses His guests and in choosing them makes them willing to attend with proper regard for the inviter! We shall never understand the mind of God in these things.

Caution: The details in a parable should not be stretched beyond the single, basic point of the lesson. Some details in these parables simply appear to round out the story adding suspense and literary colour. The point here is that as guests spurned the generosity of a king in refusing to come to his son's wedding banquet, so the nation has rejected God's grace in His Son, the Messiah. Parables are illustrative stories; they illumine and should be interpreted through the lens of the major point of the story only.

Applications

1. The lesson of the fig tree is that profession without possession is false profession. Have you met people like a fig tree, abundant in religious talk but devoid of religious life? It is not the leaves of our words that evidences life, but the fruit on the branches. Without works faith is non-existent. By their works you shall know them, not their smiles, confidence, or affirmations. Do you know people like this in your family? The characteristic of a true disciple is righteousness, fruit, and moral conformity. What kind of fruit-bearing tree are you?

2. If Jesus has the authority of heaven, as John had before Him, He deserves supremacy over our lives. His teachings are to be obeyed. The fundamental mistake of the religious leadership in Jesus' day was that they stumbled over this issue. They refused to believe that Jesus possessed the authority of heaven. They did not believe that He came from God (if He did not, He should not be embraced). The issue of truthfulness is the foundation of belief. They did not believe; do we? If Jesus came from heaven as He claimed, we must accept the truthfulness of His message. There can be no higher authority.

3. The more you read of the life of Jesus the more you have to say that He was clever and wise. He could ask questions that were penetrating and profound. He knew the art of communication as well as knowing the Holy Scriptures. From this I deduce: first, that He should be carefully heard and, second, He has a depth of wisdom unparalleled. He could dispatch people with simple questions, teach enormous lessons by drawing them out of even a hostile audience. Simply as a teacher

He is worth emulating. Do you not stand amazed at His handling of tough situations with poise and depth?

4. God will not tolerate falseness, but He has mercy and grace for those who see the error of their ways. To agree to do something but not do it is a greater sin than refusing to do something and later repenting and doing it. Is this not wonderful and encouraging? All of us have said no to God on many issues, only to repent later. God is always willing to accept a humbled heart. You and I never need fear that God will not accept our change of mind from our wrong ways to His right ways. Does this not help us appreciate, trust, and love the Lord? He will never turn away the rebel who repents! Have you repented lately?

5. God expects and demands honesty and diligence on the part of His followers. Sadly, the history of Israel is an open illustration of this in the negative. God had great mercy and grace toward the nation, caring and providing for it, but what He received in return was arrogance, disobedience, and the rejection of those He sent to warn them. He finally sent His own Son, but they killed Him. What a picture of divine grace and the harshness of the human heart! Does this have any relevancy to our own nation? Are we courting the judgment of God for spurning His goodness and rejecting His messengers? Does this have relevance in our families? What about you and me?

6. God called His people to His banqueting table, but they treated it as of trivial importance and found other things to do. Can you imagine that? An invitation from God and they had no time for it. Consequentially God broadened the invitation to include others, Gentiles. Israel's momentary and partial loss has proven gain for those far off. God wants a full banqueting table, so He broadened the guest list. Are you not glad that He opened the hearts of a multitude of others and that included you?

7. Behind the harsh warnings found in Scripture is the motive of awakening us to our peril. God in His very

nature is not vindictive, but an expression of His justice is wrath. Violation demands reparation and if not quelled by repentance it results in judgment. In the parable of the tenants, the landowner sent the prophets and his son, but all they met was rejection. In the end, the landowner came, and all that the tenants experienced was destruction. The day of grace for the nation and its religious leadership was at an end; the wrath of God was about to fall through the mighty Roman legions. God's grace has limits, even though in other ways it is limitless. Do you know people that need to be warned to use this time to repent?

8. The human, finite mind cannot grasp the infinite wisdom and ways of God. God has revealed Himself truly to His people, but not completely. Our God is incomprehensible, and His ways are beyond our finding out. What appears to us as paradoxes or conundrums in the Bible are not so to God. My plea is that we refuse to limit our beliefs to what our minds can grasp. That is the tact of rationalists, and the result of that approach is a sterile, mathematical world with little hope and a lot of anxiety. Do not reject biblical truth simply because you cannot make it fit into your small box of human understanding. God chooses His people sovereignly and does so apart from human merit. The duty that is ours is to be willing to accept His call. The question when it comes to true religion is this: Are you willing to come to Jesus?

The continued controversy with the nation's leadership (22:15-46)

The lengthy section of 21:1–22:46 consists of three trilogies. The first are three symbolic actions on the part of Jesus (21:1-27: the triumphal entry, the cleansing of the temple, and the withering of the fig tree) followed by a challenge by the leadership of the nation (21:28-32). This led to a long monologue by Jesus consisting of three parables condemning the nation's leadership (21:33–22:14: the two sons, the vineyard and tenants, and the wedding banquet).

Here in the final trilogy, three questions are posed by the nation's leadership.

Each of the questions deals with contemporary issues of theology or ethics. The first was designed as a trap, the third as a test, and the purpose of the second is not stated though the tone is derogatory and skeptical. Jesus' answer to the first question resulted in amazement, to the second silence, and to the third we are not informed, but the controversy ends with a counter question from Jesus (22:41-46). Jesus had carried the day and defeated His opponents. This leads to a long devastating critique of the nation's leadership in chapter 23.

The conflict with the Pharisees and Herodians: the issue of politics and taxes (vv. 15-22).

The Pharisees send several Herodians, pro-Roman sympathizers, to question and trick Jesus into some sort of blunder (common cause creates odd bedfellows!) The Pharisees ardently opposed the Roman occupation; Herodians were pro-Roman in sympathy because of the empire's support of Herod the Great and later his sons; the Herodians compromised for safety. The question they posed was about the viability of paying poll taxes to a wicked, oppressive government. The answer lies on the denarius, the coin required for the poll tax. Jesus' answer is that taxes should be paid to repressive governments.

The issue in question was a poll tax imposed upon Judea in A.D. 6 after the disposition of Archelaus and the appointment of Coponius (A.D. 6–9), the first of a series of procurators (the tax went directly into the coffers of Rome with no benefit to the Jews). The Jews of Judea found the tax oppressive and fiercely resented it, leading to revolts. One such rebellion occurred under the leadership of a man named Judas, a Galilean, who aligned with a Pharisee by the name of Zadok. This revolt led to the formation of the Zealot Movement and a series of clashes that culminated in the great revolt which began in A.D. 66 in Caesarea and engulfed the nation. If Jesus opposed the tax, His confession could be used against Him in the quest to find a charge that Rome would execute; if He embraced the tax, He risked falling out of favor with the people as unpatriotic. In essence, the question is a 'hot potato'. Whatever the answer may be, if there are only two answers, it put Jesus in a no-win dilemma. The motive for the question is clear (v. 15).

The approach to Jesus was a courteous one, also rather surprising since the motive was subterfuge. Four things are said concerning His character: sincerity, truthfulness, fearlessness, and kind.

By Jesus' time, 'Caesar', the family name of Julius Caesar, had become a title. The reference here is to Tiberius Caesar. A coin of the emperor would carry his portrait on one side and the words 'Pontifex Maximus' on the other. He was declared on the coinage to be the son of the divine Augustus, thus the Son of God, and a high priest. Obviously, this was offensive to the Jews, so the answer carried political and religious overtones. The Romans, culturally sensitive to the Jews, allowed them to mint a non-idolatrous denarius. Jesus asked for a Roman coin.

The assumption behind the question is that of the incompatibility between loyalty to God and loyalty to Caesar. Jesus rejected that assumption and argued for sphere sovereignty; religion has its rights of operation and so does the state. What belongs to the emperor, the right to tax, is within the sphere of the state!

It is interesting that they had to acquire a coin when Jesus asked for one ('brought,' v. 19). This was likely because religious Jews would be hesitant to carry a coin with the emperor's face on it.

The question put to Jesus was whether He felt it proper to 'give' to Caesar (v. 17). Jesus used a different verb ('render', v. 21) in His reply. His answer is not merely something of a grudging concession to the political authority; rather it is a duty. He went on to say that one's obligations are not fulfilled in paying the tax to Caesar; there are duties also to God. Actually, paying the tax was a way of honoring God (i.e., civil obedience). Jesus paid the tax for the temple (17:24) and likely to Caesar also. Jesus was not a Zealot who rejected the validity of the tax, nor like the Pharisees who did not want to pay it, nor a Sadducee or Herodian who paid it to preserve their own personal securities. In a sense, Jesus sides with the Pharisees on the issue of governmental taxation though His motive was not one of dislike or hesitancy, but duty.

The Herodian/Pharisee coalition had met their match, and were left standing amazed; Jesus emerged the victor.

The conflict with the Sadducees: the issue of marriage (vv. 23-33)

With the defeat of the Pharisees/Herodians, the spotlight shifted to the animosity of the Sadducees, likely some priests and elders within the Sanhedrin. Their question was designed with the presupposition that Jesus would agree with the Pharisees, alienating Him against the most powerful faction in the ruling party. The Sadducees rejected the notion of an afterlife believing that the memory of the dead is all that exists.[2] For them, there was no immaterial nature in mankind that exists beyond the grave and no resurrection of the material body. Jesus takes on the question of whether or not there is a resurrection.

The Sadducees, a minority party but the controlling one in Jesus' day, came with a complex question about the marriage state in heaven and the notion of resurrection, though they denied the concept of an afterlife (again, common cause creates odd bedfellows. This time it was the appearance of an idea that they themselves rejected). The error of it all is the basic assumption that there will be a marriage state in heaven. In the resurrection there will be no marriage. The Sadducees proposed a question that they did not believe to be actually valid. To the Sadducees, the levirate marriage law made the notion of eternal life incoherent; they rejected it, believing that there is no afterlife, only non-existence.

The Pharisees and Sadducees appear together in 3:7 and 16:12, but here it is clear that they had significant differences of belief. The starting point of the question is the issue of levirate marriage (Gen. 38:6-11; Deut. 25:5-6; Ruth 4:5-10). If a husband died childless in his marriage, his brother was to marry his sister-in-law and produce a son to continue the

---

2. Josephus Flavius, *The History of the Jews*, 18:1.4 ('That souls die with the bodies') and *The War of the Jews*, 2.8.14 ('They also take away the belief of the immortal duration of the soul, and the punishments and rewards in Hades').

family line. Whose wife is she who has had several brother-husbands in the afterlife?

Jesus' answer is blunt and devastating; the Sadducees, like the Pharisees (5:21-48), are simply ignorant of the Scriptures and of the ways of God! The problem with this religious party was their ignorance of Moses' teaching, though they took pride in knowing Moses. They were gross religious materialists who simply denied the reality of the supernatural as it relates to an afterlife. They did not believe that God had the power to create, out of death, a new quality of life. The argument that there is no life after death is, then, a denial of the power of God.

The reference to angels (v. 30) may also be a stab at the Sadducees since they denied the existence of angels (Acts 23:8). The Sadducees were a religiously liberal party; they were politically savvy materialists (they only embraced as revelation the Pentateuch). They did well in this life but rejected the notion of another, more important one.

To sustain the accusation, Jesus quoted from Exodus 3:6, a verse of the Pentateuch that they confessed to embrace. The verse does not strictly prove the doctrine of resurrection as it does the concept of immortality. Although the three patriarchs had died, they are still alive because God has an ongoing relationship with them. Life after death presupposes a resurrection. God's covenant with the patriarchs was not terminated with death. The use of the present tense ('is') indicating ongoing experience for Abraham, Isaac, and Jacob captures our Lord's assertion that there is an afterlife. These men live, and God is the God of the living, though they had died.

The crowds were astonished (v. 33) even as the Pharisees and Herodians had been amazed (v. 22) by Jesus' reply.

The conflict with the Pharisees: the issue of priorities
(vv. 34-40)

The Pharisees would have been pleased that Jesus had muzzled the Sadducees, so they asked Him a question without being joined by others. The question from a student of the Law (a scribe) concerned which is the greatest commandment. Jesus replied by mentioning two commandments that are actually linked together because we cannot have one without the other. His answer is that we are to love God with every facet of our being (inwardly) and have the same love for people (outwardly). This is the only time in the three-question-confrontational episodes that Jesus answers with a straight reply.

With the Sadducees defeated and the populous clearly favoring Jesus, the Pharisees determined it was time to intervene. Unlike the previous encounter with the Pharisees and Herodians, the question did not have political overtones, but religious and moral ones. A lawyer among them posed a question that likely was an attempt to show that Jesus contradicted Moses. The Mosaic code comprised 613 commandments (365 positive and 248 negative). They comprise the same in number as the numerical value of the letters in the Ten Commandments interestingly. Prioritizing of one or two above the many would certainly lead to more than one answer, opening the possibility of discrediting the Lord.

A clue, perhaps, to the precise inquiry of the scribe might be found in Mark's account of the same incident. There Jesus answered the inquiry by distinguishing two categories of commandments, the greater from a lesser. 'Much more than all burnt offerings and sacrifices' (Mark 12:33) is the command to love God wholeheartedly.

It would seem that 'scribes', students of the Scriptures, and 'lawyers', interpreters of the divine law, refer to the same profession. It would make sense that a Pharisee of this profession would raise a question of this nature.

The answer of Jesus (vv. 37-40) contains quotations from Deuteronomy 6:5 and Leviticus 19:18. This is the only time in the Scriptures that these verses are joined together. His choice of these two texts is interesting for two reasons: first, the emphasis on the governing principle of love lifts the discussion above any particular text since it is the underlying principle of all the commandments. Second, by uniting together love for God and love for others, Jesus unifies the tables of the Law, the Decalogue, into a single unit. However, the second is based on the first. Without a love for God, there can be no God-like love for one's neighbor. These two commandments summarize the intent of the Hebrew Scriptures, 'the Law and the prophets' (see 7:12).

A question from Jesus to the Pharisees (vv. 41-46)
The strident dialogue with various factions within the nation's leadership ends with Jesus silencing His opponents and posing an inquiry that they were unable to answer. However, if they answered it, they would be in trouble. The question is profound. If the Messiah is a son of David, why does David refer to Him as his Lord? 'How can he be both a son and Lord?' (a quotation from Psalm 110:1). In families, the father is greater than the son; here, however, is the reverse. Consequently, there is no answer from the religious leadership. The answer is, of course, the truth of Micah 5:2; the Messiah is both human and divine!

Jesus begins by implying that the traditional understanding of Messiah by the Jewish leadership is inadequate. Messiah must be more than a 'son' if David recognized Him as his Lord. Messiah is clearly David's greater son. This is the last time in the narrative that Jesus uses 'son of David' terminology. It seems reasonable that Jesus was making a not-so-veiled reference to Himself in asking this question of the Pharisees. The leadership revealed that they hoped for a Son of David, a politically oriented, human kingly type (v. 42).

Jesus then asks a follow-up question (vv. 43-45). He prefaces his citing of Psalm 110:1 with the phrase 'in the Spirit', indicating that David wrote the passage by divine inspiration (in that sense David was a prophet [Acts 2:30]). If David called the person, his son, 'Lord,' it must be someone greater than himself (a hint of implication that David was referring to the Messiah). Matthew is clear in his presentation of Jesus that David's greater son is the Son of God, deity (14:33, 16:16, 26:63-64, 27:43). The Pharisees were silenced!

Applications

1. The Christian lives in two 'worlds': the nation and culture of our physical existence and a new 'world' through our spiritual rebirth. Jesus clearly teaches us that we have responsibilities in each of these worlds.

We are to be faithful to the laws of both 'lands'. For example, in the earthly realm, God expects us to abide by the laws of the land even if we think we do not need to do so, even if they make no real sense at times. We are to live in the world and support the government we are under as service to God, even if our obedience is misused. Are you a good citizen of both worlds?

2. Marriage is a temporal picture of what heaven is like; it is an enduring institution, the foundation of social cohesiveness, but it is not eternal. The union of a man and a woman is a shadow of our ultimate union as believers, as the bride of Christ, to our eternal 'head'. There will only be one marriage in heaven, us to the Saviour. Is your relationship to your spouse a picture of heaven? Do people see heaven in your marriage? Do we love our mates as Christ loved His church?

3. There is life beyond the grave because God exists. He continues relationships with humans. Jesus affirmed the resurrection of the dead. He is the God of the living, such as Abraham. Though he (Abraham) died 4000 years ago, he lives. When people hear that we have died, it will not be true. Actually, in death we believers will come to life, not temporally but eternally. Does that insight help you to cope with disappointing days and derelict people? Are you looking forward to your literal rebirth?

4. The purpose of the Bible is not merely to make us more efficient in our duties; it is to transform our character into the very likeness of God. The Bible is more about character development than function, though doing is easier than being for most of us. The Bible can be summarized in one word: love. The object of love is twofold: God and mankind. Our primary duty is not to work for God; it is to love Him with all the resources of our being. Do you see that as your most important task? Do you see that care for others is how we express love for God?

5. Jesus existed before David, yet He is called a Son of David. What an amazing insight into Jesus, what a most insightful statement of Christology! Jesus is God. He existed before Israel's greatest king and David called Him Lord! He is also David's son. This shows that He is God and man! Does that insight excite you? Do you delight in thinking about the Lord Jesus?

The Rejection of the Nation by the King (23:1-39)

This chapter contains the reply of Jesus to the religious establishment of His day, specifically the scribes and Pharisees; it is a ringing negative criticism of their lives and practices. There was to be no truce between Jesus and the leadership of the nation; both had very fixed opinions. When Jesus concluded this condemnation, He would leave the temple for the last time (24:1). The fate of the building, the temple, is bound in the fate of the nation's leadership. It, thus, seems that chapters 22 and 23 are a unit. The leadership sought to publicly discredit Jesus in chapter 22, and He delivered His verdict of them in chapter 23. As Jesus entered the temple for the last time in chapters 21 and 22, He spoke to the nation's leaders for the last time prior to His trial before the Sanhedrin in chapter 26.

The setting is still in the temple courtyard. Jesus initially addresses the crowds about the practices of the scribes and Pharisees (vv. 1-12) and then addresses them directly with seven 'woe' pronouncements.

Some biblical scholars suggest that this is another of the discourses of Jesus in the book since Christ is speaking, seeing chapters 23–25 as a unit that would include the discourse of chapters 24–25. However, the characteristic concluding phrase at the end of the previous discourses is absent ('And it came to pass when Jesus had ended these sayings' [or a similar phrase, 7:28; 11:1; 13:53; 19:1]). See also 26:1. Further, Jesus speaks to the crowds in this chapter whereas His discourses are to the disciples with the crowds listening, though in the Sermon on the Mount (5–7) Jesus spoke to the crowd with the disciples around Him listening (5:1). The speech in chapter 23 occurred in the temple, while chapters 24 and 25 were given on the Mount of Olives (24:1).

Finally, there is a change of subject between chapter 23 and chapters 24 and 25, from instructing the crowd to instructing the disciples. Overall and in spite of differences, it seems to me that this is a discourse by Jesus and the phrase, 'Jesus left the temple ...' (24:1) is very similar to the other five discourses noting a conclusion and transition.

The indictment of the scribes and Pharisees (vv. 1-12)

Jesus, in addressing the crowd, openly criticized the leadership for the manner in which they executed their role, not so much their teachings *per se*. They were ignorant of the problems their teaching created for ordinary people and they placed more emphasis on outward appearances than on inward pious realities.

Michael Green has a very good summary of Jesus' complaint about the leadership: first, they practiced what they did not preach; second, they were unwilling to do what they told others to do; third, they loved to show off; fourth, they liked titles and respect; and fifth, they did not understand the nature of ministry as being that of servanthood.[3]

The gist of verses 1-3 is that the Pharisees and scribes claimed to be students of Moses (a scribe was an expert in the Law and thus referred to as a lawyer [the Jews did not separate religious law from secular law; they were one since the state was religious in nature]).

The indictment of Jesus is proven in verses 4-7. The Pharisees made rules, but did not help the weak (v. 4). While the Pharisees, being purists, sought conformity to the laws they created, they refused to help those who collapsed under their impossible rules.

The Pharisees liked to be seen as pious (v. 5). They made an outward show of piety. They lengthened the tassels on their shirts (Deut. 22:12; Num. 15:38-39) and wore large boxes (phylacteries) containing Scriptures on their foreheads and upper left arms (it being nearest the heart [Deut. 6:8; 11:18]). Tassels were attached to the outer shirt as a reminder to obey the laws of God; Jesus wore them (9:20). The practice was not being condemned here; the motivation for it was the issue.

---

3. Michael Green, *The Message of Matthew* (Westmont, IL: Inter-Varsity Press, 2020), p. 241.

The Pharisees liked to be seen as important (v. 6). They coveted the symbols of priority, seats of honor in public gatherings. The Pharisees liked titles and accolades in public (v. 7). They enjoyed the prestige of the recognition of their importance. 'Rabbi' suggested status.

Some remedial instructions are provided by Jesus in verses 8-12. He expounds on the last point of criticism, titles. The focus shifts from the leadership ('them') to His listeners ('you'). Jesus uses a trilogy of titles: rabbi (v. 8), father (v. 9), and teacher (v. 10).

First, take accolades with caution (vv. 8-10). When Jesus stated that we should not call people 'rabbi', 'father', or 'teacher', He indicates that we should not call people by titles that suggest rank, a superior in the presence of an inferior. In the New Testament, these terms are used of people, but not as official titles and not as indication of superior status. It would seem unlikely that Jesus is quibbling over external titles; the issue is not titles but attitudes. We are to call each other 'brother', suggestive of equal status. Thus, the issue of the rejection of titles is really not about titles; rather, it is about a false status often attached to the title bearer. The term 'teacher' is used properly of people (Acts 13:1, 1 Timothy 2:7, and Hebrews 5:12).

The word 'father' is interesting because Jesus refers to God as His Father. Jesus is not saying that the title is wrong to use, but the title must not be misused. Jesus was not inferior to His Father, so in using the title He was not indicating rank.

Second, seek to be a servant (v. 11). Jesus is saying that we should not pursue titles nor accolades. We should not seek to be known for what we do, but who we are in the service of others. Lowliness must mark the lives of God's servants (18:4; 20:26-28). We should pursue humility (v. 12). Jesus states the point as a moral maxim.

The condemnation of the scribes and Pharisees (vv. 13-36)
In this section Jesus delivers His most concentrated evaluation of the religious leadership of His day. He does it in the form of seven woes, seven being the perfect number; they are truly and completely all these things. 'Woe' is a

funeral lament, a form of mourning for the dead. These Pharisees may appear to be living, but they are dead!

The verbal attitude of Jesus takes a strident, caustic shift in this passage. His evaluation of the Pharisees and scribes is anything but gentle; He is direct and His language very strong. Seven times Jesus calls them 'hypocrites', three times 'blind', three times 'blind guides', once a 'son of hell', once 'fools', once 'serpents', and once a 'brood of vipers' (as did John the Baptist).

The passage is set in a chiastic pattern. This not only reveals the artistry of the writer, but it also marks out the emphasis of the paragraph (the fourth woe, a repeated assertion by Jesus).

A   First woe (v. 13): failure to recognize Jesus as the Messiah

B   Second woe (v. 15): superficial zeal and doing more harm than good

C   Third woe (vv. 16-22): misguided use of Scripture

D   Fourth woe (vv. 23-24): failure to understand the thrust of Scripture

C′   Fifth woe (vv. 25-26): misguided use of Scripture

B′   Sixth woe (vv. 27-28): superficial zeal and doing more harm than good

A′   Seventh woe (vv. 29-32): heirs of those who failed to recognize the prophets

Perhaps another way to envision the seven woes is this. The initial six woes seem to be organized in couplets (three couplets and a concluding climax). The first pair (vv. 13-15) is about their violence towards the kingdom of heaven, the second (vv. 16-24) about their truncated perspectives on ethics and religious practice, and the third (vv. 25-28) on the contrast between outward and inward purity. The seventh woe is expanded in length, bringing the condemnation-theme to a climax.

The Pharisees have rejected the Messiah and persecute His followers (v. 13). The meaning of 'hypocrite' is that of one who operates out of self-deceit. It is about a person who places the emphasis in the wrong place, a person who misconstrues what is important. In this case, the Pharisees and scribes have stressed minute details and missed the main point! The charge is not of insincerity or double standards, but of possessing a single, though perverted, standard. They keep people, and themselves, out of the kingdom.

[It is likely that verse fourteen is an interpolation, an addition by a later scribe. It is not found in our earliest manuscripts and those that do contain it are not consistent in its placement, some before and others after verse thirteen.[4]]

The Pharisees have false zeal (v. 15). They traveled widely to make a convert who often becomes more zealous than they (e.g. Saul of Tarsus). They have a great deal of enthusiasm, but it is misdirected. 'A child of hell' means one who belongs to and is destined for hell.

The Pharisees encourage evasive speech, double-talk to conceal (vv. 16-22). To make His point, Jesus cites two, later three, examples of their hair-splitting to gain advantage through deceptive and evasive speech in instances of oathtaking and promise-keeping. Their approach to religious practice was trivial and game-like, not addressing the most important matters. In each case, He condemns the action because it was a subterfuge to avoid the most important issues of life and faith. He does not condemn them for what they did but for the motives behind it, the avoidance of the important and essential.

His words here seem to be examples of deceptive speech reflective of Jesus' corrective instruction in 5:33-37. If a promise is sealed with a reference to the temple, it can be broken but not when the gold of the temple is invoked. The same is true of the altar or heaven; they are inherently non-binding according to the Pharisees!

In verses 16 and 17, Jesus makes a distinction between the temple and the gold of the temple. He describes the leaders as blind guides, fools, and blind men. The point is that they quibble over words to deceive. If the point of the temple is the presence of God, there is little difference whether one invokes the temple itself or its adornment. What is being invoked is the character and presence of God. What sanctifies the temple is God's presence.

---

4. See the Net Bible, note 1777, on the verse.

The distinction between the altar and the gift on the altar is dealt with in verses 18-21. The issue here is deceptive hair-splitting. The 'altar', the presence of God, is greater than the gift. The gift is sanctified by the 'altar'. To swear by the altar is to invoke God's name that is greater than the gift. The gift is lesser than the altar upon which it is placed!

The distinction of heaven and the throne of God in heaven is addressed in verse 22. This seems to be an additional example of Pharisaic hair-splitting and deception, an added thought. To swear by heaven or the throne of God is the same thing; the promise is based on the character of God.

The Pharisees misinterpret the Scriptures (vv. 23-24). This is the center of the seven laments; it is the key. The Pharisees ultimately misinterpret the Scriptures by adding their many rules to safeguard the commandments. In doing so, they have twisted the teachings of Moses, making them a burden to the people of God.

The complaint is not that they failed to take great care with the Scriptures; it is that they missed the point of them (v. 23). They stressed details and twisted the main point. They missed God's will! Their piety is miscued; they diligently stress minor points and have missed the major ones. To make the point that they missed the greater by emphasizing a small thing He mentions cumin, an aromatic herb used in seasoning food.

The weightier matters of the law have to do with 'justice, mercy, and faithfulness' (Gen. 18:19; Micah 6:8; Hab. 2:4). They avoided the small insect and indulged the camel (v. 24); they got little things right (tithing), but missed the more important ones (justice, mercy, love). The gnat was the smallest insect in that culture, the camel the largest animal. Both of these animals are unclean (Lev. 11:4, 41).

The Pharisees are occupied with external things, not the essence of true religion (vv. 25-26). The comment in the previous woe about purity laws is extended here. The Pharisees had over-extended the moral code to a ridiculous extreme. So concerned were they not to violate sacred law that they created laws beyond the intent of Scripture and emphasized those. What was meant to prevent disobedience became the 'new law'. The point is that the Pharisees' method of righteousness is all wrong.

The inside of the cup is a metaphor for the heart, internal attitudes; the outside of the cup suggests external behaviors. True religion springs from internal attitudes and virtues resulting in external modifications. They stressed the outward.

The Pharisees are outwardly pure but inwardly corrupt (vv. 27-28). In the month of Adar, the month before Passover, it was common to whitewash graves so that strangers coming to the land could readily identify them. To inadvertently touch a grave would mean you were defiled (Num. 19:16) and could not participate in the Passover. According to Jesus, the Pharisees were perverse and corrupt. The point is the contrast of value between the internal and the external. His language throughout this section is strident.

To say that the Pharisees are 'lawless' is ironic because they created more laws than Moses conceived. What Jesus likely meant is that they were such, not because they did not have laws, but they acted in conformity to their laws in contrast to the laws of God, which they disobeyed. Because they refused to submit to the laws of God, they were lawless!

The Pharisees are so ignorant of the Scriptures that they murdered the prophets (vv. 29-36). Yet they honor the tombs of the prophets. They honor the status of the prophets that God sent to Israel by building and safeguarding their burial places, but they sent the prophets there! Their piety is twisted; they profess to revere the prophets, but they are in the tradition of those who killed them.

A minor issue is whether 'prophets' and the 'righteous' are equivalents, 'tombs' and 'monuments' also. Is Jesus referring to two different groups or one? While this cannot be definitively determined, the point is that the Pharisees act in duplicity when they honor the past, but do not heed the message of the past just as their forefathers failed to do.

The Pharisees lie about their conduct toward the prophets (v. 30). They simply did not understand the seriousness of obedience the prophets demanded, nor the severe implications of their continued ignorance. Their response to religious truth is the same as those who failed to respond to the pleas of the prophets.

The action of the Pharisees revealed that they were as guilty as those who killed the prophets; they are heirs of murderers (vv. 31-32). They are liable to judgment; there is no alternative for them. Judgment awaits; it is inevitable. 'Fill up then the measure of your fathers' means to complete what their ancestors started. As they killed the prophets, the Pharisees will murder the greatest of them, Jesus!

The conclusion of Jesus is given in verses 33-36. He speaks about the doom of the Pharisees in verse 33. It is interesting that Jesus calls them a 'brood of vipers' as John had (3:7). 'Snakes' and 'brood of vipers' means snakes and the sons of snakes. The connection may be Jesus' observation that they rejected John, a prophet of repentance, and they are doing the same with the greatest of the prophets, Jesus. They have a long history of false piety. Being the 'sons of murderers', they will face inevitable judgment!

Their treatment of the 'new' prophets is stated in verse 34. Jesus explained to them that as they mistreated the prophets that announced His coming in the Hebrew Scriptures, they will do the same for His 'new' prophets, the apostles and their followers.

Jesus enumerates the types of treatment to be exacted upon those in the heritage of the prophets. The Jews did not crucify; that was a Roman punishment. What the text likely means is that the Jewish leadership would incite the Romans to punish by this means (as they did with Jesus [Acts 2:36; 4:10]). A lesser form of punishment was flogging, though still severe. Since the synagogues were religious and civil centers, justice was assessed in them (2 Cor. 11:24). The durative nature of Jewish persecution is noted by the phrase 'from town to town'; it would be persistent and inescapable (2 Cor. 11:21-27).

Their treatment of the prophets is illustrated in verse 35. Abel was the first to be murdered in the Hebrew Scriptures (Gen. 4:8); we do not know of 'Zechariah the son of Barachiah' being killed (Zech. 1:1). If he was the same individual as Zechariah the prophet, Jesus added a detail otherwise not recorded. That he was murdered in the temple, in a holy place between the altar and the sanctuary, highlights the horror of the injustice.

2 Chronicles 24:20-21 refers to a Zechariah, son of Jehoida, who was murdered as Jesus indicates. However, is the son

of Barachiah the same person as the son of Jehoida? If the identification of Zechariah, the son of Jehoida, is to be preferred, it is interesting that he was killed in the late ninth century BC. His story is found in 2 Chronicles, the last book in the Hebrew canon. Both Zechariah, the son of Jehoida, and Abel (Gen. 4:10) called out for revenge for their deaths (fitting the judgment theme in the next chapter).

Another suggested solution is to understand the son of Jehoida and the son of Barachiah as the same person, being named for his grandfather and his father. Zechariah is called the 'son of Berechiah' and the 'son of Iddo' (Zech. 1:1), thus likely indicating a father and grandfather. 'Whom you killed' links the Pharisees with the murderers of the prophets, a theme repeated in this paragraph.

Verse 36 concerns the near doom of the Pharisees. Since the lament that follows is over Jerusalem (vv. 37-39), Jesus must have in view the destruction of the city and temple in A.D. 70. 'This generation' most logically refers to those living in Jesus' day.

When asked why the first temple was destroyed, the later Jewish answer was 'idolatry, immorality and bloodshed'. In answer to the question concerning the second temple, it was because of 'hatred without cause'. This would suggest that groundless hatred and rebellion is as great a reason for guilt and judgment as the three reasons for the former judgment.

The lament of Jesus over the nation (vv. 37-39)

Jesus concludes by voicing a lament over Jerusalem, over the nation's lost privilege and opportunity. He now considered things as irreversible. They rejected Him and He has turned His back on them. Judgment waits for both Jesus and the nation, Christ on the cross and the nation in two Roman wars that destroyed the temple and dispersed the nation (A.D. 66–70 and A.D. 132–34, respectively), though what is most likely, though not exclusively, in view here is the first Roman destruction. These are the last words of Jesus to the inhabitants of the city as a whole.

Jesus begins with a rehearsal of what the city had done to God's servants in the past. He again charged the Pharisees and scribes with killing the prophets. Here the charge is applied to the people of Jerusalem. The repetition of 'Jerusalem' emphasizes the gravity of the error and the judgment to come. While Matthew records only this visit to Jerusalem, the final one, here is a hint of other trips to the city ('how often I would have …').

The heart-wrenching plea of Jesus is illustrated by a hen and her brood. The problem with the Jerusalemites was not their inability to respond to Jesus or the prophets, but their unwillingness to do so ('you would not'). The blame for Jerusalemite failure is squarely placed on their personal choice ('unwilling'). They had simply refused the offer of grace and mercy.

'Your house' (v. 38) is likely the temple itself since Jesus speaks these words in the temple courtyard, though He may be referring figuratively to the city since that appears to be the most immediate subject. The Romans ravished the city; the Jews set fire to the temple themselves.

The quotation in verse 39 is from Psalm 118:26, a text of greeting used by priests in the temple. The people of God will someday greet their Lord. When Jesus returns in the last day, in the consummation of the kingdom, all will acknowledge Him. Many more than the immediate audience would be part of the crowd requesting His crucifixion, but what Jesus means is that in a future day, when He returns, it is then that they will have changed their view and recognize the error of their ways, but it will be too late.

Jesus' point is that the breach between first-century Judaism and Himself is complete. The near-future destruction of the city, the symbol of national identity, indicates the emergence of a new people of God. The earthly focus of the presence of God has ended; yet God will still dwell among His people and also within them (but not in a physical building).

Applications

1. The Lord Jesus was the gentlest and most humble of people; He deeply cared for the pains and hurts that had fallen upon the people that He met. However, He did not sacrifice truth or a passive spirit when He confronted falsity. Jesus abhorred those who

twisted the Scriptures to their own advantage. He showed public disgust for false piety and religious showmanship. What a model is He to us? He was not weak and passive, but kind and gentle. He did not allow His humility to denigrate His understanding of truth, He was never concessive to error. He was soft in appearance, but not soft on selfishness. He could confront. Can you? Do you use meekness as a veil to hide unwarranted passivity?

2. Jesus could be stern with the folly of people, but He also cared deeply, even shedding tears. He could be harsh with the Pharisees, false and misleading shepherds, but He cared for the errantly led. Do you cry out for the people you know who are unwilling to come to the Saviour? Is your duty complete when you tell them, or does their rejection only spur you to deeper levels of care for them?

3. What kind of a world (home and church) would we live in if we shunned titles and prescriptions of our own importance and sought to serve others? Jesus tells us not to seek to be important, but to be a caregiver as opposed to a care consumer. He tells us that we should be characterized by humility, not forwardness. Is that true of you? Are you seeking recognition or are you seeking out people to help? Do you serve to be seen or to help? Is your life about you or others?

The Prophetic Announcements of the King (24:1–25:46)

This is the fifth and final discourse in the book, the so-called Olivet Discourse (24:3). Jesus delivered this after leaving the temple complex and crossing the Kidron Valley (it seems to be a distinctly separate section from chapter 23). The clue that this is a single unit is 26:1, 'when Jesus had finished all these sayings … .' The first discourse was addressed to the disciples and secondarily to the multitudes (Matt. 5–7); the four others were to the disciples.

In leaving the temple complex, symbolic of the conclusion of His ministry to the nation, perhaps after crossing the Kidron Valley, being on the Mount of Olives where the perspective of distance revealed the stunning beauty of the temple that Herod the Great took over forty years to remodel, Jesus made a comment that the temple, though a stunning structure in size and beauty, it would be destroyed (vv. 1-2). Jesus made the point that the disciples should not be deceived by the greatness of the architectural structure; it was temporal and merely a shadowed symbolism of a greater reality to come! It was grand. Tacitus, the Roman historian, spoke of the temple in Jerusalem saying, 'There stood a temple of immense wealth.'[5] Josephus described the temple complex in great detail; its beauty and costliness were beyond imagining.[6]

The tabernacle, the Solomonic temple, and Zerubbabel's temple were shadows of God's presence among His people. Christ is the true presence of God; the shadows have been abolished. As tabernacle worship ended, so with the advent of Christ temple worship ended ('… an hour is coming when neither in this mountain [Mount Gerizim] nor in Jerusalem, will you worship the Father' [John 4:21]). The departure from the temple complex is symbolic; in leaving it He has abandoned it. It is no longer the abode of the divine presence of God in the midst of a people. Further, when Jesus returns at the end of the age, He will enter the city through the same gate (Ezek. 44:1-3), the curse having been removed!

The language of temple destruction is ambiguous. It is important to the later trials of Jesus because He will be accused of speaking against the temple, a formidable religious charge (26:61) that will take the form of a taunt by the city's inhabitants while Jesus is upon the cross (27:40).

In leaving the temple complex by the Eastern Gate or Golden Gate and entering the Mount of Olives through the Kidron Valley, the disciples look back and are enthralled by the magnificence of the temple. It may be that Jesus' comment in 23:38, the city becoming desolate, occasioned the questions in their mind. They asked two questions (v. 3), and Jesus seems to answer them both ('these things'). Since they are future events, and prophetic statements in the Bible are subject to multiple fulfillments, one is before the other and the one is a picture

---

5. Tacitus, *History*, 5:8.

6. Josephus Flavius, *The Wars of the Jews*, 5.5.1-5.

of the later one. The destruction of the temple in A.D. 70 was a judgment as well as a picture of a final judgment in the more distant future. The distant, ultimate, and final coming of Christ can be seen in phrases like 'this gospel … shall be proclaimed throughout the whole world … to all nations, and then the end will come' (24:14). The nearer judgment is seen in the words 'this generation' (24:34). Thus, the Bible always speaks to God's people; we all experience judgments of one sort or another, but they are symbols of a much greater, final one (the one we will not experience). The first came because of an unwillingness to embrace the Saviour by the nation, the second by the nations. The first would come in 'this generation', Jesus being confident of the nearness of the event; the second was not near and Jesus makes it clear that He does not know the time of it (v. 36).

The phrase, 'end of the age,' occurs six times in the Greek Scriptures, five times in Matthew. It always looks to the final judgment and the consummation of the age. This would suggest that we have two judgments here, one in the near future ('these things' referring to the destruction of the temple) and the other at the end of time, the former being a shadow of the final one ('the sign of your coming and of the end of the age' [v. 3]). There is unity in these two questions because each deals with judgment though there is a lapse of time between them.

What makes this discourse difficult to understand is that Jesus blends the two judgments, the symbolism of the near being a shadow of a distant reality. Practical instruction in answering the first question applies to the second as well.

The initial question answered (vv. 4-31)
The 'all these' (v. 2), referring to the temple complex, causes the disciples to ask when the destruction will occur (v. 3). The disciples see the destruction of the temple and the last judgment as coterminous events. Jesus separates the two, creating a time-space between them, though both are terrific catastrophes.

In verses 4-14, Jesus tells the disciples that various signs will make the coming destruction of the temple predictable, but the final judgmental coming of the Lord at the end of the age is not. He foresees the grievous trouble that will come upon His followers in the days ahead (23:37-38), but He does not let them forget the certainty of His final triumph (v. 14). The final coming of great judgment is not subject to a discernible time frame. Jesus is saying that it is important for the disciples to separate the Jerusalem destruction from the final end-time destruction. The Jerusalem destruction could be seen as defeat for God's people, but in the final judgment there will be vindication!

External signs of the coming destruction of the temple are mentioned in verses 4-8. The times will be difficult after the Lord's ascension for the nation, as well as for the church. It will be easy to be confused by a series of tragic events and false promises of deliverance. The 'for' that begins verse 5 indicates that Jesus told the disciples about the reasons for the rise of religious deception that will characterize the era of turmoil ending in the destruction of the temple.

There will be self-proclaimed saviors (v. 5). We know from the writings of Josephus that several persons claimed to be the promised political deliverer, a prophet, in the tumultuous decades before the outbreak of the Jewish revolt in A.D. 66, which led to the destruction of Jerusalem in A.D. 70 and Masada in A.D. 73.[7] Theudas assembled four hundred deluded followers and was later killed (Acts 5:36); Judas of Galilee fomented a similar uprising (Acts 5:37). Some 30,000 followed an Egyptian according to Josephus. The point is that Jesus' warning about false prophets is validated within the Bible and from secular sources. What Jesus desires the disciples to firmly understand is that all other 'Messiahs' are false and deceptive, leading to destruction, not deliverance, for the deluded.

There will be wars, famines, and earthquakes (vv. 6-8). International conflicts will happen, Jesus assures the

---

7. Josephus Flavius, *History of the Jews*, 20:5:1. 'Now it came to pass, while Fadus was procurator of Judea, that a certain magician, whose name was Theudas, persuaded a great part of the people to take their effects with them, and follow him to the river Jordan; for he told them he was a prophet, and that he would, by his own command, divide the river, and afford them an easy passage over it; and many were deluded by his words.' Also, 'And besides this, the sons of Judas of Galilee were now slain; I mean of that Judas who caused the people to revolt, when Cyrenius came to take an account of the estates of the Jews, as we have showed in a foregoing book' (20.5.2).

disciples, but they are not to be deceived by them. They are not evidence of the end of the age, but only the approach of Jerusalem's destruction. It is often in times of uncertainty and fear that people find hope in false promises. The longing for security often comes at the expense of insight and wisdom, leading to loss. Turbulent times create false hopes!

While the Roman Empire was stable militarily between Christ's death and the outbreak of the Jewish revolt in A.D. 66, there were several clashes before and after A.D. 36 in Parthia, the eastern perimeter of the empire. Herod Antipas fought the Nabeteans (the daughter of King Aretas was divorced by Antipas who married the former wife of his brother Herod, Herodias [the issue that led to John the baptizer's murder]), and the subsequent military intervention involved the Roman legions and the defeat of Aretas, though Herod Antipas suffered defeat at his hands initially. Roman legions were required to end the revolts of Theudas and an unnamed Egyptian in Palestine in A.D. 66. Rulership in the empire destabilized in A.D. 68 with four emperors in rapid succession until Vespasian assumed the throne in A.D. 69 and who left the Jewish revolt to be quelled by his son and successor Titus.

Earthquakes occurred in Asia Minor in A.D. 61, Italy in A.D. 62, and Jerusalem in A.D. 67. Matthew mentions one at the time of Jesus' death (27:51); Luke tells us of one at Philippi (Acts 16:26). We also know that a worldwide famine occurred during the reign of Emperor Claudius around A.D. 46 (Acts 11:28). These are normal occurrences, according to Jesus, and they should not lead to panic or placing our hope in some political deliverance knowing that they are only shadows, pictures of a harsh reality in the future. 'All these are but the beginnings of birth pains' refers to the period of distress and suffering before the return of Jesus. It is the period between the advents as a whole. Persecution characterizes the age.

'All these' (v. 8) are the beginnings of the tragedy that characterizes the era between the advents of Christ. Moreover, they are evidence of the nearness of Jewish judgment (A.D. 70), but not of the end of the age and the fullest manifestation of the kingdom with Christ's return.

In speaking about life and the community of faith (vv. 9-14), Jesus applies what He had argued in verses 4-8.

Since our Lord's return in judgment is only shadowed by the destruction of Jerusalem, Jesus alerts the disciples as to what it will be like for them in the immediate years ahead (and by application to us).

There will be persecutions and defections (vv. 9-10). Jesus previously told the disciples in the instructions of chapter 10 that persecution would be their lot (v. 22a); here He makes the point once more. However, while Jesus' comment in chapter 10 was part of a Jewish mission, here it is extended to 'all nations'. Stephen was martyred (Acts 7); James, brother of John, was murdered (Acts 12:2). Peter and Paul were killed in Rome in the 60s. Hostility and rejection characterized Paul's missionary endeavors. The word translated 'nations' (v. 9) can be as easily translated as 'Gentiles'. As a result of harsh circumstances, some will apostatize from the faith entirely (v. 10). Demas is, perhaps, an example of this (2 Tim. 4:10). See Matthew 10:22. There will be deceptive prophets (v. 11) and increase of evil and flagging love (v. 12).

Yet there will be alternative sureties (vv. 13-14). Jesus makes three points: true faith is enduring faith, the message of the gospel will expand in the midst of difficulties to the ends of the earth, and when the time appointed comes, so the end of time (24:3b) with the Lord's return. Perseverance is the fruit of biblical faith since its essence is love expressed to God. We are not saved because we persist; we persist because we are saved (the phrase is also found in 10:22b). Those who stand firm in their faith possess the promise of divine safekeeping.

Despite the persecutions of our age, it will not prevent the proclamation of the gospel worldwide (v. 14). The worldwide dissemination of the gospel is not the cause of the end of time, but the accompanying circumstance. It seems inescapable that the reference here is not to A.D. 70, but to the coming final judgment since the worldwide proclamation of the gospel was not accomplished by A.D. 70 (unless we take the 'world' of that day to mean that the ministry of Paul in Spain was 'to the ends of the world'). The 'gospel' is about the content of the claims of Christ and His accomplishments at Calvary; it is bearing witness to what Christ has done, not a challenge for people to do something for themselves.

Specific signs of the coming judgment are given in verses 15-22. The Lord describes a particular time within the period when there will be intense stress. Since Jesus is speaking to the disciples ('when you see' [v. 15]), it would seem that the immediate fulfillment of judgment concerns the destruction of Jerusalem and the temple complex. Further, Jesus makes the point subsequently that there are no signs of His final coming, though there are signs of the nearness of the judgment in A.D. 70.

The beginning of the Jewish revolt against the empire began in Caesarea in A.D. 66. Vespasian, the Roman general in charge of quelling the rebellion, had conquered most of the land by A.D. 68 (the Romans later, following the Bar Kochva rebellion of 132–134, renamed the area Palestine or 'Palestina' to remove any evidence of Jewish claim and suggesting that the ancient claimants were the Philistines). Internal political unrest in Rome caused the suspension of the final operations in A.D. 68–69 with the quick succession of several emperors. During that period, the Jews struggled in civil/religious conflict over the control of the temple complex leading to internal conflict. This greatly weakened the defense of Jerusalem when the Romans returned in A.D. 69. When Vespasian became emperor, his son Titus commanded the operation in Judea.

The meaning of the 'abomination of desolation,' 'the abomination that causes desolation' (NIV), is uncertain (v. 15); it obviously refers to a horrendous event that will take place in the temple. The citation of Daniel 9:27 is interesting. It speaks of invasion from the north of an army that defiles the temple. Most scholars take the Daniel reference to be the desecration of the temple in 167 B.C. by Antiochus Epiphanes, the Syrian, who discontinued Jewish worship and installed a pagan shrine to Zeus where swine and other unclean animals were sacrificed. This outrage led to the Maccabean Revolt in 168 B.C. (1 Maccabees 1:41-61).

If so, Jesus is implying that the desecration of 167 B.C. was a shadowed prefiguring of another that is in the near future. It would most likely then refer to the desecration of the Temple in A.D. 70. The final fulfillment of the 'abomination' will be, as Daniel predicted (8:13; 9:27; 11:31), at the end of the age.

In the setting of the Jewish Revolt, the destruction of Jerusalem and the temple, the 'abominable thing' would not be the Roman desecration of the temple because at the time it would be too late to flee. The Romans built a siege wall around Jerusalem and sealed it off from any possible escape before assaulting the city (vv. 16-20). It would appear that the desolation was the internal fighting among the Jews for the temple complex (the Romans destroyed the city, but Jewish fighting among themselves destroyed the temple complex). It thus may be a reference to what the Jews themselves did to the temple through internecine strife. 'Holy place' means the temple complex.

Jesus gave specific instructions concerning the judgment's nearness (vv. 16-22). The importance of haste is stated. The description of events is not confined to A.D. 66–70, though much of the language relates to the Jewish Wars. The mentioning of 'Judea' (v. 16) suggests a time before Rome completed its conquest and sealed off Jerusalem. Apparently, there was still time to escape. The Roman siege and sealing of the city would come rapidly so the readers must move quickly to avoid it. Jesus expects this event to take place while the strict Sabbath law was in effect (v. 20).

'Mountains' (v. 16) were traditional places of refuge offering difficult places for pursuers to access. Not going 'down from the rooftop' (v. 17) might suggest haste to escape by leaping from roof to roof and avoiding the dangerous streets (a reference to chaos in the city, not the temple complex). Haste to flee means that retrieval of valuables becomes unimportant (v. 18). Here may be another clue that the instructions are prior to the siege since people are working fields. Flight is hindered if there are children (v. 19), poor weather, or Sabbath restrictions on mobility (v. 20) because distance was prohibited.

Greater devastations have occurred in subsequent holocausts than in the fall of Jerusalem, but never has such a high percentage of a single city's population been exterminated or enslaved (97,000). It seems that verse 21 refers to the final judgment ('a great tribulation' never to be repeated) while verse 20 refers to A.D. 70. Jesus mixes the judgments with an unseen time span between them. However, it must be remembered that what is used here is prophetic/apocalyptic language that is characterized by overstatement to make a point graphic (these verses may refer to the same event in A.D. 70). The world wars were horrible 'tribulations' in the twentieth century, each claiming millions of lives, sometimes in a single battle (the Russians in World War I lost over a million in a battle) or the holocausts (the Turks and over two million Armenians; the Nazis and six million Jews; Stalin and some twenty-two millions of his own people; Pol Pot and the Khmer Rouge; Rwanda's ethnic cleansing). We have had several holocausts greater than the Roman devastation of Israel. Clearly, tragedies will occur, but not quite like this one.

'And if those days had not been cut short' (v. 22) may be a reference to the Romans taking the city after it had suffered famine for five months in the siege. Because of God's people in the city, He determined to end the siege before all life was lost. We do know that the siege was momentarily lifted when Vespasian left for Rome and Titus replaced him; at that point many fled the city. However, 'had not been since the beginning of world' may hint to the great flood in Noah's day (see 24:36-39; Peter connects the final destruction with the Noahic Flood in 2 Peter 3:4-6); in such a case, the destruction of A.D. 70 was a tragic shadow of a much greater one to come at the end of this age.

The parables that follow make the point of a time lapse before the coming of Christ for the final judgment; it is not as near as A.D. 70, though A.D. 70 may have been a shadow of it. It seems that Jesus combines the judgments but does not alert the disciples to the length of time between them.

The warnings in verses 23-26 refer to the general period of distress between the advents. The near fulfillment is A.D. 70 and the final fulfillment at the end of the age. The delusion of the false prophets is mentioned in these verses. In times of desperation, people place hope in the frailest of realities, often the false. Prophets will come claiming to be able to bring deliverance, but they are not to be believed. The deliverer will not come to some obscure place in which He must be sought out. It will be apparent to all.

The suddenness of the coming judgment is stated in verses 27-28. The second, final coming of the promised One will not be a drawn-out process; it will be sudden and without warning.

There are no signs of the nearness of the final coming of Jesus in judgment. As lightning fills the sky so that everyone sees it, so when Christ returns no one will miss it. It will be manifestly bold, sudden, and inescapable. He will fill the sky with His glory. No one will need to point it out! The KJV rendering 'eagles' is correctly translated 'vultures'. Eagles are not carrion eaters. This is a proverb; as surely as you see vultures around dead animals, you will see the coming of the end of the age. The spiritually dead will attract judgment as dead animals attract vultures. 'Son of Man' is again a reference to Daniel 7:13-14 and the authority given by God to Jesus to rule. It is the term Jesus most frequently used of Himself in this gospel.

The coming judgment is described in verses 29-31. Having contrasted the near judgment with the final judgment (vv. 27-28), that there will be signs of the near one but suddenness in the distant one, Jesus speaks in more detail about the former. The point is that the disciples should not place hope in promises of deliverance from false prophets/messiahs.

The key to understanding verse 29 must begin with the referent to 'after those days'. 'Those days' contextually refer to the near destruction in A.D. 70 (v. 30); Jesus warns His disciples not to connect the near destruction with the final one. The quotations found in this verse appear to be taken from Isaiah 13:10 and 34:4, though similar imagery may be found in Ezekiel 32:7-8; Amos 8:9; and Joel 2:10, 30-31; 3:15. The Isaiah 13:10 passage describes the destruction of Babylon and 34:4 describes Edom. Such imagery as found here is used in the prophets to suggest severity of judgment; it need not be taken literally (the things described did not literally occur in the judgment of these two nations). It seems to be a reference to distress in the spiritual realm rather than literal stellar bodies. The vivid language connects the destruction of Jerusalem with Babylon and Edom; the destruction will be as thorough as that of those nations! It may be that Jesus is describing the coming destruction of Jerusalem, yet the language seems to speak of more than that. The two comings seem to be intertwined (as in verse 27).

Verse 30 speaks clearly of the final coming of Jesus. The appearance of the Son of Man and the recognition of the failure to embrace Him does not fit the destruction of

A.D. 70. Jesus, the Daniel 7:13-14 figure, the Son of Man, was enthroned as King in the triumph of His resurrection and ascension. Coming in the 'clouds' is a metaphor of victory that seems to belong to the end-of-times, the final victory (Jesus is enthroned by virtue of His triumph, but the nations have not experienced it. Jesus does not appear to be enthroned, though He is, and the nations will see it someday). Further, Jesus was not seen as the Messiah-figure by the nations in A.D. 70.

The exact meaning of 'the sign' in heaven is uncertain. It may be an outward sign, or it could be the coming of the Son of Man Himself, a view perhaps finding support in the disciples' initial question (24:3). The allusion to the mourning of the nations is to Zechariah 12:10-14. 'All the tribes of the earth' is broader than Zechariah's reference to the nation in 12:10. Zechariah 12:11 indicates that there would be widespread mourning over the rejection of the Messiah; again, there is no hint of this in A.D. 70. Prophetic literature creates a picture and is not to be read with minute literality. Jesus applies the Zechariah passage to the nations or peoples of the world.

The universal gathering of God's elect from the earth is also an end-of-times event (v. 31). Christ's coming involves judgment and redemption, one of the unwilling and the other of the chosen!

Exhortations in view of the coming judgments (24:32-44)

Jesus turns from the signs that precede the coming judgment (both near and distant) to explain the kind of conduct required of His followers in view of that certainty as they await it. The point implied is that it is not immediate, a view that plagued the disciples' thinking (Luke 19:11). The parables that follow have to do with a single theme: preparedness and diligence in light of a delay. 'Be anticipating, be working, and be prepared for a long delay' is the theme. Again, Jesus is blending the answer to the disciples' dual question (v. 3), the destruction of the temple complex and His final return at the end of the age, the first a shadow of the second.

The near judgment: the parable of the fig tree (24:32-35)

As the leafed fig tree indicates the advent of summer, be aware that the coming of the Lord is near. There are no real clues as to the exact day, but it will come with suddenness as did the flood in Noah's day (the universal flood being a picture of a later universal judgment). The suddenness of His coming should cause us to be as alert as if we knew when a thief would break into our homes (vv. 43-44).

It is a common observation that trees bud and leaf indicating the coming of summer (vv. 32-33). 'All these things' likely refer to what believers can expect in the period of distress (vv. 4-28), the period between the advents. The Jerusalem destruction will have anticipatory portent, the second coming will not; it will be sudden and complete. The lesson of the parable of the leafy fig tree is that the presence of evidence should indicate a subsequent reality (vv. 34-35); that is, as the leaf suggests fruit, so signs suggest the nearness of the judgment of A.D. 70.

'This generation' likely refers to the generation of Jesus' day. Matthew uses the term several times (see 1:17; 23:36-38) and it is literally used of those living at a particular time. This is most clearly seen in 23:36-38 where Jesus states that those who reject Him will see the destruction of the temple (v. 38). Another way to interpret 'this generation', however, is to relate the phrase to the people who see the sign of the end or final coming of Christ (v. 30). In that case, the events of A.D. 70 were a shadow of the final one. Jesus seems to mix the judgments. The distress came in the Jewish wars as stated, but it did not end with the Jewish wars; it is characteristic of the times before the final judgment.

D.A. Carson follows the thought of John Calvin suggesting that 'this generation' is best interpreted in a generic fashion as descriptive of any generation.[8] While the phrase specifically applies to the Jerusalem destruction, it is not exhausted in meaning by it. All the things described in verses 4-28 occurred in 'this generation', but were not exhausted or fully fulfilled in 'this generation'. 'This generation' experienced the signs that will be evident in every generation.

If there ever was a ground for hope in the coming of the Saviour, here it is (v. 35). Material things are not durative, but God's promises are sure! Here we also have a clear

---

8. D. A. Carson, *Matthew*, p. 507.

Christological assertion of the veracity of Jesus' character; He will keep His word!

In regard to the final coming in judgment (vv. 36-44)
The 'but' of verse 36 introduces a contrast between the two comings of Jesus in judgment (one near and predictable, the other distant and unpredictable; one in A.D. 70 and the other at the end of the age; one a shadow and the other the fulfillment, one involving the employ of a nation [Rome] to be the instrument of judgment, the other angels from heaven). The change of subject becomes apparent for the following reasons.

First, the use of the words 'but concerning'; this phrase appears in 22:31 where there is clearly a change of subject. Second, 'that day and hour' is singular (a singular event) while in verses 19, 22, and 29 the 'those days' is plural suggesting multiple events (the Roman campaign). Third, the judgment in verses 4-34 is predictable, but the event of verses 36-44 is not. Fourth, the event of verses 4-35 has temporal connections, but the event of verses 36-44 does not (there are no signs for it).

What Jesus tells us is that the time of His coming is unknown (v. 36), that it will catch people by surprise and unpreparedness (vv. 37-41), and that we should always be ready (vv. 42-44). Jesus does not answer their second question (v. 3); there are no signs of His second coming!

'That day and hour' (v. 36) refers to the second half of the disciples' two requests (v. 3). Matthew has already referred to 'the day of judgment' (10:15; 11:22, 24; 12:36) and 'that day' (7:22). Jesus is the judge in 7:22 on 'that day'. He will one day sit on His throne judging the nations (13:41; 16:27-28; 19:28). That only the Father knows the time of His Son's return in judgment is interesting, one of those things that causes us to scratch our heads in wonder!

Since the time of His coming cannot be known, it will be a surprise just as the Noahic flood judgment came upon the people in Genesis 7:6-24 (vv. 37-39). The universal, cataclysmic destruction of the flood is used as a vivid analogy of a judgment to come. Peter uses the same illustration about the scoffers of his day that denied that the Lord would come in judgment (2 Pet. 3:4). He is coming; there are no warning signs to alert people so we must be ready.

A second illustration comes from the routine of domestic life (vv. 40-42); people going about the duties of life, unaware of larger events, will be entrapped by them. The one 'taken' is not explained; it may be to judgment; it may be to rescue. It would seem, however, that the point is to judgment, fitting the flood illustration that preceded it. The point is clear; be alert and waiting for the Lord's return. The 'Son of Man' (v. 39) is here designated as the Lord, the sovereign master.

A third illustration concerns burglary (vv. 43-44). Every burglar relies on the advantage of surprise; he/she counts on the fact that the occupants are not alert for one reason or another. The message is simply that, since the coming of Christ may be at any time, we must be ready.

Duties in light of the final judgment (24:45–25:46)

Since the Lord's return in the final judgment can be at any time, the exhortation of Jesus is that His disciples should be alert and ready. In the three parables that follow Jesus tells His disciples what they should be doing as they expectantly wait.

Be doing: the faithful slave (24:45-51)

Knowledge of the any-moment, sudden coming of Christ in the final judgment should not paralyze us into inactivity, nor should the delay of His coming cause sluggishness and apathy. A good slave is one whose master finds him working when he comes. Jesus starts with a question and thereby seeks the interaction of His disciples (v. 45). They can answer the question themselves after hearing the story.

Slaves in Jewish culture often held very responsible positions; slavery did not carry the onus of racial inferiority and liability to exploitation. The obedient servant is characterized by compliance and trustworthiness. The reward of faithfulness is greater responsibility, more diligence being required (vv. 46-47). A disobedient slave is described in verses 48-51. In each of the three following parables (25:1-46), the issue of extended absenteeism is an excuse for faithless indolence.

The slave's faithlessness is revealed in disobedience to his master's orders; instead of providing for the household, he abused his charge. Absenteeism, however, does not indicate the master's failure to keep his promise of return. How are we to understand the brutal execution of the faithless slave? 'Cut to pieces' should not be taken literally because in the next phrase the slave is alive. The meaning seems to be that of severe consequences.

Remember that this is a parable; it is designed to convey a single message. In this case, it is the need for obedience while the master is absent. The faithless servant is not the point of the story and should not be used to teach doctrine. Parables illustrate a truth; they are stories that illustrate a lesson.

Applications

1. It is important that we are not beguiled by mere appearances. What seems outwardly secure, stable, and enduring whether it be buildings, marriages, or the progressive maturing of our children may be a myth. Outward circumstances may hide markedly different inward realities. The temple was truly one of the great architectural wonders of the world; it must have appeared glorious and permanent; today it is gone with only a few stones as its witness. What often appears durative is frequently a passing shadow. Are you chasing shadows that look real, but will be tomorrow's vapors? Do you see beyond the outward crust of religion to the deep realities of true religion? Where is your hope of security (a home, children, a mate, the workplace, extended family, friends, or Christ)?

2. International conflicts, persecution, false teachers, and natural disasters characterize the age between the advents of Christ; 'birth pangs' they are called. There is no specific evidence of the near coming of the Lord simply because such things have been with us since the beginning of the church (and actually before that if you read the Hebrew Scriptures). There is no political or technological remedy that will end wars, natural disasters, and catastrophic diseases. They characterize life's experiences in a fallen, corrupted, judged earth. However, there is hope; such circumstances will not last forever. The ruler of the universe will return someday,

judge His enemies, and restore life to a pre-fall, pristine state. Are you looking forward to that great day?

3. Jesus' promises will all come true, His pledges of justice as well as those of grace and mercy. He promised two judgments; one near and one far, one regional and one global, one executed by a military power and one by His angels; one was predictable because its approach could be seen and the other has no predictability, only certainty. One has come true as He stated it would, a nation collapsed, a city destroyed, the symbol of God's presence obliterated. The second is yet to come. The first is a shadow of a greater one to come. Do you believe that Jesus can come back at any moment and that He will with suddenness? If so, how has this altered how you live, the choices you make, the values that guide your life? Are you living in hope of Christ's return, or is this world your hope?

4. When the hard times come that are so much a part of life in this fallen world, where do you turn for help, perspective, and comfort? Many in our culture turn to sedatives to dull the pain of human existence such as prescription and illegal drugs, the momentary pleasures such as entertainment, credit card-funded vacations, sex, alcohol, overeating, or obsession with Facebook and Twitter. Some turn to extravagant claims of politicians, televangelists, and financial get-rich schemes offering peace and prosperity. These are all false messiahs, false objects of hope and trust. Where are you teaching your children to find their security? Where do you find yours? Jesus said that in troubled times pied pipers will be many, but do not listen to them. If it is too good to be true, it is likely not true!

5. Perseverance in the things of God is evidence that we are the children of God. Salvation is something that cannot be lost, and the grand evidence of its continuance is love for the things of God. What are we to be doing as we wait for the Lord's return, not knowing the time when it will occur (tomorrow, next year, the next century,

the next millennium)? We are to be going about the business of providing for our households. Obedience to the instructions of the absentee master is the surest sign of our loyalty to Him. We are not to be sitting on our hands or worrying about what might happen tomorrow; we are to be diligent in providing for our families. Is that true of you? Are you more heavenly minded than earthly minded? Do you see raising your children, caring for your domestic responsibilities, or making an honest living your obedience to God?

6. When Jesus returns at the end of the age, it will be to judge His enemies and gather His children. Since we do not know the day of His return, we should act with urgency to tell of Christ and what great peace there is in knowing that we no longer need to fear God's judgment. Christ bore it for us!

7. The point of the Lord's instruction, that His return can be at any moment, is to remind us of the need to be alert and diligent about how we use our days. Being prepared for His coming means being about His interests now, not our own interests. Do you find yourself often preoccupied with your temporal interests while eternity's interests slip by neglected? Temporal interests are important and necessary, but are those things all you think about regarding the filling of your days?

Be prepared: the parable of the ten virgins (25:1-13)
The point of the parable is that you cannot get ready quickly for the coming of the Lord; we must live in a state of preparedness. This parable deals with the inception of the consummated kingdom at the end of the age.

The role of the female virgins in the parable was to escort the bride and bridegroom from the bride's home to that of his parents with singing and dancing. The five foolish virgins brought oil, but not enough to illumine the torches if a delay would have occurred. They did not anticipate the length of the groom's delay. The wise virgins were prepared for the delay, bringing sufficient quantities of oil. The issue of their sleeping is not something they are reprimanded for doing, the delay making it understandable. In fact, it may have been the better part of wisdom to avoid weariness.

In the first century, the Jewish marriage ritual was composed of several stages: a parentally-arranged contract between the two families, the betrothal or engagement period of several months when the marriage was finalized but not consummated (the wife continued to live with her parents), the event when the husband came to her house to take her to his parents' house, the wedding ceremony in the bride's home, and his return to his home with his bride where the marriage would be consummated with celebrations that could last a week. By tradition this occurred on a Wednesday if the bride was a virgin, Thursday if she was a widow. The procession from the bride's home normally took place at night. This is the setting of the parable; friends accompanied the procession to the groom's home.

The procession in the night necessitated torches to light the way; obviously, without oil there could be no light. Consequently, those without oil could have no part in the big event. Sharing the oil by the wise girls would have not been prudent, since enough becomes not enough if shared. Also, the duty of alertness cannot be shared; all have the obligation to be alert.

Remember, a parable illustrates one point only with additional data to fill and make the story complete. This parable is not teaching the loss of salvation for the non-alert, but the need to be alert for His sudden coming.

Verse 13 states a command and the reason for it. Be alert; the Lord's return will be without warning.

Be diligent: the parable of the talents (25:14-30)

The third of the parables on readiness returns to the theme of the first one, slave and master relationships. It is a story about the exercise of responsibility in the interim absence of the master. It explains what it means to be alert.

While the preceding parable teaches the importance of being ready for the Lord's return, this parable teaches what readiness means. It means that we are to be actively involved in the interests of the master while he is away (vv. 14-15). The distribution of the master's wealth was in terms of responsibilities to invest in the master's interests. The amount of the responsibilities varied, but that is not the point of the story.

Scholars are not certain as to the value of a talent; obviously, it is a considerable sum. It could be a unit of weight or metallic value (gold, silver, copper, brass). The five-talent man went eagerly and skilfully about his duties and doubled his master's investment. Obedience is the outward expression of heart affection. The two-talent man did the same and the master would benefit. The one-talent man did nothing with the master's money except hide it, revealing that he had not really come to know his master. Burying the talent, a common practice to protect valuables at that time, meant there was no possibility for loss. However, preservation of the investment was not the instruction; it was to invest for the sake of gain.

The master's return and the reckoning with the servants is described in verses 19-30. The parable teaches that the way one conducts oneself in the time before the Lord returns is clear indication of one's relationship to Him. Obedience resulting in diligence indicates that we believe in the Master; indolence shows that we do not really know Him.

This parable has remarkable similarities to the parable Jesus told in Luke 19:11-27 near Jericho as He was making His last trip to Jerusalem. There the story was that of the minas; Jesus, like any itinerant teacher, told similar stories in different contexts to different crowds.

'After a long time' is a theme in each of the three parables. With regard to the rewarded five-talents man, it is interesting that though the money was large, the master's reply was that he was faithful in 'a few things'. While the achievements differed between the first two slaves, they received similar rewards. The reward for faithfulness is additional responsibility.

More detail is given about the punished one-talent man (vv. 24-30). He did not know his master except as a hard taskmaster; he knew nothing of his grace. Grace is the wellspring of obedience. He returned the talent, but nothing more. He disobeyed, revealing his lack of love for the master. Motivated by fear, he was unwilling to risk the master's investment. Exacting interest from fellow Jews was prohibited (Exod. 22:25), but not from Gentiles (Deut. 23:20).

His performance did not match his profession, which reveals an empty profession based on a misunderstanding of the master's character. It is interesting that in repeating the slave's words about the master, Jesus dropped the words 'a hard man'.

Remember that this is a story, a parable designed to teach a single lesson, but with details that fill out the story. The story is not about salvation and the loss of it through dereliction; it is about duty reflective of the Lord's instruction while He is absent. 'So' (v. 28) indicates that the judgment on the wicked slave was just.

The certainty of the final coming and the final judgment (25:31-46)

Jesus ends the Olivet Discourse by assuring the disciples of His final coming in glory and judgment at the end of the age. There will be a final judgment of the peoples of the earth and a separation: sheep and goats, wheat and tares (13:24-30, 36-43). This section is more of a discourse than a parable. In the judgment at the end of the age, there will be some surprises. The passage is about the role of works; works are the evidence of salvation, being integral to the rebirth by the Spirit of God. They are not the cause of grace, or salvation would not be by grace, but by works. This is the last public teaching of the disciples in the book.

Usually sheep and goats graze together during the day. At night, they are separated because sheep can tolerate cold, and goats do not. The idea of separation of a herd by kinds was then given deeper symbolism by Jesus.

The destiny of the sheep and goats will be verified by their treatment of the Lord through their treatment of His children. Heaven is not entered through kindness; it is entered through a change of character by the grace of God that produces kindness and innocence, not selfishness and hardness of heart (evidence of an untouched heart).

The 'Son of Man' (v. 31) is also identified as the 'king', a designation that only occurs here by Jesus in the book. Those on His right, the sheep, are invited to inherit the kingdom. Notice that the kingdom, eternal salvation, is inherited; it is not earned; it is a gift usually granted upon a parent's death.

This inheritance is sure because it was planned to be so before time; our redemption is not an afterthought!

The basis of the judgment is explained in verses 35-40. The evidence for the validity of the invitation is works; the sheep belong to the kingdom because God has implanted His life and character in them. In these verses six evidential actions are mentioned. The six examples of the action of 'the sheep' do not constitute the cause of their salvation, but the evidence of it. Works is a response to grace, not the cause of grace.

The unrighteous are doomed to eternal judgment even as the wicked angelic beings are, including Satan. The abode of 'the goats' is with those who perpetuate evil. The basis of their judgment is the same as the evidence of righteousness, though for the wicked the criteria are absent. The picture of the wicked is that of a people consumed in self-interest. They seek their own benefit by ingratiating themselves to the rich and powerful in the world, neglecting the needy.

The separation of believers from unbelievers will occur when the Lord returns in His glory, glory meaning the manifestation of His character, the former to life and the latter to unending condemnation.

Within evangelical circles of recent vintage the reality of an eternal punishment of the wicked has been challenged. It has generally taken two forms: temporal punishment followed by annihilation (the most prominent evangelical being John Stott to argue for this) and universalism (as in *Love Wins* by Rob Bell). Yet if there is no hell, there is no punishment; if there is no punishment, there is no right or wrong; if there is no right or wrong, there is no justice; if there is no justice, there is no grace; if there is no grace, there is no reason for a redeemer, if there is no redeemer, there is no holy God! Without the law, a declaration of right and wrong, there is no 'good news' because there is no sin! Without hell there is no gospel!

Applications

1. The lesson of the parable of the ten virgins is that we should live with a constant expectation of the Lord's return because there are no specific signs of its nearness. It will come with suddenness. The way to live with

preparedness is to conduct our lives in such a way that we would not be embarrassed by any action, should it be our last one. Are you living in such a manner, in some area of your life, that you would find inappropriate should the Lord return in the context of that manner of living? Are you prepared for His coming?

2. Because the Lord's return will be without any warning indicators, except perhaps for those things that characterize the tragedies of the centuries, it is easy to grow slack as the foolish virgins and not be alert. The Lord would have us live in the delightful anticipation of His return. Is there a possibility that the Lord will find you 'snoozing' when He comes? Are you enjoying this life so very much that it has dulled your anticipation of the joyful return of the Lord? What does it mean to you to be awake, not asleep, waiting for His coming?

3. A point not to miss in this trilogy of parables is the fact that what is sure is that the Lord will return. When He comes, He will judge His enemies, separate believers from unbelievers, and establish His full reign over His people in a renovated and restored world. This world is not the best of all possible worlds; it is a cursed one. Do you recognize the temporality of this world in which you are living? Do you know that a better world is coming? Are you teaching your children that this world is not heaven? Are you filling them with the implications that someday God will make for us a better place?

4. While the King is away, before He returns, we should be busy about the Lord's work, using what He has given each of us for His glory. It is clear from the parable of the talents that our duty is to take the gifts, investments, and opportunities that God has granted to each and use them for His benefiting, not merely to erect our own private kingdoms. Is that true of you? Are you using your privileges for self-gain and aggrandizement, even pleasure, and not using what you have in the service of the King? What talents have you been given that you

are not using for the King? How do you think that you can change that?

5. The use or non-use of our abilities for the Lord reveals our heart's condition. It is neither our words nor our smiles that reveal our truest commitments; it is our values lived out in our actions. Love and respect are revealed by obedience and conformity. The mark of a child of God is that they have an interest in the things that interest God. Are you busy in the interests of the Lord or are you hiding your giftedness? What should you be doing for God that you are not?

6. The reward of the Lord's pleasure on our activities is not proportionate to the productivity of our labor, but to the diligence in our labors. The Lord looks at our heart-attitudes and willingness to serve more than outcomes. We are variously gifted, and some abilities of service lend themselves to greater obvious fruit than others. God sends us to different places to serve Him; some are harder than others and fruit is far, far less. Some will never see the consequences of their labors because someone else will reap the fruit. The reward for being a Christian is eternal life with the Lord. Heaven is a classless society, not hierarchical; we will all be blessed of the Lord. How does this help you to understand your duties? How does this relate to the work that you do? Do you serve God to get rewards from Him or because you have His pleasure already?

7. There is going to be a judgment day for all of us. That judgment will be based on our works because our works are the evidence of our true values, what we consider most important. Works do not save us, the best of them being finite and blemished by selfishness; but our works tell us where our heart-affections reside. Do you seek to serve God because you have experienced His grace and desire to respond in behavioral gratitude? Or do you think that He is a hard taskmaster and are reluctant to be involved in His interests? How do you know Him, as a caring master or as a feared judge?

The Suffering and Death of the King (26:1–27:66)

Several things are striking about the passion narratives. First, while the four gospel writers select various incidences from our Lord's life and ministry to develop their particular themes, as well as their biases (Matthew clearly reveals his Galilean perspective with only one recording of a visit to Jerusalem), the recounting of the death and resurrection becomes much more uniform in perspective.

Second, the gospel writers present Jesus as in control of the events that would eventually bring about His death. He is clearly not a victim of circumstances beyond His power. He gives instructions about preparations for His last days telling the disciples what is going to happen with considerable detail.

Third, Jesus sees the events of the last week as a fulfillment of what the prophets predicted. He is confident that what would happen was completely within the divine will of God (Acts 2:22-23). The dispersal of the disciples (26:31), the disavowal of Peter (26:34), the tearing of the temple curtain (27:51), an earthquake and resurrection of saints from the graves (27:52-53), and the resurrection of the Lord (28:6) were predicted centuries before their occurrence.

The preparation for the King's suffering and death (26:1-46)

The phrase, 'when Jesus had finished all these sayings,' is Matthew's manner of alerting the reader to the conclusion of a discourse (this is the fifth occurrence of the phrase in the gospel). In this case, it not only marks the end of a discourse, but the conclusion of our Lord's earthly ministry.

This is the fourth time Jesus tells His disciples of His death (see 16:21; 17:22-23; 20:18-19). Each subsequent time He provided greater details. He made the statements here on the Mount of Olives late on Tuesday evening (the day of controversy with the religious leadership and the subsequent Olivet Discourse), which according to this timeline would be considered as Wednesday (the Jewish day is calculated from evening to morning). Preparations for the Passover began on Thursday afternoon for Galileans with the slaughter of the Passover lamb and it was celebrated that evening (considered by the Jews as Friday). 'Two days' (v. 2) do not have to be forty-eight hours, simply parts of two days. Galileans prepared and ate the Passover lamb on Thursday, Judeans on Friday. Jesus ate the Passover lamb with His disciples on Thursday and became the true Passover lamb on Friday!

The symbolism of the Passover ritual finds its fulfillment in Christ and Calvary. Passover marked the ancient deliverance from the heinous servitude of the Jewish people in Egypt; Christ has delivered us from an even greater bondage. The means of the passing over of the angel of death in Egypt, averting judgment, was the slaying of a lamb and the covering of blood; Christ has been slain for us and His atoning blood has averted the tyranny of slavery to sin and death.

The meal included roasted lamb, unleavened bread, and bitter herbs with four cups of wine mixed with water. It celebrated redemption and the hasty departure from affliction in Egypt. It is interesting that when the 'true Passover lamb' was sacrificed there was darkness (27:45).

Jesus was too popular to be arrested publicly so the leaders had to depend on stealth (vv. 3-5). The meeting in the high priest's courtyard was an informal gathering; it was an ad hoc group, not the entire Sanhedrin.

The chief priests and elders, the clerical and lay leadership of the nation, composed the Sanhedrin. The head of the Sanhedrin was the Roman appointed high priest, Joseph Caiaphas. The first of the Roman appointments was Annas ben Seth, but he was deposed in A.D. 15 after nine years in the office and his son Eleazer served from A.D. 16–17. He was replaced by Joseph Caiaphas, a son-in-law of Annas (John 18:13), who served from A.D. 18–36, suggesting that he was able to stay in the good graces of Rome. Though Annas was a deposed high priest, he still functioned with considerable authority, the Jews reckoning that position as life-long. The family of Annas provided the state-appointed high priests, seven in all, until the Jewish revolt.

The anointing of Jesus at Bethany (vv. 6-16)

The anointing of Jesus in anticipation of His death stands in marked contrast to the participants' demeanor in the episodes that immediately precede and follow. In the prior event the leadership of the nation plotted Jesus' death; in the subsequent event a disciple betrays Him to death. It is little wonder that the woman's story is to be told in the community of the faithful; she had remarkable insight and compassion.

John tells us that the woman was Mary of Bethany (John 11:1), the sister of Martha and Lazarus. The event likely occurred in the home of Simon the Leper (then deceased or healed), perhaps their father. If he were living and not healed, they would have been in violation of the Mosaic Law.

According to John 12:1, the event occurred the previous Saturday evening, 'six days before Passover' (the two days of 26:1 refers, then, to the plot). Perhaps Matthew placed the story here, not earlier, due to its connection to Jesus' death pronouncement in 26:34. It is also interesting that Mary is not named in Matthew's account.

The perfume (probably nard or spikenard from India) was very expensive. According to John 12:3-5, it was worth 300 denarii, nearly a year's income. This suggests that Mary, Martha, and Lazarus belonged to a well-to-do family. Perfume was kept sealed in a jar with a long stem. Mary broke the stem and walked between the couches (dining was by reclining with the feet away from a common table) to anoint Jesus' head. They did not sit to eat!

The disciples failed to understand the significance of what was going on (vv. 8-9), as frequently was their case. Judas led in the criticism of Mary's act (John 12:4); it is interesting in the gospel narratives that every time Mary attempted to do something for Jesus she was misunderstood! The disciples were not able to grasp the significance of the occasion.

Mary may not have grasped the significance of her anointing of Jesus. She did it out of love and respect according to John; Jesus rebukes the disciples for questioning a clearly laudable endeavor (vv. 10-13). What Mary did was an act of devotion. To the disciples, the action of Mary was intrusive and a financial waste. Jesus was not denigrating the plight of the poor (v. 11); He was taking precedence over the poor. Jesus is more important to serve at times than those in severe need. His statement is not a defense of social neglect; it is a disclosure of His superiority!

Mary's act had a spiritual meaning (v. 12). Normally the body of the deceased would be properly prepared for burial with spices and wrappings, but not so a criminal. A criminal would be thrown into a ravine or open pit. Jesus would be buried in the manner of the rich (Isa. 53:9). The emphasis is on His death as a derelict, the Jewish perspective, not the divine perspective which was that He was a sin-bearing, divine, and triumphant substitute!

Mary's act will be memorialized (v. 13). In contrast to the disciples' ignorance of the significance of her act, Jesus tells us that her endeavor would be enshrined in His story as long as the Bible is read. This 'gospel or good news' is a reference to the Lord's death for us.

The initiative for Judas' betrayal of Jesus came from him and not from the Jewish leadership, though they welcomed it (vv. 14-16). It is amazing also that Judas was the keeper of the group's finances (John 12:4-6) and that he often took from the funds. Jesus knew all of this! It is reasonable that such a person would grab for all the money he could get since the group was about to be dispersed and a source of his greed would end.

'Then' (v. 14) suggests that Judas made his plans on the same day, Wednesday, that Jesus announced His crucifixion for the fourth time (v. 2). He must have realized that Jesus was not the 'promised one' that fit his expectations. Though his motives are not revealed, it may be that he, being motivated by greed, took offence at Jesus' rebuke in Simon's home in defense of the actions of Mary.

Thirty pieces of silver was the payment for damages when a neighbor's ox accidentally gored another neighbor's slave to death (Exod. 21:32). The price was the fee for a slave! It was, however, the fulfillment of prophecy (Zech. 11:12). Jesus was betrayed for a month's wages as well. However, the text does not reveal the coin in question. If a denarius, then the above is correct. If a shekel, a Jewish coin, the price would quadruple (one shekel equaling four denarii or then four months' salary).

The tense of the verb in verse 16 suggests that Judas continuously looked for the circumstance to betray Jesus from this point on. He had to find a time when it would not be embarrassing to the leadership who feared the reaction of the crowds if Jesus were arrested publicly.

The final Passover with the disciples (vv. 17-25)

The Passover meal would be eaten Thursday evening (in Jewish reckoning, Friday). The lamb would be slain on Thursday afternoon by Galileans (Friday by Judeans). An example of the Jewish reckoning of a day is 28:1. See the comments there.

The Passover began with the Feast of Unleavened Bread on Thursday evening, a major celebration of the people's deliverance from oppression. It prefigured Christ's redemption, the redemption from Egypt being a shadow of a greater one.

Like the arrangement to get the donkey and colt for the entry into Jerusalem, there is a hint here of pre-arrangement. Finding a man carrying a water jar on his head would be easy to spot because men did not normally do this domestic task in this manner (Luke 22:10-13).

Preparations were extensive for a visitor to Jerusalem. A lamb had to be purchased, a location procured, and the meal prepared. The meal was eaten after sunset and included unleavened bread, bitter herbs, greens, roasted lamb, and four cups of wine (there is no mention of eating lamb at the Lord's final celebration. Thus, the Galileans observed the Passover meal prior to the sacrifice of a lamb in the temple). Judeans, following a temple calendar, ate it on Friday evening. Jesus was crucified Friday about the time of the sacrifice of the Passover lamb in the Temple (3:00 p.m.).

The notification of Judas as the betrayer is described in verses 20-25. Though Jesus had stated that He would be betrayed (17:22; 20:18-19; 26:2), He gave no indication of His betrayer's identity until this point (Matthew had indicated that it was Judas [10:4]). Even though Jesus passed the sop to Judas, the disciples remained clueless (v. 23). Since all participated in the Passover celebration, the disciples understood that it was one of them. Judas occupied a place of honor at the meal reclining next to Jesus at the head of the u-shaped table (Jesus in the center, John to His right since he leaned on Jesus' chest, and Judas to His back). Was Jesus suggesting that Judas had one last chance or was He identifying him so as to let him know that he was the betrayer? I think the latter. Is that not amazing! This was a fulfillment of Psalm 41:9, the one 'who ate of my bread, has lifted his heel against me.' 'He who has dipped in the bowl' (v. 23) did not identify the betrayer; it indicated that he was in the room.

Jesus' reply to Judas' inquiry was sufficiently vague that the disciples did not judge that Judas was the betrayer. Judas left immediately (John 13:30), the disciples' judgment being that he went on a mission of charity. However, Judas must have sensed that Jesus knew that he was the guilty party. It is interesting that Judas addressed Jesus as 'rabbi,' not Lord (v. 25). He did not know Him as such!

The institution of the Lord's Supper (vv. 26-30)

Jesus revealed two things in the context of the Passover meal: His betrayal by a disciple, and the reinvention of the Passover's meaning with the institution of the Lord's Supper, the focus shifting from the Egyptian deliverance to Calvary's deliverance.

In the midst of the Passover ritual (this makes it unique and unusual), Jesus instituted the Supper. He advanced the Passover ritual to a new and heightened symbolism. He took a loaf of unleavened bread and broke it, saying, 'This is my body' (v. 26). This phrase was not part of the Passover liturgy. As the loaf was broken, so the body of Christ would be broken. Just as eating the Passover lamb identified the participant with the redemption out of Egypt, the land of bondage, so eating the bread and drinking the wine declared participation in the new exodus. The cup, the third of four, was the cup of blessing symbolizing His life in death. By declaring the cup symbolic, as 'my blood of the covenant ... poured out for you,' Jesus was saying that His death was the basis or cost of a new interpretation of the Passover, the gathering of the new community of God through those associated with Jesus, the true Israel, the true source of exodus from bondage.

It is clear that the words 'this is my body' and those of the cup, 'this is my blood,' are symbolic, since Jesus was in His body at the time and blood flowed in His veins (while asserting a non-physical presence in the Lord's Supper celebration, the spiritual presence of the exalted Christ is not to be discounted). The primary reference is to Exodus 24:8. The deliverance under Moses was assured through the shedding of blood, a shadow of a later redemption promised in the New Covenant of Jeremiah 31:31-34 and Hebrews 8, and fulfilled at Calvary.

As the first Passover symbolized not only deliverance from bondage but settlement in the land, the final 'true' Passover brought deliverance from bondage and the surety of a later settlement in heaven, in the consummated kingdom. He will not drink wine, the symbol of celebration, until the final victory.

The Passover looked back to the Egyptian deliverance from which God's people were to derive strength for the journey in the 'wilderness' of life, and hope that 'tomorrow' the Messiah would come, and with Him the kingdom and rest in the '(new) Jerusalem'. A place setting was set for a guest, Elijah, who was thought to be the King's forerunner. Elijah, Jesus says, had already come in John. The Passover pivoted on the five promises of Exodus 6:6-7 ('I will bring you out ... I will deliver you ... I will redeem you ... I will take you for my people ... I will be your God ...').

The fruit of the vine was to Jesus symbolic of joy and delight. That He will yet celebrate with the disciples ('with you') suggests that Jesus is referring to the consummation of the kingdom that will be established in His return in the final day! Jesus will celebrate with us, His friends, in the Marriage Supper of the Lamb (Rev. 19:1-7).

After the fourth cup of wine, they would have sung Psalms 115 to 118. Jesus would have sung a line and the disciples would have repeated it (before the second cup, they would have sung Psalms 113 and 114). Then they departed to the Mount of Olives.

The final prediction of His death (vv. 31-35)

From the intimacy of a final dinner, the scene quickly changed to one of defection, disloyalty, and cowardice. The shepherd would be struck, and the sheep scattered (Zech. 13:7). Jesus predicted that they would be scandalized by His arrest. The shock would prove so great that they would abandon Him. Jesus quotes Zechariah 13:7. In that passage (13:1-7), God foretells a time of great apostasy during which His prophet would be cut down.

Jesus predicts His resurrection and that He would go before them to the Galilee (v. 32; 28:16-17) where they would meet (Matthew mentions no post-resurrection appearances in Jerusalem with His disciples; his interests are Galilee-focused throughout the narrative). While the disciples would abandon Jesus, He assures them that they will meet again! At the beginning of Jesus' ministry, Galilee was described as a place where the light dawned (4:15-16). It was the location of Jesus' inauguration into ministry, and it would be the place that He commissioned the disciples to carry the message to the nations (28:18-20).

Though Peter was willing to suffer even death for the Lord, the shock of Jesus' arrest disoriented him (vv. 33-35). What cannot be missed in Peter's foolish statement is his great love and loyalty for the Lord. The Romans called the third night watch (12:00–3:00 a.m., the night being divided into four three-hour watches beginning at 6:00 p.m.) the 'cock-crow watch' because it was usual for roosters to crow at 12:30 a.m., 1:30 a.m., and 2:30 a.m.. Though no one should doubt Peter's sincerity, within hours he would disown Jesus three times.

Jesus in Gethsemane (vv. 36-46)

In this section we have three prayers of Jesus and three return visits to His sleeping disciples. It is tempting to think about the pressing of olives and how it had deep symbolic significance to our Lord (the noun Gethsemane means literally 'the place of the olive press'). It is no coincidence that Jesus prayed three times in a place where olives were crushed three times. First, the initial crushing of olives produced virgin oil used for anointing kings; the second crushing produced oil for lamps and medicinal purposes; and the third was used to make a cleansing agent or soap. Jesus is the anointed one, the king; Jesus is light, the dispeller of darkness, the great healer; and the great cleanser, not from the dirt attached to the flesh, but the uncleanness of the heart. What a beautiful picture of the person and accomplishments of our Lord!

Gethsemane was located on the western slope of the Mount of Olives within a walled enclosure. Jesus left most of the disciples, choosing three of them, the inner circle, then distancing Himself from the three in the olive grove.

Jesus, facing the stark reality of what was immediately before Him, sought solace through companionship. He disclosed his anguished heart to the disciples, but all they could do was sleep (remember they had drank four cups of wine!).

Scholars have struggled to understand the meaning of the phrase, 'let this cup pass from me' (v. 39). There is general agreement that Jesus was not shying from death. The Bible bears abundant witness that Jesus came to accomplish the divine will and did so perfectly (Psalm 40:7-8 quoted in Hebrews 10:7). The issue may have been something about His death, hardly the fact of it. It was not the fact of suffering about which He prayed, but it could have been about the duration of suffering, not the physical pain, but the horror of spiritual judgment in separation from His Father. If Psalm 13:1 is in the mind of Christ while on the cross ('How long will you hide your face from me?'), it would lend some credence to the proposal of duration, not escape. 'Cup' refers not merely to suffering and death, but to the great wrath of God that He would endure.

It is interesting that when Jesus was in His great anguish, the disciples slumbered (vv. 40-41). These men did not seem to have been the best our Lord could have chosen! Peter did not lack enthusiasm for the Lord, but he did lack moral stamina to face the reality of what it means in practice. Jesus' instructions to 'watch and pray' are present tense verbs suggesting that the action should be continuous. The reference may be to the recent example of their failure so as not to repeat it, or it may have reference to future trials and difficulties.

There is a significant difference in the first two prayers of Jesus in the garden. In the first He prayed, 'If it is possible,' but in the second He prayed, 'if this cannot pass away.' In the first prayer there was a reference to the will of God, not so here. Jesus resigned Himself to the fact that the undisclosed extent of His suffering was the divine will, so He did not mention it again. He realized that there was no other way of obedience than suffering divine wrath and human malice, the length of suffering in the will of the Father. Not all things possible are the will of God and Jesus is willing to comply with His Father's will. The third instance of prayer by Jesus is the same as the second. In the second prayer He expressed submission to the Father (in the third, it is reaffirmed).

The hour of suffering is near; Jesus then tells the sleeping disciples that it is too late to gain strength for the temptations ahead. The sleepers for whom He would die have lost the opportunity! Matthew is the only writer to tell us that Jesus prayed three times; Peter will deny Him three times.

Applications

1. The fact that Jesus told His disciples several times that He would be crucified indicates that this was the focus of His mission in our world. The disciples could not fit together the glorious reign of the deliverer with disclosures of His tragic death. How could a dead Messiah rule? They chose to focus on the good part and ignore the suffering part. They did not understand that it is through pain and suffering that His glorious reign would be established. In many ways, they are little different from us. We spurn the painful path and complain when called to venture upon it, but the road to glory passes through the valley of darkness and pain. It did for Jesus, and He taught that it is the same for us. After pain comes the crown! Have you come to understand this lesson? How has it shaped your perspective on disappointment, pain, and sorrow?

2. When great events and crucial moments occur, the wise grasp their significance and respond appropriately. Mary seemed to understand that was the case when Jesus came to Bethany. Great and meaningful events call for significant sacrifice because our deepest values are those things that cause us to sacrifice gladly. She gave up her wealth to express gratitude for Jesus. Are you willing to match your priorities with your sacrificial giving? Mary wanted to express her love for the Lord and in the process did something else just as remarkable. She prepared Him for His burial and resurrection, His triumph! Are your sacrifices in proportion to your values? Perhaps a deeper insight is that your sacrifices, or lack of them, reveal your true values.

3. Some people will do anything for money, but there will always be a time when they come to regret it. In marked

contrast to Mary's sacrificial spirit is Judas' greed and disappointment in the Lord. He had an attachment to Jesus that was rooted in what he thought he could gain, not in expressing what he had gained. When his expectations did not come true, when he realized that Jesus was not the king he desired, when he realized that Jesus offered suffering without prominence and authority, he grabbed for the crusts available with a devious financial bargain. His god was himself! Can you imagine being with Jesus for over three years and missing entirely what He was really all about? What does this say about the blindness and hardness of the human heart? What insight is there about our hearts? Think of Peter!

4. It is amazing to me to see what was on Jesus' mind during the last evening with His disciples while knowing what would transpire within a few tragic hours. He wanted to be with them to comfort and prepare them. He wanted to enjoy a meal, a special meal with them, to sing and pray with them as they shared in a symbol – the Passover – of the nation's great deliverance. I find deep compassion and care expressed by Jesus and it is humbling to contemplate. In the approach of His darkest hour, He wanted to celebrate with them. I find that so unlike me when tragedy looms. I withdraw into my sorrows; He expressed His care for others. Pause to think about that as it relates to your experience. Have you come to know the overwhelming love and care that Jesus has for you?

5. Not only did Jesus desire to celebrate Israel's great feast; He wanted to give it greater meaning. He took the great ceremony of remembrance of a miraculous historic deliverance and recast it into a remembrance of the greater deliverance that He was about to accomplish. His was not a deliverance from an Egyptian bondage, but from the bondage of sin, selfishness, and death; it was accomplished through a miracle, but not merely the parting of a body of water. It was the parting of the darkened soul that by the Spirit would spring into

a well of living water. It was not through Moses, but a greater than Moses. It was more than the birth of a nation; this celebrates the birth of a new community, the new people of God. Does the Lord's Table, the Eucharist, remind you of these things? Is the Table of the Lord the occasion of thanksgiving for you?

6. We should be careful not to make promises unless we know something of the depravity of our hearts. If we know our hearts, we should not boast about our future actions; we may be doubly embarrassed later. Peter was a sincere, earnest lover of God, but he seemed to know more of the Lord's affection and care for him than his own fickle heart. We are all capable of overstatement when it comes to what we say we will do for the Lord or what we will never do. As Christians, our confidence should be in the Lord, more so than in our abilities. Have you been brought to see that your love for God is not consistent? Have you been brought to prayer and cautious conversation?

7. Jesus would have us pray, but we often sleep instead. In His deepest agony He asked His disciples to pray, but they were overcome with weariness. Does that not describe you and me at times? We must guard our days so that we have the strength to pray at the end of them. I find in the disciples such a picture of me. While I am the object of Jesus' great love, compassion, and mercy on a daily basis, I find myself preoccupied with my needs overshadowing His will and commands of me. I find myself victimized by my own selfish priorities. Is that true of you? Do you seek to enter into Jesus' concerns? Do you pray for your wants before you go about His will for the world?

8. Though the disciples appear unable to grasp the gravity of the situation, Jesus left them with commands and comforts. He tells them to proceed to the Galilee where He will meet them once more. He cares and provides for His disciples to the last moment of His temporal separation from them. What a lens for us into His care! Hear His words of compassion and love!

The arrest (26:47-56)

The betrayal money was likely for information about Jesus' movements. The leadership wanted Him secretly arrested to avoid any resistance by the crowds. A night arrest in an isolated location served their purposes and Judas knew of Jesus' habits. We are told that the arresting troops were high numerically. Other accounts tell us there were both Jewish and Roman soldiers (John 18:1-12). To say that Judas was one of the twelve, as all the gospel writers do, highlights the awfulness of his crime. An intimate betrayed Jesus!

Judas refers to Jesus with an occupational title, 'Rabbi' or 'Teacher' (see also 26:25), rather than Lord (the normal designation by the other disciples, suggesting his distance from Jesus). Judas did not know Him! The 'kiss' was a form of identification (remember, there were eleven in the group, and it was dark, so a clear sign was imperative). 'Friend' is not an intimate greeting, but a gracious one. Judas may have realized that political and material advantages would not be the lot of those who followed Jesus, only suffering and death.

John's account identifies the disciple who attempted resistance as Peter and the high priest's servant as Malchus (John 18:10). Matthew does not record the miracle that took place, nor the parties involved. Jesus intervened immediately rebuking Peter, saying to the disciple that He did not need His assistance. He could have called twelve legions of angels if He desired (a legion being about 6000 men). Protection through aggression was not the means Jesus advocated for His safety; it was trust in the will of God (this does not imply that Jesus was an advocate of pacifism [John 18:36]). The point being that one who uses the sword may have his life ended with a sword.

Though Jesus could have summoned aid, He submitted to the Father's will (His will is revealed in the Scriptures [vv. 54, 56]). Jesus' point is that to arrest Him secretly by stealth indicates more about them, their deviousness and guilt, than about Him. He taught openly, but they degenerated to intrigue to arrest Him. They acted like robbers while claiming divine warrant. What they did was a fulfillment of the prophets (e.g. Isa. 53:12, 'numbered among the transgressors'). By fleeing, the disciples fulfilled prophecy (Zech. 13:7) as Jesus had predicted (v. 31). The 'shepherd' had been stricken through an illegal arrest and the 'sheep' fled (v. 56).

The trial before the Sanhedrin (26:57-68)

From the Mount of Olives Jesus was taken to the house of Joseph Caiaphas (he succeeded his father-in-law Annas (A.D. 15-36), likely a very large structure. The Sanhedrin was composed of seventy men plus Joseph Caiaphas. It is likely that the entire body did not assemble (e.g. Joseph of Arimathea and Nicodemus would have been absent). Twenty-three members made up the necessary quorum for decision-making.

The trial of Jesus before the Sanhedrin is filled with illegalities, violations of Jewish law. Capital trials were to be held during the day, not at night; verdicts were to be rendered the following day, not immediately; trials could not be held on the eve of a feast day; witnesses were interrogated according to law; and blasphemy could only be charged for taking God's name vainly, which Jesus never did. Also, He had no defense attorney. Because of the legal improprieties it seems best to indicate that this was a serious informal hearing that required a formal reconvening early the next morning before transferral to Pilate.

Since Jesus was arrested on Thursday evening (Friday by Jewish reckoning) and the Sabbath would begin on Friday evening (Saturday by Jewish reckoning), things had to be done quickly. Further, Pilate heard cases only in the very early morning, refusing them the rest of the day.

Peter did not follow the entourage that arrested Jesus with a motive of rescuing Him (v. 58); he seems to have been interested in what would happen generally after the disturbing events in the garden.

The Mosaic Law required two confirming, creditable witnesses. The only charge the Sanhedrin could isolate was that Jesus spoke against the temple (vv. 59-61). The charge was that He was a deconstructionist determined to dismantle the great temple complex. Desecrating the temple was a capital offense. However, Jesus had only said that the temple would be destroyed, not that He would destroy it. The leadership took Jesus' words too literally because He spoke metaphorically of His own body, the true presence of God.

His body would be destroyed, but in the resurrection His body would be restored!

The intent of the Sanhedrin was to find a chargeable offence meriting death. All they could get in the confusion was a lesser charge that Jesus spoke against the temple. The charge is somewhat understandable; Jesus claimed to be the true temple, the place of meeting between God and man. Jesus ended the significance of the temple for the people of God with His presence. No longer was there a need for sacrificial lambs because the true Lamb was sacrificed. The temple was a shadow and it passed away in fulfillment in Christ!

In fulfillment of prophetic prediction (vv. 62-63), Jesus refused to answer His accusers: 'like a lamb that before its shearers is silent, so he opened not his mouth' (Isa. 53:7). In His silence, He demonstrated His claim to Messiahship! Caiaphas then demanded that Jesus answer under an oath. 'Son of God' is equivalent to being the Messiah. It was not blasphemy to claim to be the Messiah. The Messiah, according to the leaders, was a political figure, not God, so that Jesus' claim was not necessarily blasphemy. It seems that Caiaphas could not get a clear, uniform accusation from the accusers, so he asked Jesus to incriminate Himself!

The reply of Jesus was in the form of a restatement of Caiaphas' question without a direct answer (v. 64); it is more a recognition of the question than a clear reply (as also in the case of Judas [v. 25]). Jesus confesses that He is the Messiah and the Son of God; He is the promised deliverer! From Caiaphas' perspective, since he understood the Messiah to be a human, political figure, Jesus' confession was not technically blasphemy. However, it was an allusion to Psalm 110:1. Though Caiaphas would not have grasped it, Jesus was claiming from a Jewish perspective equality of authority with God.

Jesus' explanation comes from allusions to two passages: Psalm 110:1 and Daniel 7:13. The point of the citations is to qualify the nature of His Messianic claims; He is not a political deliverer in a contemporary sense so sought for by the Jews under their Roman domination. The disclosure includes a revelation and a threat. They would not see Him again until they face Him as judge. That was too much for Caiaphas.

Caiaphas took Jesus' reply as a confession of guilt (vv. 64-66). Saying that He would be sitting in the place of honor at the throne of God was blasphemous to the high priest. Tearing one's garment was a sign of disgust and abhorrence, as well as the traditional response to the charge of blasphemy (Acts 14:14). However, it was a violation of the Mosaic code for a high priest to do so (Lev. 21:10; see also Lev. 10:6). The blasphemy charge included claiming association with God such as sitting at His right hand, speaking against the temple, and criticizing the nation's leaders.

That Jesus 'deserves to die' expresses the Sanhedrin's agreement that Jesus was guilty (vv. 66-68). The Mosaic Code is clear that the penalty of blasphemy is death (Lev. 24:16). The mistreatment of Jesus was symbolic. Demanding that a blindfolded man tell who hit Him was a denial of His claim to be a prophet, spitting in His face was a denial of His authority, and blows upon Him suggested that He had no power. These are collective actions suggesting rejection and repudiation.

If Jesus was the Messiah, even though blindfolded, He should know who was abusing Him (Isa. 11:3). It was a sheer attempt at humiliation and mockery (v. 68). Here is an instance of the 'Christ' being used as a title and not as a personal name ('Prophesy to us, you Christ'). The leadership recognized His claim, yet not His person!

The denials of Peter (vv. 69-75)

On that cool night in Jerusalem, Peter joined the gathering crowd in Caiaphas' courtyard, apparently a public area, in shock and fear to learn what was happening to Jesus (vv. 69-70). Recognizing him as having been with Jesus, the servant girl asks Peter about it. Jesus is referred to in a derogatory term, 'the Galilean.' Judeans viewed the Galileans as less religious and faithful, living distant from Jerusalem in a mixed Jewish/ Gentile area with different customs. Peter's brisk reply is in the form of denial, a lie.

Peter moved toward the exit, the gate into the courtyard, perhaps sensing the hostility and personal lack of emotional equilibrium (vv. 71-72). Another servant girl pressed the issue further with another derogatory claim, saying that he was from Nazareth, a town associated with Jesus. The person with the question did not speak directly to Peter, but to the crowd. This time Peter invoked an oath with a lie (perjury).

Peter has become something of an attention-gatherer. This third assertion argues that he must have been with Jesus because his accent was Galilean (vv. 73-74). Exasperated, Peter cursed to affirm his innocence of association with the despised prophet. It is clear by the language that Peter was cursing someone other than himself; it had to be Jesus! It was his loyalty to Jesus, not his temporary repudiation of Jesus' leadership, that shows the real Peter. He who thought he could stand failed terribly. Peter had allowed his loyalty to Jesus to be severely compromised. His strident weeping was caused by his recognition that Jesus was innocent; he had dishonored his Lord.

The trial before Pilate and the condemnation (27:1-26)
Matthew's account of events is selective as is the case with each of the gospel writers. The informal interview with the aged Annas is not recorded (see John 18:13), simply the Sanhedrin's informal trial and this one before Pilate (the meeting with Herod Antipas is also passed over by Matthew, as well as the formal appearance before the Sanhedrin on the day of the crucifixion).

The Sanhedrin had found Jesus guilty of a crime worthy of death in their eyes. Since the Jews did not have the authority to execute in the manner they wanted (later they did execute Stephen by stoning on a religious charge [Acts 7:58]), here they had to prove a crime worthy of death from a Roman perspective. The charge shifted from blasphemy to political insurrection. The Jewish leadership so despised Jesus that they wanted the most humiliating death for Him that could possibly be suffered (John 18:32, 'what kind of death he was about to die'). Unwittingly, they did not know that their desire was a fulfillment of prophecy (Isa. 53)!

Pilate had been appointed governor, or prefect, in A.D. 26. Prefects were appointed to troubled areas and given authority equal to proconsuls or imperial legates over matters of life and death. Pilate was a legionnaire who married one of the emperor's granddaughters. He was vain and thirsty for position and power, but he lost his position in A.D. 36 and was transferred to Helvetica (Switzerland) where he was forced to commit suicide.

The seat of Roman governance in Palestine was in Caesarea, the great seaport city that Herod the Great had constructed and named in honor of Augustus Caesar. On Jewish feasts, Roman governors would come to Jerusalem, residing either in the Antonia Fortress, at the northwest corner of the temple complex, or in Herod's palace complex southeast of Jaffa Gate.

Verse 1 does not indicate that a second meeting was called by the Sanhedrin; it was the culmination of an all-night meeting. They had to find a charge that Pilate would deem appropriate for an execution, and it could not be a mere Jewish religious issue. The events in this chapter took place on Friday.

The remorse of Judas (vv. 3-10)

Sadly, Judas realized the mistake he had made, confessing his sin ('I have sinned'); but there was no forgiveness for him. Remorse is different from heartfelt repentance (the term here is a rare word in the New Testament referring to a change of mind but not sorrow for sin; 'seized with remorse' is perhaps a better translation).

The event of Judas' remorse could not have happened between the end of the Sanhedrin's meeting and the trial before Pilate because Jesus was incarcerated overnight, and the final Jewish trial took place early on the day of crucifixion. Judas then evidenced remorse by casting the betrayal fee in the treasury of the Temple (27:3, 5). It seems that Matthew placed it here to draw a contrast between the failure of Peter and the treachery of Judas. Peter sinned in words and for him there could be a new start; Judas sinned in a premeditated deed and there was no forgiveness. One came in a moment of weakness; the other was reflective of habitual inclinations.

Judas realized the error of being a party to the death of Jesus, though he never saw Jesus as anything other than a mere human being (vv. 3-5). His behavior, his greed, and misappropriation of funds revealed the emptiness of his soul. He retained a conscience, but it was seared by personal ambition. His actions were wrong; he was a party to innocent blood, and he knew it. Judas became a puppet caught in a web of intrigue spun out of hatred for Jesus. The leadership's disregard of Judas's plea once again mirrors the corruption of their souls and the viciousness of their actions (v. 4).

His remorse led to the return of the money, but the priests refused to put the money into the treasury, using the money to purchase a cemetery for foreigners, mostly likely for Jews who died while visiting Jerusalem for a feast (v. 5). Since Judas was not a priest, he could not enter the sanctuary, only the Court of Israel. He may have thrown the money into the sanctuary from a distance. Another account of his death is given in Acts 1:18-19. He likely hanged himself so hurriedly that the rope broke, his corpse fell, and burst apart. It is generally believed that the potter's field was at the conjunction of the Kidron and Hinnom valleys, south of the city and site of the city dump. The money could not be returned to the temple treasury because it was blood-money; it was ritualistically unclean (vv. 6-8).

The difficulty with the quotation in verses 9 and 10 is that it is attributed to Jeremiah, but part comes from Zechariah 11:12-13. It seems to be derived from both Jeremiah 19:1-13 and the Zechariah passage. It is common to fuse sources (see Mark 1:2-3). Jeremiah is alone mentioned because he is the more prominent of the two prophets. In both passages, the nation forsook the Lord and killed His people. The people of God were valued less than slaves. In Jeremiah 19 the prophet smashed a jar, symbolic of the judgment of the nation in the valley. Matthew sees in these two passages a parallel to apostasy and rejection that finds their ultimate fulfillment in the rejection of Christ and national judgment.

The interrogation by Pilate (vv. 11-26)

Pilate was brutal in his attitudes toward his Jewish subjects. However, the rebuke of Pilate by Tiberius Caesar for his cruelty caused an outward change of attitude. This accounts for Pilate's fear of the religious leadership and for the fact that while he saw Jesus as innocent of any crime worthy of death, he quickly reversed himself when he was accused of being no friend of Caesar, revealing much of his character.

With Tiberius, aged and semi-retired at this time, the power behind the throne was a man named Lucius Aelius

Sejanus. The former was more respectful of Jewish priorities than the latter who was profoundly antisemitic in attitude. Sejanus appointed Pilate procurator and also forged an assassination plot against Tiberius which was discovered, and he was executed (A.D. 31). The point in the context of our passage is that it might explain Pilate's fear of offending the Jews and his willingness to allow an innocent to be crucified. Pilate needed to show his loyalty to Tiberius to stay in his graces, meaning holding on to his position.

The location of the trial is debated. It may have taken place in Herod's palace near Jaffa Gate or the Antonia Fortress at the northwest corner of the temple complex (later Peter was imprisoned there [Acts 12:3-11] as well as Paul [Acts 21:27–23:30]). Roman trials consisted of four parts: a statement of accusations by the complainants, the interrogation of the defendant, a defense by the defendant, and the verdict by the judge. Matthew's account begins with the second phase.

A charge of claiming to be God was not one that would have concerned the Romans. That Jesus was a king, a political charge, would suggest that He was an insurrectionist, a serious charge for the Romans and grounds for death (v. 11). To ask Jesus if He was the king of the Jews is ironic. Pilate was the ruling authority over the Jewish nation. He likely was simply offering a judicial inquiry into the charges.

Jesus responded with silence (vv. 11-12), as He did to the Jewish leadership (26:63). He made no defense for Himself, replying to the question with neither yes nor no. If He had answered affirmatively, He would have indicated that the charges were valid (they were and they were not). If He answered negatively, He would be lying. Jesus fulfills Isaiah 53:7, a 'Lamb' silent before His shearers.

Pilate understood that the charges were fabrications (v. 18) and insisted on His innocence (vv. 23, 24). Since Jesus could have easily refuted the charges, His silence astonishes Pilate (vv. 13-14). The notion of 'surprise' suggests that Jesus made a favorable impression on Pilate. He knew the charges were a hoax and it is amazingly confirmed by Jesus' refusal to answer them.

Pilate is willing to contrast Jesus with a horrific criminal (vv. 15-26), probably thinking that the people would ask for

Jesus' release (an appeal to justice, but there was to be no justice for Him). There is an intriguing textual variant in the manuscripts at verse 17. Some texts of Matthew identify Barabbas as 'Jesus Barabbas'. 'Jesus' was a very common name in first-century Jewish circles. Pilate's literal words were: 'Which Jesus do you want, the son of Abba or the one known as the Messiah?' This would make more sense if there were two by the same first name, the subsequent wording clarifying which one Pilate meant.

It was a Roman custom to release a Jewish prisoner at this special season (vv. 15-18); it was not a Jewish custom. It was a gesture of goodwill toward a conquered people. 'Barabbas' does not appear to be an actual name. It means 'son of a father'. He was a condemned insurrectionist. Being a rebel engaged in guerrilla actions would have endeared him to many Jews. Thus, Pilate's attempt to release Jesus failed. Barabbas was a Judean, not a less-respected Galilean. Further, Jesus' message of loving enemies would not be popular with those who despised the Romans.

Pilate's appeal is to the people, not to the leadership, to release Jesus. His motive is unclear, but he could have done so to remain in the graces of the emperor, to humiliate the Sanhedrin in countering their wishes, or to gain Jesus' release sensing that He was innocent. He miscalculated the Jerusalemites animosity for Galileans and the Galilean prophet.

The warning of Pilate's wife is recorded in verse 19. A fifth-century Christian source identified Pilate's wife as Claudia Procula, a granddaughter of Tiberius, illegitimate at the time of birth but her mother became Tiberius' third wife. Procula was vain. Matthew may have included this incident to provide further evidence that Jesus was innocent. The situation must have been grave for Procula to interrupt her husband when he was sitting in his official capacity as a judge on the judgment seat.

Pilate was perplexed by the desire of the crowd to have Jesus crucified (vv. 22-23). His question suggests that he was seeking to get the crowd to reconsider their decision. Further, he voiced his own opinion of Jesus' innocence. Crucifixion was an execution that signified the curse of God on the subject (Deut. 21:23). This particular form of death was a Roman punishment; Jews stoned criminals. However, the leadership desired the most humiliating form of execution possible (John 18:31-32), viewing Jesus as a blasphemer of God.

Hand washing was not a Roman custom; Pilate seems to have used a Jewish custom against the Jewish leadership (vv. 24-26). He was suggesting that it was not his choice to have Jesus crucified, believing that He was innocent (even though the Jews were a subjected people, and he was the most authoritative political figure in the East). Pilate did so out of cowardice and fear of losing the graces of Rome and his position.

The religious leadership took complete responsibility for the death of Jesus and, thereby, doomed the nation (v. 25). The question of what to do with Jesus was not settled by evidence and argument, but by mob hysteria and political greed.

Matthew does not explain Jesus' scourging, simply mentioning it (perhaps it was an appeal for mercy by Pilate as the previous action was a hopeful appeal to justice). As a preliminary to crucifixion, the victim would be whipped with leather straps that had bone or metal fragments attached at the ends. The flesh would be ripped from the back of the sufferer. Sometimes salt would be placed in the open wounds to stop the bleeding that could lead to a premature death. It would have been extremely painful.

Applications

1. The arrest of Jesus by temple soldiery and a Roman contingent is truly amazing. If Jesus had desired to avoid suffering for us, it would have been an easy matter for Him. He could have called legions of angels to come to His rescue. The point is obvious: Jesus came to die. It was His high calling. His death was not the end of a pathetic figure; it was His greatest moment. It was the reason that He came. He came to give His life in our place. No one took His life from Him; He gave it freely and voluntarily for us. Does this not inspire amazement? Does this not cause a grateful response on your part? How are you responding to Jesus' gift of Himself?

2. Peter is portrayed as one whose heart is in the right place, but whose understanding is deficient. First, he tried to prevent our Lord's arrest and then his grief over the events of the evening left him in panicked fear that was expressed in moral ineptitude. When the heart and mind are separated, there will be problems. For our affections to be expressed properly requires the faculty of understanding. Have you ever let your emotions overshadow what you knew to be true? Have the results ever produced favorable or desirable consequences?

3. Peter's behavior illustrates how twisted our morals can become. While he loved his Lord deeply and would willingly give his life in sacrifice for Him, he was capable of cursing Him. Are not our hearts fickle? We are capable of significant spiritual heights (Peter walked on the sea; he confessed that Jesus was the Christ; he was willing to take on an army of soldiers to spare Jesus from arrest) and yet sink into abject cowardice. Christians are capable of very diverse and contrary morals. What does that tell us about our redemption? What does this tell you about the need to guard your heart? What do our worst moments tell us about the love of Jesus for us?

4. Bad choices may lead to sad regrets that can be irreversible. Judas recognized his moral failure, but he never recognized that Jesus was his Messiah. For unbelievers, there is a point when their rejection of the witness of the gospel seals their judgment. Judas is a classic example of misplaced repentance. He was sorry for what he did, but spurned Jesus. Do you know people who know that Jesus was a good man, though that is not enough? Judas walked with Jesus for three years and did not get the clues. What does that say about the hardness and blindness of the human heart?

5. Jesus was not a victim of circumstances beyond His control. In fact, Jesus' death was not a failure; it was His greatest accomplishment. He came to die so that, in His victory over death, we might live. He came to

die to show us that in His kingdom the crown of the victor comes after selfless servanthood. He died that we might live and to show us how to live. Have you come to realize that alliance with Jesus entails acceptance of restrictions and a life of devotion to His interests expressed in service to His people?

6. It is pitiful when a person knows what is right but fails to do it either out of fear of others or of loss of privilege. Sadly, Pilate knew that Jesus was innocent, but he lacked the moral virtue to spare Him. He loved his favorable existence and privilege more that he loved truth. He is an example of a lot of people you meet in life; self-interest and self-preservation are their primary concerns. Have you met people like that? Have you met Christians that acted like that at times? Have you ever found yourself acting out of self-interest rather than the interest of others? Did you find it in your heart to repent?

7. Jesus Barabbas was the only person in history that Jesus literally took the place of. Had he not, there could have been no redemption, for while he took the criminal's place physically, he took ours spiritually. Barabbas was an insurrectionist and murderer deserving of death; Jesus took upon Himself our misdeeds expressed in our rebellious hearts and only then deserved death, being otherwise the blameless Son of God. Barabbas was released from the just consequence of his sin; Jesus was punished when He took our place! Have you paused lately to stand in awe and wonder at the greatest story ever told? If Jesus had not taken Barabbas' place, He could have never taken ours!

8. Have you encountered people who are unwilling to come to Jesus, being willing to bear their own punishment for evil choices? The Jewish leadership, and their duped fellow Jerusalemites, were willing to accept responsibility for Jesus' murder. They were even willing to have their children endure any consequences. The failure to repent led to tragedy in the destruction and

mass annihilation following the Jewish revolt in A.D. 70. Even more sadly is the fact that physical judgment, in this case, is the outward shell of spiritual judgment. A rebellious heart is not a trite matter. If this is true of believers, those who are loved of God, how much more is it true of those who reject and despise His grace?

The crucifixion of the King (vv. 27-66)
Matthew's emphasis in the crucifixion focused on the physical and verbal abuse Jesus suffered, the abuse of the soldiery, and the spiteful crowds, and not the divine aspects of His suffering.

The Roman soldiers took Jesus into the guardhouse, perhaps the Antonia Fortress, and humiliated Him further (vv. 27-31). Since the charge was that of claiming to be a king that would pose a threat to Roman authority in the volatile region, they mocked Him as a fake potentate with a scarlet robe (likely a military garment purple in color alluding to royalty) and a crown (the crown was made of a thorny-branched plant unwittingly reflective of the curse of Genesis 3:18 and suggestive of what Jesus became for us). The thorns would indicate rays of glory, divine approval, shining down upon Him, but it was a cruel mockery inflicting pain. With the reed they beat Him on the head and 'worshiped' Him ('Hail, King of the Jews' being a mockery of 'Hail, Caesar'). The religious leadership abused Jesus for claiming to be the promised One, the Romans for claiming to be a king; from a Jewish perspective the claims were the same since their hope was in a politically militant deliverer. The Roman soldiers involved were auxiliaries; no legionaries were stationed in Palestine at the time. They were likely from the surrounding area hired as mercenaries.

Pilate had Jesus scourged using a leather whip with bone or metal fragments. Such whipping often led to death as the body was severely lacerated exposing bone and internal organs. Tied to a pole with the arms above the head and stripped of clothing, a soldier on each side would incessantly whip the victim. The Romans used whipping to weaken prisoners before crucifixion. This was a fulfillment of Jesus' words in 20:19. Whipping was limited to thirty-nine lashes by the Jews, but without limitation by the Romans. Matthew's account of what took place is pithy and factual; there is no attempt to stress Jesus' agony or pull the heartstrings. His human suffering was a shadow of the enormity of His spiritual suffering; the purchase came for us at Calvary, not on the way to Calvary.

Normally, a prisoner on the way to crucifixion would be stripped and flogged. Jesus was not, perhaps because it was thought another flogging would have killed Him. Evidence of His depleted state was His inability to carry the instrument of His execution as He exited the city gate ('as they went out,' v. 32). Simon from Cyrene in north Africa, perhaps visiting Jerusalem to celebrate the Passover (his name is Jewish in origin), was therefore compelled by the soldiers to help carry the cross of Jesus. Mark says that Simon had two sons, Alexander and Rufus (Mark 15:21). Paul later sent greetings to Rufus and his mother (Rom. 16:13).

The crucifixion of Jesus (vv. 33-56)

While instruments of crucifixion varied in shape, this one is typically envisioned as composed of two beams with the vertical post extending higher than the horizontal crossbeam (evidenced by a sign placed above Jesus' head indicating His alleged crime [v. 37]). Victims were either nailed or tied to the beams. Jesus was nailed with outstretched arms through the wrists. The legs were tucked in a fetal position with a single nail driven through the bones above the ankle. Humiliatingly naked, the sufferer's weight would be on the single nail, and the body pressing down would make breathing difficult. To gain relief the crucified would have to push up, putting his weight on the nail and gasp a breath. Victims died of drowning, their lungs filling with liquid. It could take seventy-two hours before weakness caused inability to breathe. Further, the victim was crucified near a road in a prominent place as a warning to others.

Jesus was crucified outside the city at a location called Golgotha, the place of the Skull (v. 33). The Latin equivalent is 'calvaria' from which we derive the English word 'Calvary' (the word means skull or head). This was probably the same place where Stephen was later killed (Acts 7:58-60); it was outside the Damascus Gate on a major highway for all to see and even converse with the criminal.

Jesus was given a mixture of wine and myrrh, called gall because of its bitter taste, to dull the pain and lengthen the agony (v. 34). Jesus refused to drink it. The pay of the soldiers was, in part, the clothing of the crucified (vv. 35-36). Here is another evidence that Jesus was stripped naked, a part of His humiliation. Matthew reports this in the words of Psalm 22:18, without indicating that he was quoting Scripture.

The charge against Jesus and the basis for His crucifixion was placed above the cross: insurrectionism, sedition, claiming to be a king (v. 37). Likely it was carried before the procession to Golgotha or hung around His neck. It was then placed at the top of the cross for passers-by to see.

Three groups abused Him while He was on the cross in addition to the Romans who killed Him: the people passing by (vv. 39-40), the religious leadership (vv. 41-43), and the two criminals beside Him (vv. 38, 44). One commentator stated that 'ignorant sinners', 'religious sinners,' and 'condemned sinners' derided Jesus.[9]

The two criminals were guerrilla freedom fighters, likely in the same group as the spared Barabbas. They sought to bring about the end of oppression through violence; Jesus will end violence by being violated! They joined the crowd in mocking Jesus (v. 44); according to Matthew, no one spoke in His defense. One of them did change his mind (Luke 23:40-43).

Like the Roman soldiers earlier (vv. 27-31), the citizenry held Him in contempt, speaking perversely to Him as they passed by the site (vv. 39-40). They mocked His Messianic claims (here is an allusion to Psalm 22:7; these are also the devil's word in Jesus' first temptation [Matt. 4:3, 6]). They were blaspheming the Son of God claiming they had a right to dictate to Him, that humans can direct God! It is ironic that the crowds asked Jesus to 'come down from the cross', and claimed that 'he cannot save himself', but it was His cross experience that saved us. Had He followed their instruction,

---

9. R. V. G. Tasker, *The Gospel According to St. Matthew* (Grand Rapids, MI: William B. Eerdmans Publishing Co., 1962), p. 245.

there would be no hope in life and death for us. His death brought us life; His life brought His death for us!

The chief priests, scribes, and lay elders joined the crowds in mocking Jesus (vv. 41-43). They derided His claims, evidenced by His miracles, saying that He had not the power to heal Himself. They taunted Him by saying that they would believe if He came down from the cross, if He showed Himself victorious. That God did not rescue Him revealed His falsity, they claimed. How could He be the Son of God if abandoned by God? Here is an allusion to Psalm 22:8. They understood that Jesus claimed a special relationship with God! That people of such eminence were present at the crucifixion of one condemned as a criminal suggests the depth of their animosity and hatred for Him.

Matthew turns from those who were at the cross to circumstances that transpired in the context of Jesus' sufferings on the cross. He deals with Jesus' actual death in a single sentence (v. 50). From noon until three in the afternoon darkness covered the earth (v. 45), symbolic of divine judgment, the curse that Christ bore at that time for us and for all creation. The darkness was a supernatural phenomenon in timing. While the darkness was real, it was also symbolic of the judgment that Christ endured from God because of sin and a foreboding portent of judgment on the nation for rejecting their Messiah. The background seems to be Amos 8:9-10, and to a lesser extent Exodus 10:21-22. In the Amos passage, the darkness was an evidence of divine displeasure.

Jesus quoted from Psalm 22:1, the 'suffering servant psalm' (v. 46). He was conscious of being abandoned by the Father. While Jesus spoke from the cross seven times, Matthew records only one saying, the fourth utterance. While He suffered abandonment on the cross, Jesus recognized that God was His Father; a separation had occurred but not a cessation of relationship (not a loss of faith, but a loss of contact). He agonized over the loss of intimacy with God, calling Him 'My God' twice. He seems to be imploring for the separation to end.

There is a Jewish tradition to the effect that Elijah would come and rescue the righteous in their distress, but it seems to be without biblical warrant unless a connection is made with Elijah's role as a forerunner of Christ (Mal. 4). Further, when Jesus spoke of God in Aramaic as 'Eli, Eli ...', some may have thought He was actually calling on Elijah (the words 'my God' and 'Elijah' in Hebrew being close in pronunciation). If God abandoned Him, would Elijah rescue Him?

In verses 48-49, there is an allusion to Psalm 69:21. The drink was a sour wine diluted with vinegar, commonly consumed by soldiers (likely there for the soldiers executing Jesus). It was a pain soother though it is not clear whether the motive was to prolong the agony or dull the pain. The fact that the sponge was attached to a stick and lifted to Jesus suggests that His cross was elevated above the ground. Often crucifixions were very near ground level.

That Jesus spoke 'with a loud voice' (v. 50) at His death tells us that He died in full control of His senses (He did not die exhausted or fainting). No one took His life from Him; He laid it down for the sheep! Matthew does not tell us what Jesus said in His final cry from the cross, though the following verse (v. 51) suggests that He uttered the words, 'It is finished,' and then died since the veil of the temple was rent in two, indicating access into the presence of God. Luke tells us that with a loud voice Jesus also said, 'Father, into your hands I commend my spirit' (Luke 23:46).

His death brought about unusual phenomena (vv. 51-56): the temple curtain was torn from the top down (the access into God's presence had been opened for all by God Himself), rocks split, and some of the dead rose. Roman soldiers recognized the unusual nature of the event, proclaiming Him divine (v. 54); Mary Magdalene, Mary, and Salome watched from a distance.

The curtain that barred entrance into the Holy of Holies was torn from the top. It was twenty feet high and thick. The temple's function had ended; its rending foreshadowed the true dwelling place of God, Jesus Christ. Access to God had been made available to all. Several points are important at this juncture: first, here is evidence that the temple and its ritual had fulfilled its function; second, judgment was pending as Jesus predicted (v. 40); and, third, it was a sign of a new opening of entrance into the presence of God. Jesus' death brought in a new age; a transfer of authority had taken place from a physical building to a soon-to-be living person.

The shaking of the earth here and in 28:2 suggests God's intervention. Earthquake and darkness are mentioned in Amos 8:8-10. The earthquake was the occasion for the opening of graves. It is through death that life springs forth! Matthew only mentions the earthquake as frightening the soldiers, but the language he uses is the same as that of the disciples at the transfiguration of Jesus (17:6).

This is the first time in Matthew's gospel that someone outside the Jewish environs recognizes that Jesus is the Son of God. God declared it in 3:17 and 17:5, Jesus claimed the title (11:25-27), demons recognized it (4:3, 6; 8:29), the disciples said so (14:33), and Peter confessed it (16:16). Matthew is likely helping his readers understand that the new community that Jesus gathers, the church, is not restricted to the ethnic sons of Abraham. The confession of the soldiers was the same as the disciples earlier (14:33). It is not certain if they meant that Jesus was one close to God or if they confessed His deity.

Women from Galilee traveled with Jesus and financially supported Him (vv. 55-56). Most likely the mother of James and John was Salome (Mark 15:40); she was also Mary's sister and, therefore, Jesus' aunt. Mary Magdalene was from Magdala, a town on the northwest shore of the Galilee; Jesus cast out seven demons from her (Luke 8:2). We know nothing of Mary, the mother of James and Joseph (Mark calls him Joses [15:40]). An entourage of women had followed Jesus to Jerusalem. It is interesting that there is no mention of any woman opposing Jesus, only men.

According to Jewish law, criminals could not be left on crosses overnight (Deut. 21:22-23). Late that afternoon Joseph of Arimathea, a secret follower (John 19:38), and Nicodemus (John 19:39) entombed him (vv. 57-61).

Arimathea was a Judean town some miles to the north of Jerusalem. This well-to-do man had apparently settled in Jerusalem where he constructed a family tomb. We know also that he was a member of the Sanhedrin (Mark 15:43; Luke 23:50). The mention of his wealth may be an allusion to the fulfillment of Isaiah 53:9. His position in Jewish leadership-circles is evidenced by his ability to have access to Pilate.

However, to identify with an executed criminal was a bold, declarative move on his part.

With the close of the day and Sabbath approaching, there was cause for haste in obtaining the body of Jesus and properly preparing it for burial, which Joseph accomplished. Jesus was wrapped in clean linen, suggesting respect and reverence, and placed in a new, unused tomb. If Joseph strictly followed Jewish law, the expensive tomb would no longer be useable again since Jesus was considered unclean.

Two of the women remained, the two Marys, after Joseph's departure from the tomb (v. 61). In the next chapter (28:1) Matthew describes them returning to the tomb after the Sabbath was over. Perhaps, they left as the guards were posted.

While the disciples had a hard time grasping the resurrection, the Pharisees had better memories; they attempted to prevent the stealing of the body (vv. 62-66). It is likely that Judas informed them of Jesus' prediction of His resurrection. Certainly, they did not connect resurrection with the destruction-of-the-temple comments, referring to His body, and not the building complex, that Jesus made because they believed that He was speaking against their literal temple.

The animosity of the religious leaders is apparent by the way they addressed Jesus. While Pilate is addressed politely, Jesus is referred to as 'that impostor' (v. 63). The words 'gathered before' (v. 62) are frequently used of official meetings suggesting that the appointment with Pilate was formal. It seems that there are at least two enemies of the gospel here: lying leadership and money.

The leadership did not believe that Jesus would be resurrected to life but feared the disciples would take advantage of His statements, steal the body, and create a hoax-movement (v. 66). If Jesus disappeared, they would seek to explain it away through paid, false witnesses (28:11-15) as well as an appeal to Pilate's fears.

Applications

1. That Jesus would submit to such abuse is truly amazing. He could have consumed them in His wrath, but He chose humiliation and degradation instead.

Dehumanized by vile creatures, enduring physical and emotional violence, the treatment of Him is shocking. He is the creator, lacking no power and subject to no one but the Father. Why would He allow people to do that? The answer is found in the name given to Him by Joseph – Jesus. It means deliverer. He came to deliver us from sin (1:21), to be a ransom for many. He came to pay the debt of our disobedience; He accepted our curse before God; He became sin for us! Do you not stand in awe and welcome amazement?

2. Jesus was abandoned by His friends and cursed by His enemies but remained silent before His accusers. Pilate was amazed that Jesus, whom he knew to be innocent, did not seek to defend Himself. Why did He offer no defense? Jesus' purpose was to allow His own execution. He was not concerned for His safety; He came out of interest for our safety. I do not know how anyone who looks seriously into His life would not be stunned and humbled. Have you ever met anyone so unselfish, so other-centered? Is there not a lesson in this for we who claim to be followers of Jesus?

3. Simon is worthy of meditation. This otherwise unknown Jewish man was required to literally pick up Jesus' cross and carry it. In a sense, you and I are 'Simons'. What it means to be a follower of Jesus is to carry His identity. We are to 'take up his cross and follow'. Jesus took the place of Barabbas literally and our place spiritually. We who follow Him are to take up His cross, His concerns and burdens. What burdens are you carrying for your Lord? How, in Paul's words, are you filling up the sufferings of Christ? Does being a Christian mean that all your days should be without distress? Is there not a hard side to the privilege of being a follower of the Crucified One?

4. The charge for which Jesus met crucifixion by the Romans was that He claimed to be a political insurrectionist, that He was a king. Matthew began his gospel indicating that Jesus was the Son of David, and that is the charge for which He died at the gospel's end. He is a King; He is

our King. He is not a despotic monarch ruling by threat of retribution, but a kind sovereign reigning through love, gentleness, and compassion. His kingdom has no geographic boundaries, no ethnic or cultural barriers, and no educational or health prerequisites. When other kingdoms are no more, He will reign in His kingdom forever. Does that not thrill you? Are you not driven to delight and worship to think He allowed you to be part of His kingdom?

5. When Jesus died temple worship ended, the Old Covenant era ended, the era of shadows and anticipations reached its culmination. In Jesus' triumph over death, meaning His enthronement at the right hand of God, a new era began. Access into the presence of God was purchased (the rending of the veil) and there is no longer a need for animal sacrifices. He is the final sacrifice and the true temple. God is now dwelling in His people; His presence is no longer identified with a building or a geographic center. Are you taking advantage of living in the new era, the era of the formation of a new community of the people of God? Do you know your advantages? Are you seeking to gain God's pleasure and mercies instead of realizing that in Jesus you have been given His mercies? Are you living to acquire and keep or are you seeking to live in an appropriate manner because of an appreciative spirit?

6. God's plans simply cannot be frustrated no matter how much effort people may expend. This is illustrated by the religious leadership's attempt to prevent anyone from stealing Jesus' body (that thought would generate the myth that Jesus rose from the dead). In spite of subterfuge, His truth claims were vindicated; He conquered death. He is our deliverer/redeemer. The futility of the efforts to prevent the resurrection suggests that mankind is incapable of annulling God's plans. However, when we try to prevent the truth from conquering, all such efforts are doomed to fail. Lies, cheating, and bribes are the ways of the world, but, in the end, it will accomplish nothing, but only validate the

just wrath of God in judgment. Does this realization not fill you with confidence and trust in God's promises?

7. Jesus was vindicated even before His resurrection. He was not cast into the city's rubbish dump, the destiny of criminals; He was buried among the rich, which in the Jewish mind implied the blessed. This was a fulfillment of prophecy: 'And they made his grave with the wicked, yet with a rich man in his death' (Isa. 53:9). In death, Jesus had the approval of His Father. Like Jesus, His children need not fear death; we will find blessing because He will be with us. We need not fear the grave, but we should fear the One who holds the keys to it. Do you? Paul said, 'O Death! Where is your sting?... But thanks be to God who gives us the victory through our Lord Jesus Christ' (1 Cor. 15:55-57).

11

The Conclusive Proof of the King's Claims and Person: The Resurrection

(28:1-20)

What is found here is not an account of the resurrection, but a statement of the fact of it. Each of the four gospels tells us of the empty tomb, that the discovery was made in the early morning, that it was made by a woman or women, that there was an encounter by them with an angel or angels, and that Jesus was in the tomb for three days. In spite of the teaching of Jesus, the resurrection came as a surprise!

The end of the Sabbath began after 6:00 p.m. on Saturday. A Jewish day began in the early evening, not midnight (the Roman manner of establishing time) following the pattern of the days of creation (Gen. 1:5, 'evening and … morning … the first day'). Jesus was placed in the tomb on Friday and rose early on Sunday, the third day.

Meeting the Risen Saviour (vv. 1-10)

It is interesting that Matthew places the emphasis upon the women who came to the tomb; they are the first to meet the risen Lord while the disciples, according to Matthew's account, would see Him later in the Galilee.

An earthquake will get a person's attention! The earthquake suggests the gravity of a divine intervention. However, the emphasis here is not on the earthquake, but on the angel's coming to the tomb as causing it. An angel rolled away the stone, not to let Jesus out, but to let others in! This angel appears to be robust in rolling the stone away both to the women and the guards. Those assigned to guard a corpse became as that themselves. The presence of God's holiness reflected in this angelic being caused death-like trauma, yet the One that came to show that He was alive gives life!

The angel speaks to the women, not the guards, for whose sake he came. He consoles the women with a command and recognition that Jesus had been murdered, but the comforting command was rooted in the fact that He was now alive. The angel invites the women to see that the tomb is empty. The angel knew that he must have startled and confused them.

From comfort the angel quickly turned to instruction (v. 7). The message was twofold: to tell the disciples that Jesus was alive and that they were to meet Him in Galilee. The tense of the verb is instructive ('has [been] risen'). It tells us that Jesus was raised by someone other than Himself (passive voice, something done to Him by another). The Father brought Jesus to life because He had paid the penalty that sin imposed (death)! The point is that the verb explains more than a fact; it points to the agent of the fact. With a combination of fear and delightful exuberance, the women left the tomb, having heard the angel's message and seen the evidence (v. 8). The place of sorrow and the terror of death no longer had that meaning for them!

Matthew's recounting of Jesus' meeting with the women is rather low key, succinct, and matter of fact. They had been at the crucifixion, first at the tomb, and now, the first in Matthew's account to see the risen Lord. Grasping the feet is a symbol of worship. Matthew makes the point that Jesus' resurrection was physical, real! Jesus' instructions to the women are the same as the angel's earlier. They were not to fear, but to tell the disciples to return to the Galilee where He would see them once more.

The Falsification by the Chief Priests (vv. 11-15)

The guards were bribed to lie about what happened and were promised that the Jewish leaders would deal with Pilate should the failure to guard the body come to his attention. Here is another evidence of Pilate's moral weakness and his fear of the Jewish leadership. It also demonstrates that Jesus rose from the dead, since the leadership had to invent a lie to deal with it.

The women came with a message of profound delight to the disciples; the guards came to the leadership with a message that caused confusion and shock. That the guards reported to the chief priests, not the Romans, tells us that these were under the authority of the Sanhedrin, rather than Pilate. If they had been under Roman authority and lost a prisoner, they would have paid with their lives. These men were protected from Roman retaliation for dereliction of duty. This would seem to have been Pilate's point when he said to the leadership, 'you have a guard …' (27:65).

This is the second time the leadership gathered, paying money to protect their interests (cf. 26:15). It is ironic that they went to extraordinary measures to ensure that the body was not stolen, yet that is what they claimed had happened. Here is evidence of what the religious leadership thought of Pilate (v. 14). They saw him as weak and gullible to pressure, a puppet easily manipulated to concede to their pressure. If the guards had been sleeping, how could they know what had happened to the body? It was something of a good day for the guards; they escaped the consequences of duty and made a pocketful of money! (v. 15).

The Appearance of the King to the Disciples in Galilee: the Beginning of the Messianic Mission (vv. 16-20)

As was evident in the arrangements for the colt that carried Jesus in the triumphal entry and the location of the Passover meal/Lord's Supper, there was some planning here. Some worshiped and some could not believe what they were seeing, forgetting who they had been with for three years as well as His instructions on the issue. Perhaps, it was simply too good to be true! The 'twelve' disciples are now the eleven. As with the women at the tomb, the initial response to the risen Lord was worship.

The gospel ends with the Great Commission. Jesus made four statements: He promised His disciples a source of power and authority; He gave them a command; He instructed them how to carry out the command; and He promised them His presence. They were commissioned in His power, commissioned to His program, and commissioned with His presence. An interesting feature of this section is the fourfold repetition of words suggesting universality ('all authority', 'all nations', 'all that I commanded you', and 'always'). Further, the disciples utter no words; Jesus does all the talking!

The authority of Jesus is mentioned in verse 18. By the resurrection, His Father in heaven, from whence He rules triumphantly, enthroned Jesus with majesty and power to rule as Lord and King. The 'Son of Man' now rules; Daniel 7:13-14 has been fulfilled! Jesus now rules over heaven and the earth, the universe. His universal authority achieved through His obedience and suffering, though not as yet fully manifest until His return, is the basis of the command that immediately follows.

The essential command in the commissioning is to 'make disciples'; the three participles (going, baptizing, and teaching) suggest the methods to be employed to accomplish it (vv. 19-20). It would seem that the sequence of the participles has meaning. The first of these is 'going'. We are told that discipleship-making is about carrying the message of Jesus to people. The second is 'baptizing' (the outward rite seems to be water baptism, but the inward reality is Spirit baptism; it bears witness to the fact of entrance into His life); it is the outward affirmation of a prior entrance into the family of God. Disciples are made of those who are part of a community of faith where 'teaching' occurs. Through teaching, disciples are brought to maturity, but first they must know the Lord and become a part of His visible family. It is interesting that Jesus instructs them to baptize in a name, yet defines that name as three existences (one but three!). Here is a strong evidence of Trinitarianism.

The promise of His presence is not merely to the eleven; it is for the church through the centuries until the end of the age (v. 20). The disciples did not live to the 'end of the age', indicating that Jesus' promise of His presence is for all Christians.

Matthew began the ministry of Christ with the insight that light had come to the 'Galilee of the Gentiles' (4:15); it ends with Jesus' command to take His message to the Gentiles ('all nations')!

What a wonderful way to end the gospel: 'I am with you always.' In chapter 1, the gospel began with a promise (v. 23) that the coming One will be Immanuel ('God with us'). It ends with a promise that He will be with us forever. It is clear that Matthew wants us to know that God came to us and will be with us.

The intent of Matthew in summarizing the person and claims of Jesus, if my thesis is correct, was to address the reticence of Jewish believers to carry the news of Jesus to the Gentiles (28:20). The social climate of the 40s to the 60s, the rising Jewish hostility to Gentile-Roman oppression in the name of patriotic passion, made the duty to reach out to Gentiles a difficult endeavor. The largely Jewish constituency in the early decades of the church coupled with religious ethnic prejudice made it difficult to understand that in the progressive revelation of God's people Gentiles were included, though it certainly was mentioned in the terms of the Abrahamic Covenant.

A wonderful summary of the claims and implications of the startling advance of the divine disclosure of God's redemptive program has been given to us by Josephus in his summary of the crucifixion and its consequence:

> Now there was about this time Jesus, a wise man; if it be lawful to call him a man. For he was a doer of wonderful works; a teacher of such men as receive the truth with pleasure. He drew over to him both many of the Jews, and many of the Gentiles. He was [the] Christ. And when Pilate, at the suggestion of the principal men among us, had condemned him to the cross; those that loved him at the first did not forsake him. For he appeared to them alive again, the third day: as the divine prophets had foretold these and ten thousand other wonderful things concerning him. And the tribe of Christians, so named from him, are not extinct at this day.[1]

Applications

1. The point of the resurrection is that Jesus accomplished His mission. He came to conquer death. The proof that

---

1. Josephus Flavius, *The History of the Jews*, 18.3.3.

He paid our penalty in becoming sin is that He is alive! Jesus' resurrection should fill us with hope. He is alive; He has conquered our last enemy. We, too, shall live! The Easter event validates the Calvary event. Have you pondered the importance of the resurrection in the Christian gospel? Have you thought about what it means to you?

2. God's enemies never cease in their efforts to discredit what Jesus has done, but they will always fail. They use coercion, deception, and lies, but it is all futile. People are not able to frustrate the plans and will of God. Does this not offer hope to you? We should not fear what mankind can do to us. Do you realize that God will have the last word, that He will triumph over all corruption and corrupters? How does this truth alter the way you look upon your circumstances?

3. The first words that Jesus spoke after His resurrection were 'do not be afraid' (v. 5). Jesus knows that anxiety, born of disappointment and uncertainty, is a valid and significant human emotion. He does not reprimand the women for failing to grasp the reality of the resurrection; He has comforting words for them. Jesus always has our welfare in mind, even if the shadows of pain and trauma overwhelm us. Is it not comforting to know that Jesus cares and knows when we are afraid? If we know Jesus, we should heed His words to us. Is your life characterized by trust or do you find that fear and anxiety often grip you?

4. Do not miss the truth that Jesus initially entrusted the message of His resurrection to a coterie of ladies. He showed respect for them and rewarded their affection for Him by being the first to whom He appeared, the first to carry the message other than an angel. As Jesus was not bothered by the interruptions of children, He had time and respect for the marginalized in Jewish culture. Jesus was no bigot or male chauvinist. He respected the contribution of women and often spoke of them in positive terms. His love had no cultural

boundaries or limits. He is a person we should all get to know better!

5. Jesus' last word in the book was the command to carry the gospel by making disciples of all the nations. The command before us is 'make disciples' and we do this by going, baptizing, and teaching. We all listen to the last words of respected and cherished people. Since no one is more worthy to hear, it seems that Jesus' final words should be our marching orders. Do you prioritize your life to make followers of Jesus? Are you working to make disciples of your children? Are there neighbors that you need to go to and tell them the most important story in all the world?

6. It is worth thinking about what it means for you and me that 'all authority' has been given to Jesus in heaven and earth. The devil when he tempted Jesus promised Him universal authority, but it would have come through submission to him; it would not have been over heaven since his rule does not extend there. Jesus chose submission to God and His obedience brought His enthronement over a kingdom that will have no end. He teaches us by His action that submission is the way to victory. God's way is the best way; actually, it is the only way. Have you learned that lesson in the matter of your personal choices? The nation's leadership plotted their own rebellious course in rejecting Jesus and the nation fell into judgment and destruction. Jesus was the 'true Israel', the One obedient to God, and His life led to triumph. Is there not a lesson for you and me? Jesus now reigns and possesses all authority to rule over His kingdom. The way to triumph is obedience; victory comes after suffering, the crown after the cross. Have you learned that lesson yet?

7. God's commands are always tied to His promises. The promises of God give us encouragement, strength, and confidence to endure; the commands of God tell us our duties. The command is to make followers of Jesus and the comfort promised in executing the instruction is

grand. Jesus promises to be with us in the process, the One of universal authority and power, every day in every circumstance until each of us comes to the end of our journey and until time shall end. Wow! Does that not give you confidence and assurance?

Subject Index

C

D

H

Scripture Index